CAMBRIDGE LIBRAR

Books of enduring schc

Archaeology

The discovery of material remains from the recent or the ancient past has always been a source of fascination, but the development of archaeology as an academic discipline which interpreted such finds is relatively recent. It was the work of Winckelmann at Pompeii in the 1760s which first revealed the potential of systematic excavation to scholars and the wider public. Pioneering figures of the nineteenth century such as Schliemann, Layard and Petrie transformed archaeology from a search for ancient artifacts, by means as crude as using gunpowder to break into a tomb, to a science which drew from a wide range of disciplines - ancient languages and literature, geology, chemistry, social history - to increase our understanding of human life and society in the remote past.

Travels and Researches in Asia Minor, Mesopotamia, Chaldea, and Armenia

The surgeon William Ainsworth (1807–96) acted as the geologist of the 1835 Euphrates Expedition, his account of which is also reissued in this series. Great interest was aroused by the scientific and archaeological findings of that journey, and a further expedition was funded, ostensibly to make contact with the Nestorian Christians of the region, but covertly to make further mineralogical investigations. Ainsworth was the leader of the expedition, and his two-volume account was published in 1842. Starting from Istanbul in 1839, Ainsworth took a route through Asia Minor, northern Syria, Kurdistan, Persia and Armenia, returning to Istanbul in 1840. The expedition was regarded as unsuccessful, as Ainsworth had massively overspent on the budget originally allotted by the sponsors, and his secret activities were discovered by the Ottoman authorities, but the work remains a vivid account of the area. Volume 1 covers events up to the battle of Nezib in 1839.

Travels and Researches in Asia Minor, Mesopotamia, Chaldea, and Armenia

Volume 1

William F. Ainsworth

CAMBRIDGE
UNIVERSITY PRESS

University Printing House, Cambridge, CB2 8BS, United Kingdom

Cambridge University Press is part of the University of Cambridge.
It furthers the University's mission by disseminating knowledge in the pursuit of education, learning and research at the highest international levels of excellence.

www.cambridge.org
Information on this title: www.cambridge.org/9781108080989

This edition first published 1842
This digitally printed version 2015

ISBN 978-1-108-08098-9 Paperback

The original edition of this book contains a number of colour plates, which have been reproduced in black and white. Colour versions of these images can be found online at www.cambridge.org/9781108080989

The original edition of this book contains a number of oversize plates which it has not been possible to reproduce to scale in this edition. They can be found online at www.cambridge.org/9781108080989

Battle of Nizib.

TRAVELS AND RESEARCHES

IN

ASIA MINOR, MESOPOTAMIA,

CHALDEA, AND ARMENIA.

BY

WILLIAM FRANCIS AINSWORTH, F.G.S., F.R.G.S.

IN CHARGE OF THE EXPEDITION SENT BY THE ROYAL GEOGRAPHICAL SOCIETY,
AND THE SOCIETY FOR PROMOTING CHRISTIAN KNOWLEDGE,
TO THE CHRISTIAN TRIBES IN CHALDEA.

IN TWO VOLUMES.

VOL. I.

LONDON:
JOHN W. PARKER, WEST STRAND.

M.DCCC.XLII.

CONTENTS

OF

THE FIRST VOLUME.

CHAPTER VIII.

CHAPTER IX.

CHAPTER X.

CHAPTER XI.

CHAPTER XII.

CHAPTER XIII.

CHAPTER XIV.

CHAPTER XV.

CHAPTER XVI.

CHAPTER XVII.

CHAPTER XVIII.

CHAPTER XIX.

CHAPTER XX.

CHAPTER XXI.

CHAPTER XXII.

CHAPTER XXIII.

CHAPTER XXIV.

CHAPTER XXV.

ILLUSTRATIONS.

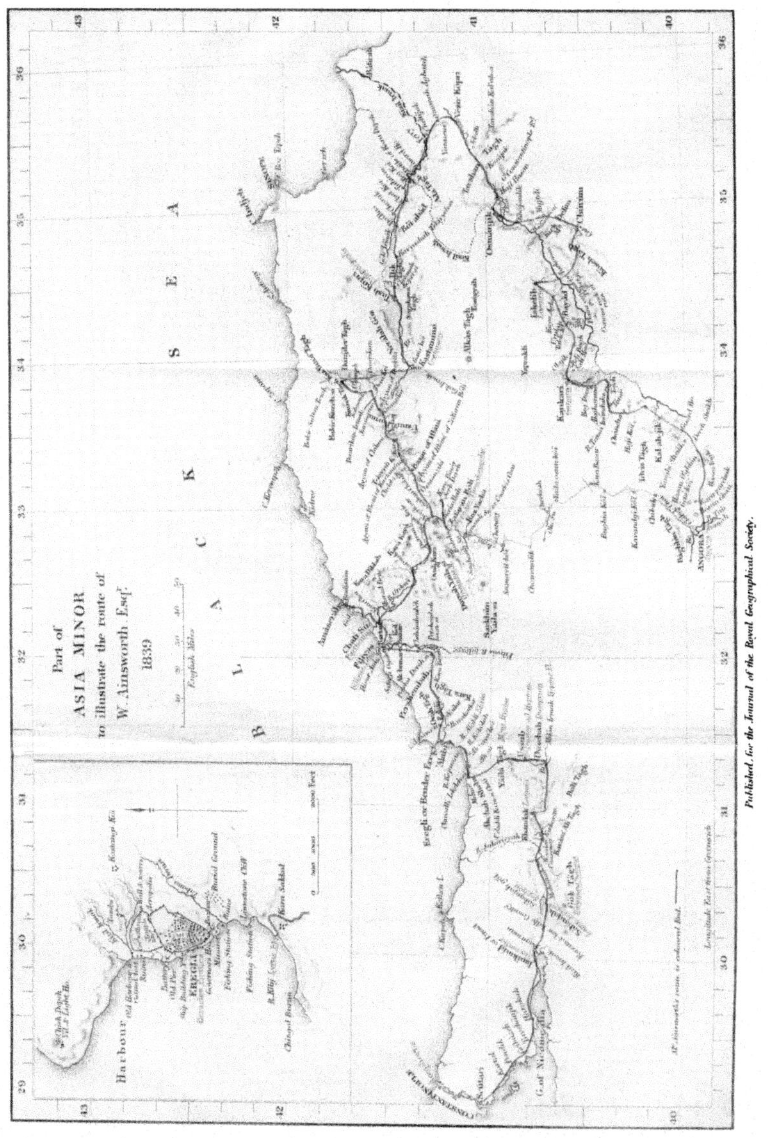

The material originally positioned here is too large for reproduction in this reissue. A PDF can be downloaded from the web address given on page ivof this book, by clicking on 'Resources Available'.

TRAVELS IN ASIA MINOR.

INTRODUCTORY CHAPTER.

On the return of the Euphrates Expedition to this country in the year 1837, a strong desire was excited among many, to become acquainted with the actual condition of the mountaineer Chaldean Christians, of whom much had been heard during that Expedition, but whose isolated position, and country difficult of access, had placed them beyond the reach of the exploratory excursions of the officers.

Under these circumstances, the Royal Geographical Society, and the Society for Promoting Christian Knowledge, united to bear the expenses of an expedition, which should specially visit these interesting tribes, and the Author of the present Narrative, and Mr. Rassam, having been selected by the Geographical Society for the undertaking, were approved of by the Society for Promoting Christian Knowledge.

The Author had accompanied the Euphrates Expedition as Surgeon and Geologist, and had communicated several papers to the *Transactions of the Geographical Society*, besides publishing the result of his scientific researches in a separate volume.

Mr. Rassam was a Chaldean, native of Musul, who had been educated by the missionaries at Cairo, and had joined the Euphrates Expedition at Malta, where he was at that time the chief Arabic Translator to the Board of Missions. He had returned with the author through Kurdistan and Asia Minor, a long exploratory trip made in search of coal, by order of Colonel Chesney, the able and enlightened Commander of the Euphrates Expedition. His travelling experience, his knowledge of the Turkish and Arabic languages, his previous connection with missionary societies, and his claims of relationship among the Chaldeans, rendered him peculiarly fitted for the undertaking generally, and the task of making the inquiries suggested by the Society for Promoting Christian Knowledge accordingly devolved chiefly upon him.

To these gentlemen was subsequently joined Mr. Thomas M. Russell, whose abilities as a mathematician rendered him of the highest value to the Expedition, so long as he continued with it. After the retreat from Nizib, he was compelled, by protracted illness, to return home, and the astronomical portion of its labours suffered much from his loss.

A considerable extent of territory, variously inhabited, lay between the confines of Europe and the country of the Chaldeans, many parts of which presented a most interesting field for geographical and general exploration; the Societies, therefore, drew up a form of Instructions as to what were to constitute the objects of research, of exploration, or of actual survey, on the route. These comprised labours, of such magnitude as can only be appreciated by those who have been personally upon the ground.

The primary instructions regarded the exploration of that portion of Lesser Asia which lay between Heraclea Pontica and Angora, and in the midst of which there were supposed to exist ancient sites, and even modern cities, as Zaferan Boli, very little known to our maps or geographical treatises.

The next great object was the survey of the celebrated Halys, or Salt River, of the Ancients,—the Kizil Irmak, or Red River, of the Turks. Then to enter into, and ascertain whether roads existed in the Haimaneh, a central district of Lesser Asia, tenanted by Kurds and Turkomans. To visit the mines of Central Asia, and more especially the salt mines of Hajji Bektash. Thence to explore the Great Salt Lake—the Tattea Palus of the Ancients, and to fix its northern and southern boundaries. To ascertain the elevation of as many points, especially high table-lands and their principal summits, as possible. To visit Kaiseriyeh, and to determine the course and sources of the Melas — a long-debated question.

Proceeding into Cataonian Cappadocia, the Expedition was to identify in that country the ancient sites of Castabala, Ariarathia, Commana Cappadocia, and others.

Arrived at Malatiyeh, it was left to the urgencies of the moment, whether the Expedition should proceed direct to Musul, by Dyarbekr and the valley of the Tigris, or whether, after examining the passage of Euphrates through Taurus, and the cataracts above Someïsat, it should enter Mesopotamia and penetrate at once into the Sinjar.

The presence of the Serasker of the Turkish army at the time on the frontiers of Syria and Mesopotamia, presented a favourable opportunity for attempting the second line, under his protection. Unfortunately, however, the Expedition arrived at the moment of the advance of the Egyptian army; the battle of Nizib followed, and by the disastrous results of that action, it was thrown back, with many losses and privations, upon Constantinople.

Mesopotamia was ultimately reached by an interesting line through Lesser Asia, the passes of Taurus, and

North Syria. It was traversed by a new road, on the line of which the ruins of an ancient Christian Chaldean city were met with, and Musul itself was reached in the spring of 1840.

Excursions were made thence, according to the instructions, to visit the remarkable city of Atra, in the Desert, and the Babylonian ruin of Ur of the Persians. Nineveh, Eski Musul, and the field of Arbela, were also explored.

During the same summer the Author, accompanied by Mr. Rassam, effected an entrance into the Kurdistan mountains, and the country of the Chaldean Christians. The instructions demanded an exploration and determination of the sites of Amadiyeh, Julamerik, and Rowandiz; information regarding the Chaldean mountaineers of the Tiyari, Hakari and other tribes; and friendly and religious communications with their patriarch, bishops and priests. All this was happily accomplished.

The reports concerning the Izedis, or Devil-Worshippers, were also to be examined into, and their chief seat of worship was visited with this view.

If, by means of a caravan or otherwise, the Expedition could cross the intervening mountains into Persia, it was to be done, and the Lake of Urimiyeh to be explored. This was also carried into execution, and the party returned by the pass of Keli-shin and the peak of Rowandiz, which was ascended, and its height determined. The city of the same name was also visited.

Quitting Musul shortly after their return from the mountains, the party proceeded according to instructions to the pass where the Tigris is hemmed in by the Kurdistan mountains, so celebrated for the resistance made at that point to the retreat of the ten thousand Greeks. Some interesting ruins were found there.

The site of Tigranocerta, and the rivers of Se'rt and Betlis, were then explored, the cities of the same names were also visited, and thence the Expedition proceeded into Greater Armenia.

Finally the party returned by the lofty upland of Mush, and the still more elevated and cold regions of Khinis Kalehsi, and the commercial sites of Erzrum and Trebizond, to Constantinople, where they arrived in the fall of the year 1840.

With the exception of that part of the travels which extended over the country between Musul and Trebizond,—comprising the Passes of Xenophon, the site of Tigranocerta, the discussion regarding the easterly feeders of the Tigris, and the description of the uplands of Armenia,—the scientific and geographical results of the Expedition have already been communicated to the Royal Geographical Society. It is not proposed, therefore, in the work now offered to the public, to dwell upon the various matters which more properly formed the subject of those reports, but, as far as possible, to convey a general idea of the character of the countries visited, of the peculiarities of their inhabitants, their scenery and antiquities, and, still more especially, to present a succinct narrative, in the form of a journal, of the intercourse held with the Chaldean Christians, and of the various adventures and mishaps which the party had to encounter while travelling through countries at all times of little security, but rendered still less so by the disturbed period in which the Expedition was undertaken.

Mr. Rassam quitted London in the spring of 1838 for Malta, and Mr. Russell and the Author shortly afterwards left this country, with a view to carry a series of observations on terrestrial magnetism across the Continent of Europe. These were subsequently printed, and favourably commented upon, by the reporter, Colonel Sabine, F.R.S., in the *Journal of the Royal Geographical Society*.

On their journey they consulted the libraries of Paris, that of the Armenians near Venice, and the libraries of Vienna, on subjects connected with the countries they were about to visit. Soon after their arrival at Constantinople, where they were joined by Mr. Rassam and a friend of his, Mr. Pulsford, a young Englishman travelling for information, and who was to accompany the Expedition a short distance into Asia Minor, they left that city, to commence their exploratory travels: having been previously, through the kindness of Lord Ponsonby, provided with a firman of considerable length and great power, and bearing the Sultan's sign manual.

The Sultan's Sign Manual.

CHAPTER I.

The Tomb of Hannibal.

Suburb of Constantinople. The Lyre, why used in Illuminations. Mehemet Ali Pasha. Scutari, the Golden City. Fountain of Hermagora. The Giant Amycus. City of Chalcedon. Shores the Propontis. Its Isles. Description of Harakah, or Libyssa. Tomb of Hannibal. Character of the Carthaginian Hero. His Death.

On leaving Pera, which was the portion of Constantinople devoted to the residence of foreigners, as early as the time of Michael Paleologus, for Uskudar, or Scutari, the caique, starting from the point of Top Khani, or the Arsenal, did not wend its way directly out of the Golden Horn across to Scutari. In order to gain the advantage of a strong back current, it kept along the European shore, passing first the Arsenal itself, and then the suburb of Fundukli, remarkable for its red painted houses, a distinction of bright from sombre colours, which the Turks arrogate to themselves in all that concerns them; but which they show especially, in their houses and garments, their tombs and their turbans.

The suburb of Fundukli was formerly the seat of the country house of Hussein Agha, one of the richest Osmanlis of the time of Mohammed IV.; and scarcely a week elapsed, according to Oriental chroniclers, without a visit from the Sultan, who enjoyed the amusement of fishing from windows which advanced upon the Bosphorus. The Osmanlis appear to have progressed in the luxurious appliances of that noble stream since those days; for not only several palaces of the Sultan, but those of beys and aghas innumerable, have in the present day apartments, beneath which its clear deep waters flow undisturbed.

Fundukli is considered by Constantinopolitan topographers to be the site of the ancient Aianteon, where was the tomb erected by Chalcis in honour of a dolphin, or what I fear might with equal propriety, although little poetic beauty, be designated a porpoise. Chalcis, according to mythologists, was a shepherd who played upon the lyre with so much skill, that one of these ungainly fish, like seals on the coasts of Caledonia, was wooed and won by his harmony. A certain Charandas, jealous of the talent of Chalcis, killed the porpoise, when the sorrowing musician erected a monument*, to his finny admirer. These edifices of ancient times are now passed away, and not a vestige of such structures remain; but what is interesting in the narrative, and

* It appears that sheep-tending in those early and pastoral times was a lucrative as well as poetic and artistic employment.

what, indeed, has induced us, *en passant*, to refer to it, is, that, as in many other cases in the East, the mythological tradition has continued to be transmitted, only in another manner; for whenever Mohammedan joys or festivities demand an illumination for the night, the shores of the Bosphorus may be seen from Fundukli to Buyuk Dereh, sparkling with radiant lyres.

Beyond Fundukli is the suburb called Dolma Baktchi (the Garden of Dolmas*), which was the favourite quarter of Selim III. The palace of the Sultan is now supplanted by a cannon foundry, and the little port in front of this appears to be the same as that formerly called Pentecontoricos, from the galleys with fifty oars, which Taurus led there when he left Scythia on his way to Crete. The Argonauts also landed at this point.

Constantinople is divided into four governments or pashaliks, each of the pashas being a member of the ministry. The suburbs of Galata, Pera, and Fundukli constitute one of these governments, and are at the present moment ruled by Mehemet Ali Pasha, a young man of very gentlemanly manners, who was a great favourite of the late as well as of the present Sultan. At the death of Mahmud, he was only Mehemet Ali Bey, a young courtier, and was the person despatched before the battle of Nizib to carry the firman and insignia of Serasker of the East to Hafiz Pasha. In his hurry he outstripped his escort, and proceeded onwards with a single tatar; when in the passes of Taurus, he was

* Dolmas are beydenjams, also called egg-plant (*Solanum Melongena*), filled with rice and chopped meat, or the same admirable compound enveloped in vine-leaves and boiled.

attacked by some Kurds, who intended to rob him. It was in vain that he proclaimed his high office of chamberlain to the Sultan, and bearer of despatches from the Father of Kings; the Kurds did not pay the slightest attention to his asseverations. "What!" he said, turning with mingled apprehension and astonishment to the tatar, "do not these people know the Sultan?" "No, my lord, not in the least," was the quiet but significant reply. So he was obliged to fee his master's faithful and submissive subjects, before he was allowed to continue his journey.

Mehemet Ali Pasha has many of the faults of an Oriental, but he cannot be considered as belonging to the old school; and although he has not made himself acquainted with any European language, he is by no means hostile to Franks, or to the introduction of European ameliorations. His fortune has for some years past been always in the ascendant, and he is at the present moment one of the most rising men in Constantinople.

The caique having reached as far as the stairs of Dolma Baktchi, struck across the Thracian Bosphorus, the course of whose currents has exercised the ingenuity of many geographers, among them our own celebrated Rennell. They appear, however, to be mainly regulated by the alternate salient and re-entering angles of the shore. There are seven of these, producing as many different currents, and which are felt in different directions. Englishmen who, while at Constantinople, may have business to transact with the ambassador, run a good chance of becoming intimately acquainted with them.

As we were rowed across the Bosphorus, Scutari, the "Golden City" of the Greeks, extended before us almost to its extreme southerly point, its houses rising in the rear to the cypress-clad heights of the Necropolis on the one side, and to the acclivities of Burghalu on the other. With a population of from 30,000 to 35,000 souls, it may be truly said, that it would be considered a large town but for the presence of Constantinople on the other side.

Porters having been put in requisition, we ascended the narrow streets, till we reached an open space at the back of the town, where we found the menzil-khan, or post-house. We had provided ourselves with an especial firman for horses, as the service from Scutari to Ismid is performed in rude carts, driven along at great speed, each with four horses, and not at all adapted for the transport of mathematical instruments.

The baggage being loaded, we rode across the vast burial-ground, like a cemetery in a forest, which is the admiration of all Oriental travellers, till a gentle descent brought us upon the beautiful vale of Kawak Serai, with the village of Kadi Keuy, the Propontis, and its rocky islets before us, and the great quadrangular barracks of Scutari advancing upon the promontory of Bos to our right.

The poplars from whence the valley of Kawak Serai (Poplar Palace) obtained its name, have disappeared, and the same may also be said of the Kiosk of Murad, which formerly existed in the same place. The valley is watered by a small rivulet, which has its sources at a short distance up the vale, a place which once had the high-sounding title of Fons Hermagora. Near where this rivulet flows into the sea is a raised place of Mohammedan prayer, overshadowed by some fine plane-trees, and beyond is a modern guard-house. Here was once a temple to Venus, and a smaller one to the hero Eurostes, and at the bottom of the same valley is the bay anciently of Amycus, afterwards of Chalcedon.

Amycus is a semi-fabulous personage, pourtrayed by the poets as the son of Neptune and of the nymph Meles, and who reigned in the most remote times over Bebrycia. This king is said by Apollodorus to have challenged the Argonauts to a wrestling match, and Pollux accepting the challenge killed him. He is also described as a giant by the ancient poets, more especially Valerius Flaccus; and a mountain at the head of the Bosphorus is recorded to the present day by tradition as the burial-place of this giant of old, as consecrated in its name of Giant's Mountain.

It appears from Hierocles that at the head of the harbour of Amycus was Necropolis (The City of the Dead). This is an interesting notice, as it assists in fixing the relative position of places, and shows also that while ages go by, names change, and races of men succeed to one another; that the uses and purposes of things may remain the same; and that Osmanlis lie now in all the pride of marble and gold, on crumbling dust, where Bebrycians, Athenians, and Romans have mouldered away before.

Passing the vale of Kawak Serai, we found ourselves abreast of the small but pretty village of Kadi Keuy, the site of ancient Chalcedon, a city which enjoys no less celebrity from its antiquity, the great men to whom it gave birth, and the various fortune which fell to its lot, than from the monuments which adorned it; and in particular that famous temple of Apollo, whose oracles scarcely yielded the palm to those of Delphi. The Megareans, the founders of Chalcedon, were long the object of derision to their neighbours, and the wit expended on their misinterpretation of an oracle, which dates from the most remote period of ancient Greece, was not too old to be revived by the sarcasm-loving pen of Gibbon.

The ride from Chalcedon along the shores of the Propontis, even as far as to Ismid, is at once interesting from the number of historical recollections, and remarkably beautiful in its soft and varied scenery. It is everywhere covered with verdure, diversified by gardens and groves, and embellished by extensive landscapes, embracing the Propontis and its islands, and the high and wooded coast of Mediterranean Bithynia, backed by the cloud-capped summits of Olympus.

The gulf which follows that of Chalcedon, now called Mundi Burnu, is the ancient harbour of Eutropas. The remains of walls and other fragments of antiquity are still to be observed. It was here that Phocas destroyed Maurice and his four sons.

A little beyond this we came to a bridge called that of the Bostangi Bashi, or head of the Gardens. There was here a guard and a government-station, where passports are examined, and quarantine is sometimes enforced. Not far from hence, and near the shore, are the ruins of the monastery of St. George, close to which is a mineral spring. The islands, called those of the Princes—the Propontides of Pliny—open upon the right in all their beauty. They are six in number, four large and two small. Two of the larger, Protea and Antigonea, are sterile, while in those of Prinkipo and Kalkis are several monasteries, and a school of some repute. Pierre Gilles, one of the oldest and best topographers of Constantinople, found the remains here of the mine which gave to the island its name of Kalkis. This traveller was sent into the Levant by Francis I., but being forgotten by his ministers, he was reduced to the necessity of enlisting in the Turkish service, and in the quality of a military man made several campaigns in Persia. He at last got away and reached Rome, where he published his valuable researches. Happy it is that in our days of intelligence wedded to philanthropy, such a termination to the toil and labour of several years can in very few cases be expected to occur.

Leaving Mount Aidos to the left, and passing the hills of Yaka Juk, we went no farther on the first day of our journey (the 18th of September, 1838,) than Kartal, a village chiefly tenanted by Greeks, and surrounded by gardens of vegetables for the Constantinopolitan market. The first day the traveller leaves the metropolis in this half-civilized country, he has to take a lesson in spreading his carpet on the floor, and sleeping under his cloak,—a practice to which he soon becomes inured.

The next day we rode through Pandikhi, the Pantichium of old, a fishing-village, also of Greeks, and where are the remains of a castle, in part constructed out of the the ruins of a still more ancient edifice. The road from hence begins to ascend to the large village of Geybuseh, leaving Cape Acritan, with the little isle of Nyssa beyond, to the right.

Geybuseh, the ancient Dacibyza, has a handsome

jami, and is surrounded by burial-grounds, shaded with the customary cypresses. At the menzil-khan there is a marble sarcophagus, which now serves as a trough for watering horses; and numerous other fragmentary remains attest the antiquity of the site. This small town, which is provided with a tolerable market, and contains a population of 1500 souls, is built on a hill of trap rocks succeeded by cretaceous limestones, the latter of which constitute a hilly country from hence to Tavshanjik (The Little Hare), a pretty village of Osmanli Turks, surrounded by gardens, and groves of fruit-trees, and vineyards, which extend from thence along the shore to Harakah, a menzil-khan and ferry to Ersek, on the opposite side of the gulf of Astacus or Nicomedia.

After exploring the ruins around, we passed the night in this last place, in a small but clean mesjid*; the only inconvenience of such a peculiar resting-place being, that they turned us out an hour before day-break for the sabah-namazi, or morning-prayer.

---

* The terms *mosque* and *jami* are very indiscriminately used by travellers in the East, nor are the natives themselves always particular in their application. Mosque is a French word adopted in our language, and corrupted from the Spanish *mesquita*, or the Turkish *mesjid;* a term generally applied to a place of Mohammedan worship not having a *menareh*, commonly written from the French, *minaret*. Such as have the latter appendages are called Jamis, from Jumah-namazi," the place of Friday's devotions," so that a mesjid is also sometimes called by the same name. A royal jami is called Selatyn. Some natives have asserted that no place of worship is, strictly speaking, a jami, unless it has two menarehs, a mesjid having one. I have adopted, however, the first and most general acceptation.

Harakah is a remarkably beautiful spot. It is situated in a bay or inlet of the sea, from which the road rises gradually, among vineyards and plantations of apricots and cherries, to the west. To the east it is carried along a more difficult way hewn in the face of steep precipices of limestone; in the rear is a high artificial mound, with ruins on its summit, overtopped by rocky cliffs, and washed at its base by a rivulet whose banks are clothed with a luxuriant vegetation, which spreads thence over the whole vale.

To the east of the rivulet are ruins of walls and buildings, the interior of which are now occupied by gardens and vineyards, but which fully indicate the former existence of a small town. In front, and near to the shore, the rivulet is crossed by a low moss-clad bridge; above which, at a small distance, and on the right bank, is a mill; while to the left is the picturesque little mesjid which constituted our temporary home.

Beyond the mesjid is the post-house; a khan, or kerwanserai, and a single shop occupy the opposite side of the road; and there are, besides, two or three houses in the gardens. These are all the habitations of Harakah, while in front of the khan, and drawn up upon the beach, are a few boats, the proprietors of which are engaged upon the ferry hence to Ersek; for this is the point where the great road from Scutari to Ismid comes from the interior uplands, after cutting the promontory of Acritan down to the sea-coast.

There can be no doubt from the comparison of ancient data with existing distances, that Harakah is on the site of the ancient Libyssa.

From the unchanging (at least without the lapse of

very long periods of time) circumstances of physical configuration, the ancient road was necessitated to follow the same line as it does at present. The same deep valley which separates the hill of Geybuseh from that of Tavshanjik in the present day, becoming deep and impassably abrupt on the sea-side, offered the same obstacles to the road being carried along the coast in ancient times, as it does at present; while the southerly prolongation of Cape Acritan rendered it also equally advisable, for brevity sake, as well as for the facilities offered by the road, to carry it from Pandikhi inward to Geybuseh rather than along the shore.

Libyssa was distinguished from the numerous mansions, stations, and changes along the great road in a very particular manner, by its being the burial-place of the distinguished but unfortunate Hannibal*. It has, therefore, been much sought after by comparative geographers. Colonel Leake has identified it with Malsum, a village to which he turned off from the great road to be ferried across to Ersek; but which neither is, nor ever was, upon the ancient or modern great road. Others have identified it with Geybuseh. There is some connexion of name between the two latter places; but two circumstances are fatal to the identification: first, that the distances are not the same; and secondly, that the tumulus of Hannibal was on the sea-shore, from which Geybuseh, and the tumulus near it, are distant some miles.

The descriptions left to us by writers of olden time,

---

* Helena, the mother of Constantine, to whom she gave birth in our good city of York, is said to have been the daughter of an innkeeper at Libyssa.

more especially those of the middle ages, are very complete. Stephanus, called the Byzantine, quoting Alexander Polyhistoris, says this site, Libyssa, is a maritime castle of Bithynia, and I have described ruins as of a castle in a position eminently maritime. Ptolemy says, "near the sea;" and Cellarius very properly deduces that from a statement of such latitude, it might be from three to four miles from the sea, if other circumstances favoured such an idea; but there are no such circumstances. Plutarch makes a very descriptive statement. "There is a place in Bithynia," says this valuable historian, "where are tumuli of sand, and a certain village of no great size, which is called Libyssa." This description does apply itself partially to Harakah, but not at all to Geybuseh. The account, however, of tumuli of sand appears to be an addition concerning the tumulus, over which, according to others, the sand was drifted, or refers to little heaps of drift-sand piled up in the bay. Pliny the Younger, who was long prefect of Nicomedia, records that the grave of Hannibal is marked by a tumulus.

Among other curious statements is one made by Appianus Alexandrinus, who says that Libyssa is neither a town nor a village, but a river, from which the neighbouring district is named; this does not certify that if a village sprang up, it might not be called after the river or district; and at Harakah there is a rivulet, at Geybuseh there is none. Eutropius describes Hannibal as being buried *near* Libyssa, and on the confines of the district of Nicomedia.

Libyssa is so written by all authorities, except by Ptolemy, who spells it Libissa. The Jerusalem Itinerary, in alluding to this place, swells up the titles of the Carthaginian hero to an amplitude which goes in advance of the truth.

Ibi positus est Rex Annibalianus qui fuit Afrorum.

The resting-place of a body, in which was enshrined a spirit so briefly successful, and so long unfortunate, is truly full of interest. The circumstances of the death of Hannibal are involved in the same melancholy sadness as the history of his whole life. A modern French author, poet, and politician,—who cannot view Hannibal but as "an East India Company's General," carrying on a mercantile campaign,—"a brilliant and heroic operation of commerce on the plains of Thrasymene,"—still contemplates the death of the Carthaginian as pathetic; and complacently remarks, that it reconciles him to his triumphs.

But how much deeper is the interest felt in the fate of such a man, by those who view him in the light of one who was engaged in combating, not for the liberty of his country only, but for that of the whole world; whose genius made a small centre of industry, the enemy all but triumphant of the most potent republic that ever existed; and who died, still stirring up the spirit of the East to resist a tyranny which at that moment threatened to overwhelm the whole world. "History," says Heeren, "in relating the incredible ill-treatment experienced by Carthage previous to her fall, appears to have wished to offer to people, who can appreciate it, an example of what they may expect from the domination of a powerful republic."

It is well known, that when the policy of Rome succeeded in effecting the disgrace of Hannibal, that, firm to his original principles, and attached even in misfortune to the real interests of his country, he repaired to the court of Antiochus the Great, and urged that monarch to carry war into the interior of Italy itself. "How fortunate for Rome," says another philosophical historian, "that two such men as Hannibal and Antiochus could not agree!"

When this last opportunity of redeeming the liberty of the world was lost, Hannibal, still resolute in attempting something for the falling nations of the East and West, repaired to the court of Prusias II., who reigned at Nicomedia, and engaged that king as a last resource in a war with Eumenes II., king of Pegamus, and an ally of the Romans. But the paltry monarch of the Bithynian forests, awed by the power of Rome, or jealous of the abilities of his guest, treacherously intended to give him up; when, without a home, betrayed by those whose cause he had espoused, and with the prospect around him of the proximate subjugation of the whole of the civilized world, Hannibal withdrew himself from a no longer useful existence by a self-inflicted and miserable death*.

It is difficult not to conceive, that as Lesser Asia promises to become a country which will be much frequented by travellers and tourists, more especially such

* The battle of Magnesia decided the fate of the old nations of the Asiatic peninsula, and acquired to the Romans all of Asia on this side of Taurus. Eumenes, in return for his friendship for the Romans, had large possessions added to his kingdom, but these were soon afterwards given up by Attalus, and reduced to a Roman province, under the name of Asia.

as are prepared by study and reading to enjoy and appreciate the scenery and the never-fading reminiscences which belong to these once favoured lands, that there will be many like ourselves, to whom a knowledge of the facts by which to guide themselves to so interesting a spot as the tomb of Hannibal will be acceptable; and who may rejoice in an excuse which will enable them to spend a few pensive hours by the ever-glorious and brilliant shores of the Propontis—moments which will not be less hallowed if passed over a grave which contains all that remains, save a virtuous memory, of "I, the conqueror of Spain and Gaul, and not only of the Alpine nations, but, which is greater yet, of the Alps themselves" (Hannibal to his soldiers: LIVY)—"The greatest enemy to the Roman name" (PLUTARCH, Life of Lucullus)—"This tremendous Hannibal" (Scipio to the Roman army: HOOKE).

CHAPTER II.

Harakli—Heraclea Pontica.

Ismid, the ancient Nicomedia. Its present Condition. Old Canal. Village and Lake of Sabanjah. Ancient Bridge. Tradition of the Natives. Plain of Duz-cha, or Duseprum. Mohammedan horror of Pork. Visit to Uskub, the ancient Prusa ad Hypium. Mountains of the Summer Quarters. Ancient mode of felling Trees. Difficulties and Misadventures on the shores of the Black Sea. Alabli. Heraclea Pontica. Hercules' Labours. Acherusian Peninsula. Temple of Diospolin. Wolf or Sword River.

A PLEASANT ride of six hours from Harakah took us to Izmid, or Nicomedia. The intervening country is hilly, but for the most part cultivated: the scenery delightful.

Nicomedia, so long the capital of a kingdom, has been truly said to occupy a most imperial situation, both with respect to the scenery about it, and to its political and commercial advantages. It is at the head of the gulf called that of Astacus, or after the city itself, Nicomedia. There is deep water for shipping of any burthen, and a perfectly safe and secure anchorage. The town stretches along the water's edge, and rises up the verdant acclivities of a hill, the summit of which was formerly crowned by the castle of its kings. Every house has its garden, and the mixture of buildings and foliage softens the scene. The valley of the gulf is prolonged by green lawns and dreamy groves; while opposite, the bold outline of the Bithynian Olympus, now called the Gök Tagh (Cerulean or Heavenly Mountains), starts out in high relief, above the water and valley scenery.

This city was founded by Nicomedes Zypoetas, who died B.C. 281. It was twice besieged by the Osmanlis before it was taken from the Greeks. On the last occasion, the Greek governor fled to a place, called probably in derision from that event, "Lamb's Castle," whither he was pursued, and being slain, his head was held up to the affrighted inhabitants, who capitulated at once.

In its present condition Ismid is still a large town, and has a population of about 30,000 inhabitants, a port frequented by small craft for trade, and first-class frigates come here for timber for government. There is a dockyard and building-slip west of the town. The Christian residents are numerous, and the Greek Church has still its apostolical representative at this ancient see. The remains of antiquity consist chiefly of fragments, there being no perfect buildings extant. The traces of the castle, and of an aqueduct, are still evident on the hill, and monuments of antiquity are daily converted in the artisan's yard into tomb-stones for Mohammedans. A small steamer might ply between Ismid and Constantinople with great probabilities of profit.

September 22nd. We rode this day to Sabanjah, a small post-town on the lake of the same name. The country at the head of the gulf of Astacus, and between the Gök Tagh and the northern hilly districts, is at first low and level, watered by the Kizil Irmak, and cultivated with rice and melons. Further inland, are pastures diversified by hedges covered with wild vines, hops, and virgin's bower, the luxuriant creepers of these climates. On approaching the lake of Sabanjah, the northern and southern hills prolong their rocky declivities into the plain, which is thus raised above its ordinary level, and is covered at first with a low and shrubby vegetation of evergreen oaks, &c., which soon, however, attain the growth and magnitude of forest trees. Pliny the Younger, in one of his letters to Trajan, proposed to convey a canal along this line, from the lake of Sabanjah to the gulf of Astacus, where he said there were already indications of a previous attempt to dig one, and I have, since my first report to the Royal Geographical Society, and on a subsequent journey, ascertained the actual existence of an old canal bed, which in some places still contains water. Plans for the same purpose have been formed by the Osmanlis, one in 1490, as noticed by Rennell (vol. ii., p. 104); others in 1505 and 1563, are noticed by Von Hammer (*Reise Nach Bressa*, s. 171). Pliny reports that the difference of the levels between the lake Sophon (Sabanjah) and the gulf of Nicomedia was 40 cubits, or about 58 feet; and the Turkish account is 30 liras, also about 60 feet. The lake is reported as being 35 feet above the Sangarius. Such a communication would still be of very high value, for the facilities which it would afford of conveying timber to Ismid, and from thence to the Constantinopolitan market.

Sabanjah, the Sophon of the Greeks, is a mere travelling station, full of coffee-houses and stables, of which the inhabitants vary every day, and has about 500 houses, a jami and a mesjid. We came in contact here with a young Nubian, who was in want of a place. Mr. Pulsford had a servant, a Greek of the Morea, but our party had none, and as this youth appeared willing and active, we took him into our service.

This small town is situated on a most beautiful site, adorned with plane-trees of gigantic dimensions, and surrounded by most inviting lake and forest scenery. There are many remnants of the Byzantine era. Fragments of columns, cornices, and architraves, highly wrought and profusely ornamented, are scattered about in the streets and the adjoining groves.

In the evening, we went and sat on the shady borders of the lake, which is upwards of eight miles in length by four in width, and of an oval form. At some seasons of the year, it is said to overflow, and pour its waters into the gulf of Astacus; but there is a constant communication between it and the Sangarius by a rivulet called Kilis. The lake has but few pretensions to beauty; the hills to the north are low; on which side there is also little woodland and few villages, nor even any rocky scenery, to give relief to the shores; but to the south, woods of noble growth and extent rise from the water's edge to at least 1000 feet above its level. The sides and summits of these hills are covered with a noble expanse of forest trees, of different tints and varied forms and foliage.

September 23*rd.* We travelled at first along the banks of the lake, and thence across plains, in part cultivated. About twelve miles from Sabanjah we came to the almost perfect remains of a handsome bridge of seven arches, 1087 feet in length, and carried over an old bed of the Sangarius, from which a small stream still finds its way along the valley to the north. The Sangarius, or Sakkariyeh, as it is now called, which flows in the neighbourhood, appears to have had its ancient bed here, and this to have been the bridge over it. The traditions of the natives favour this idea, which is substantiated by physical appearances, as well as by the remains of the bridge, now called Mahamah, and of a causeway contiguous to it.

Mr. Rassam obtained from the natives a tradition in verse, which relates that a dervish coming to the bridge was required to pay toll, which he refused to do, on the principle that he was by the rules of his order forbidden to carry money about him. The collector was, however, like most of his race, inexorable, and the dervish, incapable of proceeding on his journey, prayed that God would change the bed of the river, that taxes might no longer be collected at the bridge. His prayers were heard, and since then, the Sakkariyeh deserted its old bed.

While examining the environs of the old bridge, I lost my way, and following one too much to the east, got some distance beyond the present bridge on the Sakkariyeh, before I found out my error. I had then to retrace my steps, and succeeded in finding the remainder of the party there, who had been detained by my non-appearance. The present bridge is a wooden structure. The river is here 372 feet wide, with an average depth of two feet, and a rate of about three miles an hour. It is liable, however, to considerable rises.

From the river the road is carried through luxuriant orchards, which terminate in a marshy land, with a sluggish stream; and, although there is a wooden causeway, of nearly a mile in length, this place is scarcely passable at some seasons of the year. I have seen bullocks drawing timber-waggons through this marsh, up to their middle in mire, and the efforts by which they extricated the waggons were almost incredible. There is a great deal of fever in such a spot. At a guard-house, situated on the confines of the marsh, all the inmates were labouring under malaria. I prescribed for them at the time, little expecting to visit them again the next year. Such, however, was my fate, when I found them labouring under the same persistent malady. They said on this occasion that they scarcely knew any relief from it.

A little beyond the country improves, and low hills lead the way to the wooded heights of Khandak, which place we reached the same evening, and were lodged in an empty room over the entrance of a kerwanserai.

Khandak (a Foss or Ditch) is not improperly so called, as a little rivulet of clear water flows down the principal and only street in the place. It is a mere posting village in the forest, containing about 200 houses, and a jami. There are few remains of antiquity, but occasional fragments of columns and antique hewn stones are to be seen, sufficient to attest a former station. In the evening, we took a walk in the forest, in search of game, but did not find any. At night we fixed our instruments in an open space, near the jami, and were soon surrounded by a crowd of persons, curious to know why we were looking at the stars and taking time. They were, however, respectful, and put us to no inconvenience.

September 25*th*. We left Khandak by a circuitous route through forests of oak and beech, and after a ride of nearly four hours, came to the plain of Duseprum, now Duz-cha, about twelve miles in length by six in width. This place surpasses all the others in Bithynia, or perhaps in Asia Minor, in beauty. It is shut up on all sides, and completely surrounded by hills, which are clad from foot to summit with forest trees of various foliage. Below, it is also everywhere verdant with green sward, ferns, shrubs, or trees: not an inch of the plain but what is fertile, and yet but few spots are cultivated. Indeed no portion of this neglected country suggests such painful regrets as this place, so favoured by nature, and so disregarded by man.

The posting village of Duz-cha contains hardly more than twenty houses: numbers of columns, and other fragments of Byzantine architecture, are met with around: the capital of a column, which forms the head of a well, near the menzil-khan, is ornamented with well-sculptured doves, encircled by wreaths. Duseprum, like many others, is a site without a history.

A ridiculous circumstance occurred here, which, however trivial in appearance, had nigh been productive of serious consequences to us. Mr. Russell and myself had gone, while the horses were loading in the morning, to measure a base, in order to determine the height of the surrounding hills, when we were alarmed by a violent altercation. It appeared that while loading the horses, an unfortunate ham had fallen to the ground, and so scandalized were the Osmanlis at this appropriation of their steeds, to carry desecrated food, that they positively refused to let them go with us, and the seruji, or driver, to stir a step. It was only with great difficulty that they were pacified, and we hastened to get rid, as quick as possible, of the abhorred pig's flesh.

September 26th. We travelled across the plain by a circuitous road, fording the Milan Su, to Eski Bagh, or Uskub, about four miles from Duseprum. We found this place to have been once the site of a considerable town, part of which is still contained within a strong circular wall, round the hill, and in tolerable preservation, while the remainder was *extra muros:* to the south, and upon the hill, was also an aqueduct, but of modern construction. The modern village is for the most part within the old walls, and many of the streets are approached by narrow gateways, evidently belonging to a style of building which is generally designated as

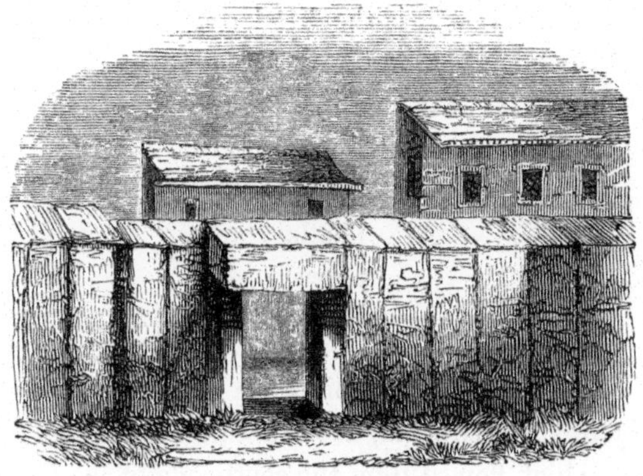

Pelasgian Gateway.

Pelasgian, or Cyclopean. The slab over one of these massive gateways was twelve feet long, and eight and three in thickness.

Excavations had been carried on in some sort of outwork or temple, where was an inscription, on a stone which appeared to have been the basis of a statue. All that was legible was

ΑΝΤΙΝΩ
ΘΑΛΛΩΛ
ΚΛΑΡΙΣΗ
ΑΝΕΣΤΗΕ

It is only a sepulchral monument to some obscure individual, but possesses an interest in determining the former inhabitants of this site. The Reverend Dr. Wait on reading this inscription, remarked truly that it may be classed among the *monumenta sequioris ævi.* From many examples, he says, "I know Antony to be intended. And the occurrence of Clarissa with one sigma betrays a modern date. The Lambda, which follows the Omega in *ΘΑΛΛΩ*, is the first letter of an obliteration, which, if capable of restoration, might have determined whose daughter or wife this Clarissa was.

The words are

To Antony
Thallus
Clarissa
Erected:

On leaving Prusa ad Hypium we found further ruins in a very dilapidated state, about a mile up the banks of a rivulet, which flowed from the south side of the Chileh Tagh or Yaila Tagh (Hills of Summer Pasture).

The ascent and passage of these forest-clad hills was rendered difficult from late severe rains. The mud was very deep, the labour to the horses excessive. We soon met two kawasses who had crossed the hills, but both the steeds and their riders had been thrown in the mud, and presented an uninviting appearance. This did not promise well for us who had baggage horses, but we ultimately, and after several hours' toil, got over without any accident, and only a few tumbles.

It was interesting to us to observe in these forests, in practice in the present day, the very same usages as were noticed by Xenophon centuries ago: trees being still, as then, fired at their base and then felled; while small waggons, yoked with male buffaloes, came from the shore to carry away the timber. There are no huts in the forest, and the driver sleeps in his cloak till his work is done; and the carts are so constructed that, although the roads are almost as bad as roads can be, the slope may become excessive without causing the vehicle to fall over. The forest trees were chiefly beech and oak.

So difficult was our ride that it had been dark some time ere we began to ford the Uskubli Su, which we did several times, as we rode along its course, before we reached the port designated as Chuvalli Iskeleh-si (Baystairs), and which consisted of a long range of wooden houses, with a beach upon which small coasting vessels are drawn up. A mile beyond this we came to Akchah Shehr (Money Town), the residence of an ayyan, and with slips for repairing or building small craft. We were lodged here in a tolerable house on the sea-shore, which was fortunate, as it came on to rain hard with a strong north wind for the next two days, by which we were detained in this solitary place without the chance of removal. They were building a small brig at the time of our visit, and there was also a Greek boat from Varna, loaded with dried beef, drawn up on shore. The journey from Uskub to Akchah Shehr occupied us nine hours.

September 29th. We took advantage of a momentary cessation of rain after mid-day, to start along the coast, passing the river of Uskubli, now much swollen. We then ascended a wooded hill by a narrow pathway, our horses slipping, and our heads striking against the trees, which also formed at times so great an obstacle to the baggage horses that we were obliged to unload and load them again. We descended to the valley of Ak Su (White Water), also much swollen; and turned up this, to where we gained a village called Ak Kaya Keuy (Village of the White Rock). The inhabitants of the place spoke Turkish, but had nothing of the Osmanli character about them, and appeared to be descended from a different race of people, probably some of the older tenants of the country.

September 30th. We started early in the morning, the day cloudy, with rain, and a strong wind from the north, bringing in the sea very high upon the coast. We first ascended a forest-clad hill, with steep and slippery clayey road, much obstructed by branches of trees, and climbing plants. The number of goat-suckers in these woods is very great; we disturbed one at almost every step. We afterwards forded the Kojaman Su (Old Man's River); we then crossed another small stream, and, a little beyond this, the road continuing along the sea-shore, we had to ascend the side of a clayey cliff, by a path so narrow that the first loaded horse that attempted it rolled over, but was saved without hurt. We were thus obliged to unload and all lend a hand in carrying the baggage on our backs, for some distance; this delayed us about two hours. Shortly afterwards we again descended to the foot of the cliffs, where the heavy swell of the sea rendered our progress very insecure. At length, in attempting to get round a rocky point, two baggage horses, one belonging to Mr. Pulsford, which we made always go first so as to be at hand to give assistance, and Mr. P.'s servant and horse, were overthrown by the sea. Mr. Russell and myself, disembarrassing ourselves of our coats, took to the water, and, after much trouble, succeeded in rescuing horses and baggage. The man got out himself. We were all, however, tumbled and thrown with great violence, sometimes upon the horses and the horses sometimes upon us.

As it was impossible to double the point in the present state of the sea, we were forced to put back again, but the horses being now fatigued and broken-spirited, did not effect their return so well as they started, and Mr. Pulsford's baggage horse, in fording the Kojaman Su, was carried away by the stream, and only saved from going out to sea by stranding upon the bar, at the mouth of the river. Mr. P. was, during these occurrences, looking on with great apparent indifference, and, as Mr. Russell's and my clothes were already well saturated, and we were very cold, we did not feel inclined to venture to the rescue again. At length the poor beast was delivered from its perilous situation, by two hardy countrymen, who came to our assistance.

We afterwards repaired to the kind Aborigines, of the village of the white rock, and found no want of wood to dry ourselves and our baggage. But our poor Nubian, whose constitution nor clothing were neither of them adapted to such exposure and such severe weather, fell very ill with malaria, and after stopping all next day vainly attempting to bring him round, so far as to give him strength even to get to Heraclea, where we intended staying a few days, we were obliged to leave him behind, with sufficient money to keep him till his recovery, and find his way back. The second day of our detention a messenger came from the ayyan of Akchah Shehr, who had heard of our misfortunes, requesting us to return to that place, but we were determined to persevere, as indeed there was no other road, except by recrossing the Yaila Tagh.

October 2nd. The weather had cleared up and the wind fell during the night, and we started with the early morning. The Kojaman Su had fallen half a foot since the preceding day, and we got, without difficulty, round the prominent cliff, which had discomfited us on the previous journey. Beyond this we came to a large river called Kokalah, and we were a long time before we could find a spot at which it could be forded. The river flowed through a beautiful well-wooded vale, but without habitations.

Our road throughout lay over a country of similar character, hilly and covered with wood. The trees were beech, chestnut, oak, and pistachio, with a beautiful undergrowth of rhododendrons, oleander, myrtle, daphne, box, cistus, &c. Nearer to the sea were more naked valleys of heath and fern. Goat-suckers continued to flit from beneath the shadowy glades, quails sprang from the heaths and grass. We feasted ourselves upon abundant chestnuts. In fine weather these luxuriant forests must be very agreeable.

As we approached the valley of the Alabli Su, the country opened and the prospect became more extensive; to the south the lofty and wooded mountains of the Yaila Tagh terminate the view, to the east a succession of hills rise up with the course of the Lycus, as far as to the pine-clad and trachytic summits of the Kara Tagh, while, to the north-east, the peninsula of Posideum with its light-house, and the walls and towers of Heraclea, lying in the shore of a calm and well-protected bay, shade off well, the wide landscape of forest and mountain, into an equally far-stretching expanse of sea.

We descended to the Alabli Su, the ancient Elæus, a small river which is crossed by a wooden bridge in so bad a state of repair that the horses had to be forded, and we then entered into Alabli, a fishing village, and port for small coasters, with not more than fifty houses, but with a residence of an ayyan of much greater pretensions. In this we were at once hospitably and kindly received for the night, the old ayyan himself paying us a visit in the evening to see that all was comfortable, and to smoke a pipe of peace.

October 3rd. The ayyan could not provide us with horses, so that, although I was anxious not to lose any distance, whether by travelling by night or by water, which would cause an hiatus in the geological recognition of the country that we travelled over, we had on the present occasion no alternative left but to get on in a boat. Starting early in the morning, before the wind got up, we soon doubled the headland called Chingal Burnu (Hook Point), and passing the mouth of the

Kilij (Sword River, the ancient Lycus), we brought to beneath the walls of Harakli before mid-day, but it was evening before, after waiting upon the governor, the researches of the kawasses had obtained for us a domicile in the Christian quarter of the town.

Heraclea, surnamed Pontica, if not the greatest, has always been one of the most remarkable, cities of Bithynia. It was one of those antique colonies, founded by the Ante-Hellenic Greeks, which were destined to bring a new order of things into the primitive countries in which they were established. It certainly was a curious spectacle, at the first breaking up of the great nations, then only first assembled in the land which was to be for a time mistress of the world, to see the Dorians allied to the Etolians, and led only by the Heraclides, take possession of the Peloponnesus, and found colonies all along the coasts of Lesser Asia, the Propontis, and the Black Sea, without regard to the original possessors of the soil—in independence and in firm reliance on their own strength—and bring them to a degree of power and prosperity which was unknown to any of the towns or cities belonging to the native chieftains.

We spent four days at this place, engaged in astronomical observations, in making a plan of the city, and in examining the ruins.

The present town occupies only the south-west corner of the extent of the former city, and contains 250 houses of Mohammedans, and 40 houses of Greek Christians, who have a church and attached school. According to Mr. Rassam, who took great pains to ascertain its present name, it is called Harakli, which is corrupted by ignorant boatmen and serujis (muleteers) into Eregli, as the port or harbour is generally designated Bend Eregli.

The walls of the town extend along the sea shore, then ascend a hill which they about divide in half, up to its highest point, where they encircle the ruins of an acropolis, having a Greek inscription of the Byzantine era in front. The wall then returns along the side of the valley called Tabanah Derehsi, which has a small rivulet in its centre, flowing into the sea immediately beyond their south-west extremity. These walls are in a ruinous condition, and constructed chiefly from the remains of older ramparts. There occur in them numerous fragments of columns, hewn stones with crosses, cornices, and tablets, with Greek inscriptions, showing that they were erected since the Byzantine era.

In that part of the wall which fronts the sea there are the remains of another and outer wall, which is chiefly composed of vast irregular masses of basalt and limestone, cemented by mortar. This wall contains no fragments of Byzantine architecture. It probably, therefore, defended the city anterior to that period, and the encroachment of the sea necessitated that when rebuilt, it should be built further inland. Connected with the outer wall are the remains of a long and rude mole, which advances from its northern end into the sea.

The present wall only extends, we have previously observed, half the length of the hill, which is bounded to the south by the Tabanah Derehsi, and to the north by the valley of the Gawur Irmak (Infidel River). But there are traces of a double wall, which was prolonged to the northern extremity of the same hill as far as to the borders of the valley of Gawur Irmak.

In the space included within this more ancient portion of Heraclea are more particularly to be observed, what appear to be the remains of a Roman temple; and several beautiful tessellated pavements are also to be seen.

The valley of the Gawur Irmak, a mere brook, appears once to have been filled by the waters of the sea, and the harbour for galleys so formed, was defended by towers of very strong construction.

As this is the most ancient part of Heraclea, we have probably here, the key to one of the poetically described labours of Hercules, who, if he wrought at the improvement of this ancient city, could not have done a more serviceable act than to dig a place of refuge for the galleys of those periods of early navigation. Such an operation may not without justice, be described as digging Cerberus from the depths below. Xenophon, who notices this as the locality of the tradition, writes it as if Hercules had reduced or subjected the animal, which would give the idea of rendering the port safe by the construction of another, but most of the ancients view it in the other light. Pomponius Mela says, "And there he extracted or drew forth Cerberus." Eustathius also, "He extracted or drew out Cerberus from the infernal regions." It is probable, in this and in other cases, if such is a correct view of this mythological tradition, that the early progress of civilization, as obscured in the fabulous history of the Greeks, would admit of gradual elucidation, by the extension of topographical knowledge more than by unassisted classical studies.

Beyond this antique harbour, which may thus be traced back to the times of Hercules, is a hill and promontory, now called Chase Teppeh, formerly the Acherusian peninsula. It rises immediately above the valley of the Gawur Irmak, and hence Hercules' labours were said to be on that peninsula itself. At its foot, and on the inner side, is a modern gun battery, and on its summit an insufficient light-house, around which are a few cottagers' houses, whose inhabitants are exempted from taxes upon the condition of keeping a lamp burning before mirrors which they suffer to be darkened with accumulated soot.

On the south side of Heraclea, beyond the valley called Tabanah Derehsi, and between it and the valley of the Kilij Irmak, is a low rounded hill, now almost covered with the grave-stones of Mohammedans; in the centre of which are traces of a former edifice which appears to have been the temple of Diospolin, noticed by old writers as occupying such a situation.

Beyond this, and at the bottom of the bay of Heraclea, is the embouchure of the Lycus,

Huc Lycus, huc Sagaris.

Ovid, Lib. iv., Epist. x., vers. 47.

The name of Wolf river was, as in other cases, given to this stream from its sudden risings and impetuosity. The modern name, Kilij Irmak (Sword River), has reference to the same character.

It is recorded by Apollodorus that the Argonauts were kindly received at Heraclea by a King Lycus, which probably means that their galleys were sheltered in this river, for it is not likely that Lycus was the name of a king, afterwards given to the river, especially as the modern name has a somewhat similar signification, and both have an origin in the long-enduring features of nature.

CHAPTER III.

The Hero's Stone.

The Hero's Stone. Pass of Blessings. Aspect of Country. Ascent of the Kara Tagh (Black Mountains). Valley of the Filiyas, or Billæus. Endemic Character of the Plague. Ruins of Stations and Guard-houses. Roman Road. Great Plane-tree. Ruins of Tium. Rivers of Bartan. Inscription and Sculptures. Tomb of Queen Amastria. Description of the Town, and origin of Amaserah, the ancient Amastrius.

On the afternoon of October 8th we started up the valley of the Lycus, our road lying at first along a causeway paved with slabs of sandstone, from two to eight feet in length and from one to two in width; this evidently was a work of olden times.

About five and a-half miles from Heraclea, we fell in on the road side with a monument of large hewn stones of an oblong form and hollow within. It was situated upon an eminence, near which was a small grove of pine-trees; beyond to the right a village; and farther to the left, higher hills. It had all the characters of a sepulchral monument, and from its extreme massiveness and great simplicity of structure, appeared to us all to belong to a very remote era. In the present day it is known by tradition only, as the Kochak Tash (the Hero's Stone or Monument).

Three miles beyond this, we came to where the river forced its way through rocks of sandstone, rising with nearly vertical precipices, over which numerous streamlets of water poured from the hills above. This pass is called Barakatlar (the Pass of Blessings), it being a duty with the Mohammedan to bless difficulties, which too many of our countrymen would curse.

Immediately beyond the pass, a large mass of rock ninety feet high and overgrown with wood, except in its most precipitous sides, has become islanded in the centre of the stream, and constitutes a singular and picturesque object. It rained hard all the afternoon, and we were not able to get farther than the village of Yal-chilar (of Masons), about twelve miles from Harakli, not far from which, in the forest to the north, are some cliffs with hewn sepulchral caverns, and now called Bal Kayasi (the Cliff of the Rock).

October 9th. It rained in torrents all night, and the Lycus rose nearly four feet, overflowing great part of the plain, which had now assumed the appearance of a lake covered with trunks of trees and drifted wood. It is, evidently, from these sudden and rapid rises, that this river obtained its ancient and modern names. The Pass of Blessings was no longer practicable.

We started near mid-day, during a momentary

cessation of rain, and were soon turned out of our path by the river side, and obliged to ascend the hills. After an hour's journey through a picturesque country, we arrived at a point where the river made a considerable bend, beyond which we crossed by a wooden bridge, and arrived at the foot of hills, which we ascended till we came to a small village, called Yaila (Summer-Quarters), from whence we had a commanding view of the Lycus, flowing at first through a rocky country, and then through a fertile valley backed by the hills of Ovah Tagh (Mount of the Plain), which were partly wooded and partly composed of white rocky cliffs.

To the south, the country consisted of alternate valleys and rounded hills, on one of which a spot was pointed out, said to contain an old iron mine. We continued along its crest for some time, then skirted round another hill, descending gradually again to the valley of the Lycus, on the banks of which we found a village of only four houses, one of which was luckily empty, and this we took possession of as a refuge from the rain that poured all night.

The next day our road still lay up the valley of the Lycus, which we again crossed by a wooden bridge, above which are the remains of an older construction in stone; we were now again on the right bank. The path we followed was carried along the acclivities of wooded hills.

After a journey of eleven miles up the same valley, during which the horses suffered much from the slippery state of the pathway, we began the ascent of the Kara Tagh (Black Mountains), at a point where two tributaries effected their junction, and near an untenanted khan situated in the midst of an orchard, and where we fed *ad libitum* on fruit that appeared to have no owner.

The ascent lasted nearly an hour, when we attained the crest of the hills, near the village of Kara-bunar (the Black Spring). The barometer indicated an elevation of 1500 feet, and the mountains around did not rise more than 500 feet above this point. The view from the summit was varied and extensive, and carried the eye down the Kara Dereh (Black Valley), and over the hilly country of Pershembah, to the valleys of the Filiyas and Bartan rivers, with the intervening district of Kol Bazar, and was only limited by the lofty and bold alpine summits of the Kaya Dibbah and the mountains and wooded outline of the Ich-el-ler and Yaila mountains.

We descended the so-called Black Valley, and then turned out of the road to the south, to the village of Bash Boghaz (Head of the Pass), situated at the foot of the Ipsili Tagh, probably from the Greek Hypsile, a spur of the Kara Tagh, and where there are said to be ruins of a castle. We were received, in the ayyan's absence, in his house; but he made his appearance in the evening, and came to smoke the usual pipe of introduction and acquaintanceship.

October 11*th*. Having procured, this morning, change of horses, which had to be collected from the pastures and distant farms, we started again down the Black Valley, which we left before mid-day, at an assemblage of uninhabited buildings used as a market once a week, and called Beg Jumah-si (Bey's Friday Market). Hence we ascended by a gentle acclivity to the residence of the ayyan of the district of Penj-shenbeh (Four days' Market). This was rather a showy place at a distance, from its white-washed jami, and large agha's mansion, but scarcely contained thirty dwelling-houses.

We did not stop here, but travelled onwards over low hills covered with underwood of deciduous oak and juniper, stopping a short time, as it was fine, to get a meridian altitude of the sun. We then descended into a deep valley, where we refreshed ourselves with wild grapes, which grew luxuriantly, supported by the aged trees around. We ascended again through a wood, and passing two or three small villages, came to the open valley of Abd Allah Pasha Derehsi, so called from a tomb with sepulchral chapel bearing that name, and which is at the point where the Black Valley terminates in that of the Filiyas.

After about an hour's ride along the vale, we came to this latter river, which we found to be a noble stream divided at this point into five different channels, separated by islands of pebbles, in some places covered with plane, sycamore, tamarisk, and oleander, but in others stony and naked. The occasional floods of the river, to judge from its bed, upwards of half a mile in width, must be very great*, but it is soon confined in one channel; and at Tium, where it empties itself into the sea, although deep, is only about a hundred yards in width.

The beautiful valley of the Filiyas, the ancient Billæus, was crowded with villages, and the views on every side varied and extensive. The river is seen flowing in nearly a straight line from where it issues from

* It was not known previous to this journey, that this important river was the receptacle of the rivers of Tcherkesh, of Hamamli or Bayandir, of Araj, and of Zafaran Boli, as well as of that of Boli, a comparatively insignificant stream.

the gloomy forests that stretch along the foot of the Yaila or Boli Tagh. To the east is a hilly country, either cultivated or covered with wood, and interspersed with villages belonging to a second Pershembah district, where the plague was at this time raging. Our road lay down the left bank of the river, to Charshembah (Wednesday Market), the chief place of another kazilik, or jurisdiction, and surrounded by well-cultivated fields of alluvial soil. Several persons, and among others, the son of the ayyan, who visited us in the course of the afternoon, were just recovering from the effects of the plague, and were in dismally low spirits.

The local origin and circumscribed developement of this malady, among the villages of Asia Minor, tend to show that it has become endemic in the country. As typhus fever and Asiatic cholera came to Western Europe—as travelling and epidemic, if not contagious disorders—and have remained there ever since, exhibiting themselves in sporadic or endemic forms, so the plague is now in Egypt, Syria, and Lesser Asia, a disease which often springs up from local causes, more especially, as may be often seen from epidemics among cattle, when the afflicted villages are full of carcases that are never removed by the peasants. We had many examples of the local prevalence of this disorder in the course of our travels; as here, in the Haimaneh, at Samsun, and in Armenia. It appears also to dwell with great pertinacity along the course and in the deep valleys of rivers, as in this case, where the disease lasted so long as actually to awaken the attention of the Osmanli authorities at Zafaran Boli, and an European medical officer was sent to ascertain the extent of the malady. Mr. Thomson, of the British legation of Persia, found the same disease raging locally in a journey he made along the banks of the river of Batum.

October 12*th*. We changed horses at Charshembah, and proceeded down the valley of the Filiyas, cultivated, or covered with sycamore or tamarisk. On both sides of this beautiful vale rose up hills of limestone, to a height of from 600 to 700 feet, densely clad with forest trees of various foliage, with cottages seen peeping here and there from among the trees.

Hemp is much cultivated both on the islands and on the banks of the river.

At a point where the river, after making a long bend, approaches the hills on its left bank, we found a small village called Chaye Keuy, which was built in part upon a mound of ruins, and there were also many large hewn stones, which make it likely that this was formerly a station on the great Roman road which followed the line of the valley of the Billæus.

At Golmekchi-ler (the Village of Potters), with about thirty houses, built upon an ancient site and artificial mound by the river side, we also found many fragments of large hewn stones and marble columns, and our road continued over what was evidently the remains of an ancient causeway.

A short way from the latter place, a dyke of basaltic rocks advances from the hills to the left, to the border of the river, narrowing its bed considerably, and thus forming a kind of defile. Here are the remains of a former gateway, and close to it a mound of ruins, overgrown with underwood, which may have been an attached guard-house.

The great road, the indication of which is thus preserved, by means of stations or villages, and of gateways and guard-houses, extended from Tium by Claudianopolis, in the valley of the Parthenius, as far as to Ancyra; and the details of this road have been preserved in the Antonine Itinerary. It is curious that this great road lies through what has been hitherto a very unfrequented and quite misunderstood part of the Asiatic peninsula, but which presents great advantages to the movements of an army in its natural facilities, its population and fertility, and its long hoarded resources *.

Not far from the gateway previously described was a noble plane-tree which measured eight yards round its trunk, in a perfectly healthy condition, and still more remarkable for its loftiness, and symmetrical form, than even for its dimensions.

The river winding round about two miles, tnrns suddenly to the west before reaching the sea, washing the foot of a hill, which bears a castellated structure of considerable size, and various architecture, and which

* Mr. Russell, in a *Memoir on the Defences of Asia Minor*, published in the *United Service Journal*, very properly notices the north-east end of the Bosphorus and the mouth of the Billæus as almost the only two points which offer comparatively easy access to the interior, in that portion of Asia Minor. It is true, as Mr. R. remarks, that Heraclea has been the scene of invasion and conquest, and it still remains a point of ingress, but the natural obstacles of bog, woodland, and hills, and the want of roads, render that line a very difficult one. Indeed, Mr. R. himself admits—"the importance of Heraclea, or *Harakli*, was, and has doubtless been, owing to the excellence of its harbour,—that of Tium; or, to speak in the phrase of modern geography, the mouth of the Filiyas,—and to the easy access afforded from thence to the interior."

announces itself as the castle of Tium. Below this, and close to the river, is the little village and harbour called Jaferji Oghlu. There were here several vessels of small burthen.

Crossing over the hill, we passed by an ancient gateway and entered upon the picturesque ruins of Tium, beyond which, after passing a large village (Beglarun Keuy), we came to a second, called Hisar Anlu (the Village attached to the Castle), and the residence of an ayyan, who assigned us a house for the night, and soon afterwards paid us a visit, the sole object of which was to obtain the common spirit of the country (araki) from us; nor did he attempt to hide his vexation and disappointment when he found that we had none.

We walked the same evening to the site of Tium, by an ancient causeway, hedged in on both sides by bay-trees, probably sprung from older roots, as such plantations are rarely, if ever, to be met with among the Mohammedans, but occur on ancient roads, as on that from Antioch to Daphne.

Passing over the walls, we found everything covered with a dense and almost impenetrable shrubbery, out of which every footstep turned up something curious and interesting, while above all rose here and there fragments of pillars, pilasters and buildings, and at wider intervals massive piles of greater pretensions.

This ancient city occupied a splendid situation, stretching along the coast, and rising in successive terraces, backed by low but picturesque heights, in the wooded recesses of which are the numerous mansions of the dead; while the castle is perched upon a promontory that juts out into the sea, towering over the depths of the Billæus on the one side, and encircling in its embrace the sculptured beauties of the city on the other.

The most remarkable remains still existing are an ancient temple of pleasing form and proportions, but now an ivy and shrub-clad ruin. An extensive palace occupied the high ground, and had an open platform and terrace in front of it, which descended in steps to the city.

We found a small but nearly perfect amphitheatre in the south-east part of the ruins, buried under a profusion of shrubs and trees. A few arches of an aqueduct also remain upright. The walls can be distinctly traced, as well as several gateways, portions of which, composed of massive hewn stones, still remain erect. Fragments of more common edifices rise up everywhere, amidst the dense and variegated foliage.

The castle is a vast, irregular pile of building, belonging to various ages, and possessing neither the simplicity nor effective beauty of the Greek monuments below. The tombs at Tium are curious, as being only hemi-sarcophagi; the lid is perfect, and has a Byzantine character, being very large, with raised corners, while the body is made *in sitû*, not of hewn stone, but merely of pieces of pink-coloured and slaty limestone.

We spent the evening and the next morning in examining these ruins, and laying down a plan of the place, and we left it with regret, for it is a spot, where not only the antiquarian or archæologist, but the simple lover of natural beauty, would delight to spend a month.

The history of this little gem of the Euxine is almost unknown. It was originally an Ionian colony, one of the Greek families, who appear to have carried the taste for the fine arts into their smallest possessions. Philotærus, from whom sprang the race of Attalian kings, was born here. It was also much favoured by the Romans, and it was made to contribute to the embellishment of Amastrius.

About mid-day we were ferried over the Filiyas. Our road lay over the delta of alluvium deposited by the river. It was, as usual, full of lagoons and marshes, amid which we lost our way; some of the horses got bogged, and we had much trouble to extricate them.

We at length reached the borders of a forest, and began to ascend. We were now in the district of Kol Bazar, but there were few villages; and in the evening, after travelling about sixteen and a half miles, the latter part always over a hilly, thickly wooded country, we arrived at Kizil Elmah (Red Apple), a village prettily situated in a valley, which extended northward about three miles, as far as the sea shore. We were as usual accommodated at the house of the ayyan, who had formerly been the skipper of a coasting vessel, and was more intelligent and entertaining than the generality of these smoke-enveloped and rustic governors. The next day we continued our journey over a similar country, low, hilly, and wooded, for about nine miles, when we came to the crest of some chalk hills, from the summit of which, the valley of the Parthenius, and the town of Bartan, burst upon our view in inviting beauty. We had still a marshy plain, impassable on foot, to ride over, before we got to the town, and on our arrival there, we waited on the governor, who assigned to us quarters in the khan.

Bartan is a town little visited by Europeans, and,

till our visit, was always marked on the maps as being situated upon a single large river. It is, however, at the junction of two rivers, which, when they unite, are called Su Chati, and this is the same as the Parthenius which separated Bithynia from Paphlagonia, and was said by Strabo to be so called, from the cheerful meadows through which it flows.

> And where Parthenius rolled through banks of flowers.
>
> POPE'S *Homer's Iliad,* book ii. 1041.

There is one stone bridge over the Kojahnas, or westerly river, and a wooden one replaces another that existed formerly on the same river at the north-west end of the town. The communication over the other river, or Ordeiri, is kept up by the ferry. There were several vessels building at Bartan, some of which were upwards of one hundred tons burthen; but the port is two miles below the town, which is four hours or fifteen miles from the sea, by the river, and three hours by land.

The town of Bartan, which is the ancient Claudianopolis, also called Bithynium, has 650 houses, out of which there are eight houses of Christians, who have no church. The Mohammedans have five mosques. The houses, on account of the marshy character of the surrounding country, are all built of two stories, the upper one alone of which is inhabited. For the same reason the town is carefully paved with large limestone slabs, better so than any Turkish town I have seen. The streets extend over two low hills, and into the valley between these hills, stretching from the banks of the Kojahnas on the one side, to those of the Ordeiri on the other, and rising up the hill side again to the north of the river.

After staying a day at Bartan, we hired horses to take us to Amaserah, a distance of twelve miles, and back again the same day, leaving the luggage and servant in the khan. At starting, we crossed the Ordeiri, and then turned up a narrow valley, with a rivulet designated as the Kara Chai (Black River). The valley soon narrowed, and was nearly blocked up by cliffs, which presented a rude rocky outline with fantastic forms, and in one place a rocking stone was curiously perched upon an isolated pinnacle.

We now began to ascend wooded hills, and continued along these till we came within view of the sea, when we turned to the east, by a steep descent, with steps hewn out of the solid rock. This is the only approach to Amaserah from the land side, and a remarkably difficult one, and it would have required little sagacity in a country where public spirit in the way of internal improvement is so exceedingly rare as in Turkey, to determine that this road hewn out of the rock, had been executed by another nation of workmen; but it was not long before we came to a small niche in the rock, destined apparently to hold a figure, and beyond was a tablet bearing an inscription in Latin, of which we could make out a few words, as follows :—

PROTAGE NORENTI CLAUDI GERMANICI*.

A little beyond this is a tablet basement, supporting an arched frame-work, with the upright figure of a Roman

* Evidently referring to the Emperor Claudius Cæsar, who assumed the title of Germanicus, and who was thus apparently engaged in works of public utility, in opening a road between the seat of his colony, Claudianopolis, and the adjoining port of Amastrius.

in his toga, much mutilated, and his head broken off; but the attitude is graceful, and the details good.

Close by was a column and pedestal, cut in solid rock, and supporting a colossal eagle, of which also the head had been struck off. There were two other tablets, of which the inscriptions were quite illegible. The column was twelve feet high, and the statue of natural size. The base of the frame was seven feet wide, the height twelve. The eagle was four feet six inches in height.

Further on the road side was a semicircular arch, formed of one ring of solid masonry, fourteen feet by seven high, and running back fifteen feet; and half a mile beyond, upon an elevated site, and commanding the sea, were the remains of a handsome mausoleum, an oblong monument of massive structure, and apparently of great antiquity. It appeared to have contained a sarcophagus, as the lid of one, and which was not of the middle ages, was lying near. We were now approaching the city of Queen Amastria, the Semiramis of Asia Minor; might not this be her tomb? Justinian describes it as being on a hill, overlooking the city and bay: nothing could answer this description of its situation more correctly. A slope of richly verdant foliage, interspersed with tall ruins of aqueducts and other buildings stretched from the tomb down to the city, lofty trees bowed their graceful branches around and above, while the restless sea spread its wide expanse below.

This queen, who so long gave her name to this sweet spot, was a Persian by birth, and daughter of a brother of Darius, called by the Byzantines Oxyathreæ. She was given in marriage by Alexander to Craterus, who divorced her, and she was afterwards married to—or, according to Strabo, who is very ungallant upon the occasion, only tolerated by—Dionysius, tyrant or king of Heraclea. Again divorced by Lysimachus, she repaired to the present site, which she embellished at the expense of three other cities, Tium, Cytorus, and Cromna, and established as the seat of her power, calling it after her name, and styling herself queen, for Spanheimus refers to a coin with the inscription *ΑΜΑΣΤΡΙΟΣ ΒΑΣΙΛΙΣΣΗΣ*, "Queen of Amastrius."

The fate of this woman of various fortunes was melancholy. She is said to have been miserably drowned by her own sons.

Amastrius has, however, a more ancient history than that of the epoch which has for a moment arrested our attention. It is noticed by Homer, under the name of Sesamus, as existing in the time of the Trojan war, or 1200 years before Christ. Scylax called it a Greek city, and it was probably, like the neighbouring colony of Sinope, founded by the Milesians.

The modern history of Amaserah is involved in obscurity. It occupies no place in the Byzantine or Turkish annals. The character of its ruins attests that it belonged to the Genoese, and that, like Sinope and Trebizond, it was once one of their active and prosperous commercial entrepôts.

The modern town consists of only 145 houses, and has a population of about 900 souls. From its difficulty of access it is used by the Turks as a place of detention for deposed beys and governors. It is built upon a rocky peninsula that has two necks, the first formed by a lesser and greater bay of the sea; the second by a small inlet, over which a narrow causeway leads to what was formerly the castellated or military portion of the town.

The cape called Diwan Burnu (Point of the Divan), is formed of rude and nearly perpendicular rocks, which rise above the little bay to the south-west, the whole of which was formerly built in with large hewn stones, like a well kept harbour.

The bay to the east is wide and capacious, and beyond the town there is a rocky mass, which forms an untenanted island; and to the east a lesser rock is connected with the mainland, by a wall, which is now in a ruinous and dilapidated condition.

The whole of that part of the ancient and modern town which occupies the peninsula is surrounded by a wall, defended by towers, which appear to have been renewed at various times, but to have received their chief regeneration from the Genoese, whose escutcheons are over the gateways, and whose preference of utility to ornament is well exhibited by their irreverent intermingling of Gothic tracery and Byzantine wreaths amid the solid blocks of Roman architecture; and even eagles, carefully sculptured in bas-relief on slabs of white marble, are to be seen prostrate at the angles or corners of the walls which they once adorned.

The town fronts the sea to the north, in its whole extent, but owing to the advance of the bays previously described, it is joined to the mainland only by a neck of land. In this direction, or that of the coast, it is approached by a well wooded and most picturesque valley, bounded on all sides by lofty hills, covered with dense forests.

This vale is replete with ruins of various character. One of the most extensive of these is a large building of red tiles, supporting, in an unscientific manner, huge blocks of stone, and cut up by numerous irregularly disposed and irregularly formed arches. This place is called Badistan by the natives: it was approached by a handsome gateway with a semicircular arch, and appears to have been a monastery.

At the foot of the mountains, to the west, is a fragment of wall, with two tiers of arches, which belonged to an aqueduct. On the hill side are other ruins, overgrown with shrubbery, amid which they were just discernible, while the massive mausoleum, before described, stands prominent, high up on the hill side, and assists in filling up a picture such as Asia Minor is almost unrivalled in producing, and in which monuments of bygone times, belonging to varied epochs and people, are gathered together in the same little centre of unchanging beauty.

Tomb of Amastria.

CHAPTER IV.

Zafaran Boli—Flaviopolis.

The Hollow Rock. Mountain Pass. Mesjid in the Forest. Baggage in Arrear. Turkish Hospitality. Ascent of the Orminius. Sclavonian Mountaineers. Town of Zafaran Boli. Church of St. Stephen. Empress Theodora. Environs of Zafaran Boli. Injustice to a Greek Boy. Osmanli misrule.

We quitted Bartan on the 18th of October, and pursued our journey, travelling up the course of the Ordeiri in a south-easterly direction. A rugged and mountainous district, that of the Kaya Dibbah (Hollow Rock), lay to our left; in this little alpine and picturesque group of hills a total difference is observed, from the generally tame outline of the Bithynian Olympus.

The same craggy steeps extend by the Kara Kaya (Black Rock), another lofty precipice, as far as to the Durnah Yailasi, in a south-easterly direction, while they are united to the Orminius to the south, by a lofty range with rounded outline, and wooded acclivities, named

I'ch-il-ler Tagh, and which attained, by our admeasurements, an elevation of 1966 feet above the plain of the river.

The Ordeiri forces its way through a pass in this latter range, which we reached after a ride of four hours and a half. The mountains were clad on each side to the summit, with a dense vegetation of forest-trees of varied and beautiful verdure, while the river, now a mountain torrent, rolled over a stony bed below.

This pass opened into a pretty uninhabited plain, embosomed in the forest, then narrowed again, being filled up with huge masses of fallen rock, overshadowed by a profusion of shrubs, among which laurel, myrtle, ivy, and box, were most conspicuous. Beyond, we came to a forest of birch, and then forded the river, amid plane-trees, sycamore, and some pines, the seeds of which had been brought down by the torrents, from the mountain heights.

A short time afterwards we reached a poor hamlet called Sarnish, which is situated in the kazilik of Oluz. We were obliged to put up with sorry accommodation, while we dispatched a kawass, who had been sent so far with us by the governor of Bartan, to the residence of the ayyan, to procure horses for the next morning.

October 19*th*. After waiting a long time, no horses making their appearance, we mounted the few wretched animals that could be procured, and put the baggage into waggons drawn by buffaloes.

After about an hour's ride we came to a mesjid in the forest without a single house near it, but, as this was the Mohammedan Sabbath, the woodmen and hutsmen had collected from around, and two large sheep were roasting in the burial-ground, to be feasted upon, after divine service.

Crossing the river at this point we commenced an ascent through a forest, the road being made of logs of wood, laid transversely. The lofty precipice of the Black Rock lay not far from us to the left; the scenery around was very beautiful, and a tributary to the Ordeiri came tumbling through a rocky pass, near its base; while the yaila, or summer quarters of some pastoral people, occupied a patch of greensward, high above our heads.

Descending hence again into the well-wooded valley of the Ordeiri, we passed several saw-mills; and, turning up a valley to the south, reached the residence of the ayyan of Dursanli, a word corrupted from Durt Hasanli (the Four of Hasan). The name of the kazilik is, however, Ovah Kasa Si (the Kazilik of the Plain), apparently an egregious misnomer.

The ayyan was not at home, but, in his absence, the ladies sent a servant from the harem to offer their services, and with an extremely polite message that whatever we should order should be prepared for us; as we always made a rule of paying for whatever was given to us, we made no scruple of ordering the customary pilau of boiled fowls and rice.

While waiting for this, night came on apace, and we became so anxious for the fate of the baggage, in the buffalo waggons, that after a farther lapse of time, we resolved to issue forth in search of it. So we mounted our horses and began to retrace our steps; but we found it a very different thing to threading these intricate woods and steep paths in the day-time, as we were thumped against trees or the horse stumbled almost every moment.

We soon, however, came up with the tedious quadrupeds; no one had disturbed their progress, and we now assisted in driving them into their quarters for the night.

On our return supper was served up, but the pilau was represented by four eggs, swimming in butter. An egg a-piece, after a long day's work, was a very unsatisfactory affair; so we went forth in search of fowls, of which we soon captured two, and these were already transfixed upon a long stick, and Mr. Pulsford was very ably turning them before a noble expanse of flame, when the ayyan and his brother made their appearance; we accordingly took the opportunity of thanking them for their hospitality, and they were delighted that we were satisfied; we could help not feeling, however, that our expressions of gratitude, and theirs of satisfaction, were somewhat hyperbolical.

October 20th. Our road the next day still lay up the head waters of the Ordeiri, and, after a short ride through woods of plane and cork oak, with underwood and coarse grapes, we arrived at the mesjid and village of Bagh Jevis (Walnut Garden).

Everything now was upon a large scale, and truly alpine: at the head of the valley was the mountain of Durnah Yailasi, the ancient Orminius, with a forest of pine fringing its rude acclivities, but with a bald summit rising above all. To the south were wild crags and precipices, the home of the mountain antelope and the ibex. These alternated with dark wooded recesses, that appeared almost inaccessible.

There was here and there a village in the bottom of the valley, and a few houses (more indeed than could have been expected in so secluded a spot,) were scattered along the acclivities of the hills. But what most interested us and excited our curiosity was, that these hamlets were tenanted by a race of people who, excepting in their language, (which was a very corrupt Turkish,) had not a feature in common with that race. They were dark and swarthy, their hair long, their forehead indented, their features sharp and distinct, and altogether different from the round Turkish physiognomy. They appeared to belong to aboriginal races, driven from the coast into the mountains, and there degenerated; for their hair was uncombed, and their fierce and harsh features looked as if smoke-dried.

It is well known that there was a Sclavonian race in these parts. They are noticed by Homer, as the Ἑνετοι or Heneti, and were a family of the same Sclavonians called *Venetæ* by the Romans, and *Winden*, or *Wenden*, by the Germans. They were described by Strabo, as living beyond the Parthenius, and as occupying a considerable portion of maritime Paphlagonia.

This is the only case that I know of, of the existence, on the Asiatic peninsula, of a nation, which, under the name of Servians, Bulgarians, Bosnians, &c., &c., constitute so large a portion of the population of Turkey in Europe.

It took us exactly four hours and forty minutes from the time we left Dursanli, to gain the crest of the Orminius. The two barometers indicated for this point an elevation of 3200 feet, but, although we had been continuously ascending since we left Bartan, it was very different with the country now before us, which, named by Rennell, after an Oriental authority, "the stony Iflani," extended to the east, as an elevated upland of pine forests, stony plains, and continuous moorlands. On our descent, and at an elevation of upwards of 3000 feet above the sea, we met with beds of large fossil oysters, and in the limestones below, cones and spiral univalves, generally of a gigantic size.

In the evening we arrived at the town of Zafaran Boli. We were at first received in the khan attached to the post-house, but being exposed to much disturbance there, from travelling and boisterous tatars and kawasses, Mr. Rassam went personally to request from the governor that lodgings might be given to us in the Christian quarter, a suburb which is called Kuran Keuy (the King's Village). This was acceded to, and we were glad to enjoy the repose which the next day, being the Sabbath, offered to us among these remnants of the Paphlagonian Greeks, confining our researches to visiting their church and perambulating the town.

Zafaran Boli, a place hitherto little known to Europeans, is situated at the junction of two small streams, the united waters of which flow under the lofty arch of an ivy-clad bridge, and thence down deep rocky dells.

The upland above terminates over the town, in several distinct tongues of land, having rock terraces at the summit, and steep acclivities descending into the town. The most easterly of these headlands is occupied by a new barrack, and its attached jami; the next bears the ruinous walls of an ancient fortress; the third is the seat of the governor's house, and on the fourth and last is Kuran Keuy, the Christian quarter; while the lower town itself, with its numerous menarehs, khans, colleges, and hammams, stretches along the foot of the hills and up the valleys between them.

The town contains about 3000 houses of Mohammedans and 250 houses of Christians. It has a good market, four handsome jamis, several mesjids, colleges, tekiyyehs (monasteries of dervishes), two large khans, and four public baths.

The chief trade is in saffron, the large production of which has rendered the place so flourishing, and gave to it its ancient name of Flaviopolis, and its modern one of Zafaran Boli.

At the Greek church, consecrated to St. Stephen, we were shown a limb of the martyr, preserved as a most invaluable relic, said to have been brought from Syria, and presented to that church by Theodora, wife of Justinian.

It is related that this empress—the frail object of Gibbon's just but unsparing sarcasm, dreamed her first visions of future greatness in Paphlagonia, which she is said to have last left with the pleasing assurance, that she was destined to be the wife of a potent monarch. The memory of such an event led her, in after periods of devotion, as is recorded by her historians, to distribute liberal alms and benefactions to many churches both of Paphlagonia and Bithynia.

October 22nd. We made an excursion to Kara Bunar (the Black Spring), a spot in the stony upland, seven miles from the town, where we had been led to believe were some curious remnants of antiquity. We passed, on this excursion, a remarkably narrow and deep ravine, which cut the upland across for several miles. Beyond this we fell in with a party of travelling Zinganis, or Gipsies, who, in total violation of Oriental decency, sent their women to beg of us. We then turned off to an isolated grove of dark pines, where amidst numerous Mohammedan tombs, we found fragments and capitals of columns of the Byzantine era, and among them a slab of limestone, which bore the rude effigy of a female figure with wings, probably an angel. This appeared to be the site of some early Christian church or monastery.

The ensuing day, we started early in the morning to visit the junction of the Soghanli Su (Onion River) with the Filiyas—a question of hydrography which it was important to settle. Our road lay along the Bulak Dereh, a ravine as picturesque as the others, and then by the more open banks of the river, till, at about seven miles from the town, we arrived at its junction with the Filiyas, where a wooden bridge is carried over the united streams.

We returned by another route, over well-cultivated fields, many of which were now covered with flowering saffron, to the village of Bulak, from whence, crossing a rocky ridge, we entered upon a mountain-inclosed vale at the foot of Orminius, covered with vineyards, and diversified by small country houses. A mile up this valley led us to a more secluded and rocky spot, where a stream of water flowed from an open cave in the limestone rock.

The good people of Zafaran Boli make frequent pleasure parties to this place, where are stated to have been, in former times, two monasteries, one consecrated to St. John, the other to Theodora. We returned to the town by the suburb of Boghazlu, so that we had now encompassed it in every direction, and certainly we never expected to find anything so tasteful and comfortable as the country mansions are, which constitute these suburbs, and which belong chiefly to the native Greek merchants.

While we were at Zafaran Boli, a Greek boy came to offer his services to us to replace our lost Nubian servant. He was then in the service of a Frank doctor attached to the regiment at that time quartered in the town; he could obtain no pay, and though a long arrear was due to him, preferred sacrificing the past, to continuing in such unproductive employment. The day of our departure, however, his master reported his desertion to the governor, and got a kawass sent to our house to claim him. We exerted ourselves to our utmost to free the lad from such slavery, but without effect. We waited upon the governor and represented how inconsistent it was with justice, that the boy should be forced to remain in a service which he did not like, more especially when long arrears of wages were due and insufficient food was given to him; that the lad had a right to choose his own master, and that being a Greek, and not a Rayah, and having voluntarily entered into our service, he had placed himself under our protection, which we were resolved to extend to him as far as in our power. The governor, however, gave it against us, and persisted in attributing to the master a right over all the actions of his servant, and we had the pain, at the end of the discussion, of seeing the boy led forcibly away by the kawasses, when he was by his master's inhuman order, whipped in his prison cell. Emancipation was not, however, long in coming, for on our arrival at Angora we immediately represented the whole transaction to Izzet Mehemet Pasha, who sent for the lad, and he remained in our service till we returned to Constantinople.

We lost the company of Mr. Pulsford at this place. He proceeded by the direct road to Angora, while we continued down the valley of the Gök Irmak (Sky-blue River), with the intention of exploring the lower part of Halys, up to the parallel of the same city, a labour which we hoped to accomplish before the winter set in.

Zafaran Boli, it may be remarked, is one of the very few towns in Lesser Asia that has preserved its ancient prosperity under the Mohammedan rule. Almost universally the opposite is the case. Iconium, Cæsarea, Angora, Sebaste, Tigranocerta, Edessa, and a host of places rendered illustrious by their former prosperity and greatness, are now in the most prostrate and fallen condition, while others also of celebrity, as Nisibin, Anazarba, Issus, Amorium, &c., are mere heaps of ruins. In Paphlagonia, as in Bithynia, we find a brighter period, even in its half-savage condition, and at the remote epoch of the Greek colonies, than in modern times. The history of wars with the kings of Pontus is relieved by the account of the founding and embellishment of cities; its bishops were seated at the councils of the Church; its towns were the homes of the noblest Asiatic Greeks. It remained to be prostrated, with the other fair provinces of the peninsula, under Mohammedan misrule and lethargy.

It is a curious fact that the Osmanli conquerors of Lesser Asia cannot claim the foundation of a single town or city. For four centuries they have neither established new ports, nor formed new roads, nor have they originated any new branches of industry or of commercial intercommunication. Even the Saracens did more by their inroads. The Turkomans of the Seljukiyan dynasty constructed a road from Koniyeh eastward; but, beyond a few bridges and causeways, and numerous religious edifices, the Osmanli sultans have done nothing for the interior. With one of the finest countries in the world to pour its tribute into the coffers of the Sublime Porte, the sultans have built jamis, a fleet, tombs innumerable, and have adorned the shore of the Thracian Bosphorus with wooden palaces, while agriculture, commerce, and industry, have sunk to the very lowest ebb, in a climate and country favourable to each; and at the same time all the intellectual and tasteful pursuits of mankind have been banished by the hideous form of a baneful religion, from the earliest home of literature and science, of music and the fine arts.

CHAPTER V.

Tash Kupri—Pompeiopolis.

Upland of Iflani. The Black Forest. Muleteer runs away. New mode of procuring Horses. Trouble with the Muleteers. Visit to the Copper Mines. Cupidity of a Turkish Governor. City of Kastamuni. Evils of farmed Governments. Trade of Kastamuni. Its Castle. Persecutions of Christians. Town of Tash Kupri—Pompeiopolis. Antiquities. Splendid Sarcophagus. Greek Metropolis.

October 25th. Retracing our steps towards the upland of Iflani, we found ourselves on gaining those high levels in the midst of winter, and our road lay through a pine forest where the snow tumbled upon us from the overladen branches. Beyond this the moorland was nearly continuous and little diversified: when cultivated, there were a few villages; when not, it was a continuous waste or forest land.

It was late in the evening before we arrived at an

isolated house, where the ayyan of that portion of Iflani which is under the jurisdiction of Zafaran Boli resides. There were several robbers stalking about the house in chains. We had an apartment assigned to ourselves, the ayyan as usual visiting us with his suite in the evening.

October 26*th*. There was a great delay in procuring horses this morning, and it was late before we started. Crossing over some low hills, we came to the valley of Bedil, with five villages, and then another which expanded into a plain, cultivated in almost every part, and studded with villages, in the midst of which, as is common in cultivated and populous districts of this character, was the market village, a series of untenanted shops, open only one day in the week, and that generally the Mohammedan Sabbath, the day on which business is transacted.

After a short journey of four hours we came to a stony spot, where was the residence of the ayyan of Iflani under the jurisdiction of Kastamuni; hence the two Iflanis are always distinguished as Iflani of Zafaran Boli, and Iflani of Kastamuni. We were to obtain a relay of horses at this place, but experienced so much delay, that we were forced to remain all night. When night came on, as it was clear and frosty, Mr. Russell and myself went out to shoot wild duck, which abound in the rivulets of the moorlands, on which excursion we rambled a long distance from the village and enjoyed considerable sport. Near to the village is a mound and some ruins, where, according to the tradition of the natives, a great battle was once fought.

On the upland of Iflani, at a mean elevation of

2800 feet, the cultivation consists almost entirely of wheat and barley; indeed it may be considered among the most productive wheat countries of Anatolia; besides this, the natives also cultivate a species of polygonum in the fields, and a chenopodium in their gardens, principally to feed fowls, the eggs of which form a large item in their diet; but these seeds are also ground and used in making bread. The gardens also furnish a little maize in sunny exposures, and plenty of cabbages and pumpkins. The climate and soil are well adapted for potatoes. The appearance of the fields, with their short stubble, the marshy spots covered with their sedges, and the greensward with its long festucas, is very similar to those of many parts of Ireland. The land is both manured and regularly top-dressed. As a general average, 80 okahs, or 220 pounds, of wheat, fetch 25 piastres, or five shillings, the same measure of barley three shillings.

October 27th. Crossing the limestone rocks of Iflani, we came upon the cultivated valley of Sighir (Ox), beyond which was a small plain with five villages, under one court (divan), held at Tekiyyeh Keuy (the Village of the Dervishes' Monastery). Beyond this, the character of the country completely changed, from a continuous upland, intersected by nearly circular plains and valleys, with gentle slopes, to a mountainous district and wooded heights with conical and sharpened summits, rapid but not abrupt acclivities, and deep and narrow valleys, clothed at the base with forests of fir, which on the acclivities and at the summits alternated with, or were replaced by, equally prolific but now leafless woods of birch.

One of these narrow valleys now opened before us, having only small patches of cultivation and corresponding groups of hamlets like eyries on its side, while a dark-looking forest spread out below. This district is called the Kara Aghaj (Black Forest). It is in the ayyanlik of Chilani, where we arrived after about half an hour's farther ride. Our muleteers, who were two in number, wanted to obtain a relay of horses here, but the ayyan was absent, and as none were to be obtained, we obliged them after much altercation to go on with us.

An hour's journey from Chilani brought us to the foot of the mountains of Uzún Burun, on entering the forests of which, one of our muleteers decamped; in another hour we reached the summit-level or mean of crest, for which the barometer indicated an elevation of 3600 feet. This mountain chain extends nearly north-east and south-west, and is formed of rounded mountains with gentle acclivities, covered with wood from the base to the summit.

The descent was more rapid than the ascent, yet night overtook us before we reached the plain of Dadahi, and we had still to travel some distance before we arrived at the ayyan's house, making in all four hours from the crest of the Uzún Burun. The ayyan was not at home, but we were received in his house and treated to a large fire, and the next morning at an early hour the notables of the place came to see us.

The ayyanlik of Dadahi has under its jurisdiction about twenty-four villages. The cultivation is nearly the same, at an elevation of 2500 feet, as that of the Iflani district, but maize, tobacco, and French beans are added to their productions; vines do not succeed.

The plain of Dadahi is extensive and studded with villages, with the market as usual apart from the rest. This district corresponds to the episcopate of Dadybra under the Byzantine empire.

October 28th. The next day we started over the Gerish Tagh, a range of hills covered with forests of oak and fir, and descended by a lovely vale sheltered by cranberry trees, upon the ripe berries of which, numerous jays, blackbirds, and fieldfares were feasting. From hence we gained the more open valley of the Daurikhan Irmak, up which we travelled but a short distance to the village of Jurimaran, where we were again to change horses, and beyond which we in vain attempted to get the muleteers to proceed. Their orders were not to go beyond the jurisdiction of the ayyan of Dadahi. The customary observations and labours of the day over, we spent the evening fishing in the river of Daurikhan, and so little experience in hooks had the poor fish of this remote district, and so plentiful were they, that they allowed themselves to be caught by the fins, when not captured by the mouth.

October 29th. It was in vain next day that we looked out for horses coming. There was not an attempt made to bring us one. The ayyan, who was a young man, had not power to enforce our firman; so after bringing our baggage out of our house, Messrs. Russell and Rassam went into the pastures to secure horses, while I remained in charge of them, as they were brought in, and of the arms and baggage. This detained us nearly all the morning, and was only accomplished amidst the shouts and vilification of the peasants, more especially the female portion, who exclaimed loudly against mares with foal and unshod colts being pressed into the service, but we had difficulty enough to secure these, without being particular in our choice. Had we had a tatar or kawass with us, probably these inconveniences would not have been met with, but still, when off the great road, the supply of horses is always very uncertain and attended with great delays.

At length the steeds were loaded and ourselves mounted, when the reluctant villagers found themselves obliged to provide two of their number to accompany us and bring them back from the next change. Our road lay up the valley of the river, till we came to Dereh Keuy the Village in the Valley, a small village prettily situated in a deep glen surrounded by precipices, and where, as in several villages around, the peasants were engaged in the manufacture of gun-flints.

Hence we travelled over the upland of Salmanli, having hills to the north, on one of which were the remains of a castellated building, and to the south the extensive, level, and cultivated district of Daurikhan, abounding in villages. Our muleteers, forced upon the service against their will, would give us no information, nor even name a village for us; so that we were obliged at the next houses we came to, to seek for some more communicative guide, and we were lucky enough to obtain as such a willing and good-tempered youth, who was of infinite service to us at night.

Entering a forest shortly before night-fall, we met with some armed and travelling Turks, whom our muleteers endeavoured to enlist in their cause, by false representations of our being Gawurs who had illegally forced them and their horses into our service: we kept driving them on, however, in spite of their hostile epithets, and the boy showed us the way. At length night overtook us, and, under other circumstances, we would have bivouacked, to spare the poor beasts; but we had no option now, for had we unloaded, the peasants would certainly have stolen away in the darkness, and left us with our baggage in the forest, as it would have been impossible to have kept guard upon all the horses when turned out to grass.

Our road lay over a mountain forest, the track scarcely distinguishable, and very steep, the mud deep and slippery. As the men would lend no assistance to the laden horses, the toil of the ascent was increased for all of us; but we persevered in our efforts, and gained the crest of the hills, where we found a guard-house. We were too fatigued and cross to pay attention to the summons made as to our *personnel* and purport, so rode on, and soon afterwards, but late at night, arrived at the mountain-inclosed town of Bakir Kurehsi (Copper Furnaces), where a comfortable room and fire were assigned us, and we rewarded our faithful young guide.

October 30th. This morning we waited upon the governor, and exhibited our firman, which authorized us to explore and examine into the state of the mines in the Osmanli empire. This did not appear to be at all agreeable to him, but finding that we were bent upon immediate proceedings, he proposed to accompany us, and we accordingly issued forth with a train of kawasses, &c., to examine in the first place the furnaces, which are sixteen in number, small, and the bellows worked by water-wheels, which themselves are turned by a small stream that flows along the centre of the valley. We then went to the piles of scoriæ and refuse of former years, which were being turned over and sifted, so that every bit of any promise whatsoever might be now turned to account. The persons employed in this labour were chiefly convicts, or forced labourers. None of the veins of metal are now wrought, nor could we even obtain a specimen of the original ore in the town; but this no doubt was owing to orders from the governor to that effect, for he all along showed much anxious jealousy at our explorations.

We next proceeded to the shafts; they were mostly either fallen in, or full of water. One of them Mr. Russell and myself explored to a considerable depth, but without reaching the vein of metal. This accomplished, we requested Mr. Rassam to accompany the governor home, while Mr. Russell and myself examined the acclivities of the mountain, and ascended to its summit, where was a tomb, called Bakir Sultan (Copper Sultan), and the residence of an attached dervish, who must have a rather singular home.

The view from this point was very grand, and presented in every direction a continuous succession of mountains, rounded, but with steep acclivities to the west and east, broken into bold rocky cliffs to the north, and overtopped by the more distant snowy summits of the Alkas Tagh to the south-east, while a vast accumulation of cloud lay over the Black Sea, like a great white shroud spread at our feet.

The town of Bakir Kurehsi is pleasingly situated in the hollow, but is now in a state of great poverty and general dilapidation. It contains a handsome jami, and upwards of 200 houses, half of which are untenanted.

That these mines were formerly very productive, may be inferred from the fact mentioned by Gibbon, that in the time of Mohammed II., Ismael Bey, the Turkoman prince of Sinope, yielded to the conqueror of Constantinople, on his summons, a city, and a revenue of 200,000 ducats, derived, it is said, chiefly from the copper mines; an amount which the historian remarks appears enormous. The author of the Jehan Numa has said after Strabo that the people employed in these mines emit a horrible stench from their bodies when they come to the surface. We did not, however, perceive anything of the kind in the old galleries.

In the evening, the governor being upon a visit to us, Mr. Rassam excited his wonder by the exhibition of so finished a piece of workmanship as a gold chronometer of Molyneux's, which had been presented to him by the Honourable the Board of Directors of the East India Company, whereupon Mr. Russell told the Turk, whose eyes and looks were beaming with cupidity, that it was meant as a present for him. This had nearly been more than a joke, for it was afterwards with great difficulty that he was made to relinquish his claim to it, and that only by the loss of his good graces,—no great loss after our business with him was over,—and he retired in high dudgeon.

November 1*st.* We left Bakir Kurehsi by a gap in the mountain, called Kirnak Taghi, and continued to travel for three hours along a rocky mountain and forest country, at times by the rude banks of a stony torrent, at others over the muddy and branch-strewn pathway of the forest glades. It rained hard all the morning. Beyond this the country opened, and a few miles farther we entered upon the extensive plain of Daurikhan, covered with villages.

On our arrival at the head village of the district, we found the ayyan absent, and no one, after our long ride in a pitiless rain, would afford us shelter, or give us a resting-place, so that we were ultimately obliged to take possession of the furnished house of a respectable Mohammedan, who happened to be from home. This determination on our part, to help ourselves, had a good effect, for the next morning we obtained horses and a seruji, without more than the usual trouble.

November 2nd. We continued our route over woodless hills, crossing two different ranges, with their intervening valleys, both belonging to the Yerala Goz chains, when we came to a low, wooded crest, with a ravine, where was a guard-house, and a little beyond this the valley of the Gök Irmak burst upon our view, stretching far away beneath our feet, dotted with villages and plantations, and backed by the city of Kastamuni, over which towered the patrimonial castle of the Comneni, and of the Isfindaberg princes of the Turkomans.

From Zafaran Boli to this place, except in the low valley of the Daurikhan river, our elevation had never been much less than 2000 feet above the sea, at Bakir Kurehs2800 feet, and on the high uplands of the Yerala Goz 3240 feet. This fact, which had hitherto only been rendered apparent by the indications of the barometer, and by climate and vegetation, became now actually visible, for, without having made any ascent from the general level of our road, the valley of the Blue River, which stream had still to flow some distance before it joined the Halys, was many hundred feet below us.

We arrived, early in the afternoon, at the crowded and bustling city of Kastamuni. Our Daurikhan muleteer was so afraid of being detained as a soldier, that he would not go to the Serai, or governor's house; so Mr. Rassam had to go on first, and as we were to follow, we missed him, and had to wander about the town nearly two hours, till, directed by some Christians in the market-place, we luckily found him in the Greek quarter, where he had secured a comfortable apartment in the house of a member of that persuasion.

The next day we visited the governor, who was in ill health. I prescribed for him, and sent him the medicines in the evening, visiting him frequently afterwards during our short stay, so that we had many opportunities for conversation upon the state of the mines, as well as of the adjacent country. He agreed with us in the necessity of new works to carry on the former, and of the introduction of a new system; but he said, who will advance the money? In the present system of things, where local governments are farmed out, the governors often changed, and only making use of their time to realize as much money as possible, it can never be expected that any labour will be undertaken that requires the outlay of capital, and time for remuneration.

During our stay, besides our observations astronomical and magnetic, we explored the city, which is of considerable magnitude, and examined and laid down a plan of its castle, an ancient ruin of much historical interest.

The present name of the town is a corruption of Castra Comneni, of which family this place was a patrimonial estate, if not an independent kingdom, before it attained the power and eminence which arrested for awhile the fate of a sinking empire. It became, at the fall of the Comneni, the residence of an independent race of Turkoman princes. Among these was Kutrum Bayazid, who, about A.D. 1393, laid waste the Turkish provinces, although himself paralytic and disabled. His son Isfindaberg became one of the most powerful and most persevering enemies of the then rising Osmanlis. He was succeeded by a race of princes who bore the same name.

In the intestine broils which followed the defeat and death of Bayazid I., and the conquests of Tamerlane, Musa Chelebi, one of the sons of Bayazid, flying before his more successful brother Suleiman, took refuge in this castle, and at the court of the prince of Kastamuni.

In the time of Mohammed I. the then representative of the Isfindaberg family allied himself to Karaman Oghlu (the patronymic of the princes of Koniyeh), and they marched together against the Sultan of the Osmanlis; but the latter was victorious, and Bakir Kurehsi and Tosiyeh, but not Kastamuni, are noticed by Oriental historians as among the places that fell into the hands of the Osmanlis, while Isfindaberg, like the former kings of Paphlagonia, when driven before the Romans, took refuge at Changri.

Sinope and the adjacent country being reduced by Mohammed II., conqueror of Constantinople, the whole of the principality fell into the hands of the Osmanlis; and in the time of Murad III. (A.D. 1585), we find his vizir, Osman, wintering his forces at the castle and town of Kastamuni.

Under Osmanli government, Kastamuni has always

been the capital of a province or sanjak, and the residence of a pasha (mushir), till under the economical reforms of the late Sultan, it was made the seat of a mutesellim, or governor, under the mushir of Angora.

Kastamuni is situated in a valley, from one-half to three-fourths of a mile in width, and this it completely fills up; a break in the hills that bound the city to the west gives origin to another valley, which is filled up by the suburb, called Hisar Ardi, while upon the rocky cliff which separates the two valleys, stand the ruins of the castle.

The total number of houses is said to amount to 12,000, giving a population of 48,000 persons. The Greeks have out of this only 160 houses, and the Armenians 20. The former have a small church, dedicated to St. John the Baptist. The Armenians meet for prayers in a khan. In the Mohammedan city we counted thirty-six menarehs, and there are twenty-four public baths. There are also in the city four monasteries of resident or stationary, and two of itinerant, dervishes.

The principal trade of Kastamuni is in wool; that produced in the neighbourhood is said to be nearly as good as that of Angora. The men also work largely in copper, and the women in cotton brought from Adanah, and of which sails for shipping are made, and sent to Constantinople: they also print cottons, and tan leather, but in the latter article Tash Kupri excels them. There are said to be thirty-two printing houses, having from four to eight presses each, also twenty-two dyeing houses, of which six are for red and sixteen for blue dyes. Thus this city, like many others in Lesser Asia, owes its existence to the demands and necessities of a large, fertile, and populous neighbourhood; wherever such exists, there must be one point where the products of art and industry are to be found, to supply the wants of villagers and peasants. This will create a population, which will again have its own wants, and cities of such origin are propagated through an indefinite period of time, and are always available, although too often neglected, outlets for the products (cutlery wares, cottons, prints, &c.,) of more favoured manufacturing countries, and which can always undersell the tradesman in localities where not only the arts are at their very lowest ebb, but where also, from want of capital and enterprise, the transport of goods from other places is almost totally neglected.

The castle of Kastamuni is a rude structure, built of the same coarse sandstone as the rock on which it stands. The mortar is a mixture of lime and pebbles. Some of the towers, three of which are round, are nearly fifty feet in height: one is partly built of tiles, and some square ones, more especially such as flank the outer wall, are of better construction than the rest, and formed of large stones; they probably belong to a more remote era. A plan was made, from which it appears that the castle is of an oblong form, 414 feet long by 60 wide.

Little more than a century ago the Christian inhabitants of Kastamuni were expelled from the city, and forced to take up their residence in a village on the Gök Irmak, which is still designated as Gawur Keuy (Infidel Village). When re-admitted to live and trade within the precincts of the town, they had no church, and only their old burial-ground, till under the late Sultan a firman was granted, allowing them to build a church, and to bury their dead, near the abodes of their forefathers.

Although the commerce of Kastamuni is inconsiderable, its population and extent claim for it some attention. Some of the jamis and the new barracks rise above surrounding buildings; but the houses generally, although of two stories, are ill built; the streets are also narrow and dirty, and the centre of the town, washed by the river of Kastamuni, is but a deep kennel, into which the filth of the whole place is collected. There are no open quays to enliven the scene, and only here and there a wooden bridge, across which the Mohammedan has to pick his way, lest he should wake the sleeping dogs, and be defiled by touching them.

Kastamuni is not unfrequently visited by the plague, and is always liable to bad fevers, more particularly malaria, which is said often to assume a very fatal type. At an altitude of 2350 feet above the sea, the snow is said to lie two months upon the ground, and the summer to be very hot.

November 6th. This day we continued our journey, proceeding along the valley of the Gök Irmak, five miles and a half, to where it makes a bend to the eastward, and flows along a pleasant valley, full of villages, plantations, and gardens.

After a ride of seven miles along this vale, we came to a point where the river enters into a rocky ravine, and we at the same time crossed over some low hills, beyond which was the basin-like hollow in which stands town of Tash Kupri, in a most beautiful situation, surrounded by low wooded hills, and crowded with grove-embosomed villages.

We entered the town, which stands on the right bank of the river, by a bridge seventy-five yards long, and which formerly consisted of four arches, two of which now remain, but the two others, which were carried away, are replaced by three low and badly-constructed modern arches. We then rode to the governor's house, where a divan had just been held, and the governor himself was standing under the porch with a number of respectable-looking old Turks, inhabitants of the place. After the preliminary salutes and inquiries, our firman was produced, and it became evident to the governor and the old gentlemen who also stood by to hear it perused, that we were, in virtue of said document, entitled to a lodging for the night in the good town of Tash Kupri. The governor, however, seemed puzzled to know what to do with us, and turned round inquiringly to his friends; but each and all shook their heads, and slunk quietly away, when the governor good-humouredly ushered us into his own house, and assigned to us an apartment, in which we had not been long installed before he and his brother came in search of araki, with which, had we permitted him, he would at once have drank himself into a senseless condition.

Early next morning, while Mr. Rassam was getting the horses and baggage ready, Mr. Russell and myself went to explore the antiquities of the town. We first visited a small building, used as a madreseh, or college, and which is one entire collection of hewn stones and remains of antiquity, put together in the form of a parallelogram, with an open space in the centre, and two rows of ancient pillars, no two of which had capitals of the same order.

Near this building was a magnificent sarcophagus, of white marble, which was seven feet nine inches long, four feet wide, and three feet six inches high, and ornamented at the sides with exquisitely-wrought wreaths encircling a human face that was unfortunately mutilated. Sculptured bulls' heads also adorned the side, and rams' heads the corners, with bunches of grapes beneath.

We copied several Greek inscriptions in various parts of the town, one from the gateway of the college, one from a fountain, and another in the interior of a tanner's house, near the bridge. One of these inscriptions was decisive as to the identity of Tash Kupri with the ancient Pompeiopolis: it ran as follows: "*To Good Fortune; Caius Claudius Gallitianus, the son of Pallicus, the kind administrator of the country, the senate and people of Pompeiopolis, the metropolis, have dedicated on account of his courage.*"

The modern town of Tash Kupri contains 1500 houses, all inhabited by Mohammedans. We counted ten menarehs, two khans, and two public baths. Tanners and blacksmiths form a large portion of the community. It was formerly, not only a Christian town, but, as we see by the inscription above, a metropolis, and its episcopal representative at the council of Ephesus subscribed himself Arginus.

CHAPTER VI.

Pass of the Black Valley.

Virgin's Castle. Gate of Flints. Pine Forest. Jackalls. Town of Boïabad. Castle of the Sipahis. Valley of the Blue River. The Black Valley. Guard-house in the Defile. Town of Vizir Kupri. Greek Sepulchral Monument. Hare Mountains. Charcoal Burners. Attempt at Robbery. Practical Justice.

On our return to the Serai we found the horses ready, and, although it rained hard, we mounted, and, bidding adieu to our imprudent but good-tempered host, we started over cultivated lands, leaving the river, which a little below the town is lost in a ravine, to the left.

After ascending a short distance, we observed before us the dismantled walls and crumbling fragments of a castle, which occupied the summit of a nearly insulated rock. This place is known to the natives by the name of Kíz Kalehsi (the Virgin's Castle), a name not uncommon in the East, and significative of "unconquered."

The weather had cleared up, and Mr. Russell and myself cantered over the fields towards the castle, so as to examine the ruins, and not delay the loaded horses, but, after a ride of upwards of a mile, we found ourselves separated by a deep and almost inaccessible ravine from the object of our wishes, and had to return as quick as we came in order to obtain the sun's meridian altitude, which was done within a few seconds of the time.

We afterwards descended into a ravine, with a rivulet, where we found fragments apparently of arches, now called Chekmak Kapusi (Gate of Flints); and it certainly does appear more like a gate or defence of the pass, than a bridge over the rivulet.

Our ascent of the Ilik Tak, renowned for its pine timber, commenced at this point. The road was rocky and steep, and the horses which had been collected at Tash Kupri turned out very bad indeed, and toiled up with difficulty. We had not reached the crest of the hills before Mr. Russell's horse, which had unfortunately had a sharp ride over heavy ground, gave up entirely, and could not be prevailed upon to move a step in advance. In this dilemma we observed a Turk coming down the same road with a horse, carrying a load of wood. Our seruji assured us, that he had left the town early that morning, under pretence of getting a load of wood, but, in reality, to avoid his horse being pressed into our service; so, waiting quietly till he came up, we appropriated to ourselves his horse, leaving him Mr. R.'s, which was willing to go back, although obstinate as to proceeding further, to carry his fuel to the town, and promising to send him his horse back by the seruji.

As we gained the tops of the hills we entered upon

extensive pine forests. The chief species, and the one most remarkable for its growth, was the Pinus pinea. Some trees, which we measured, were upwards of 100 feet high, and 3 feet 4 inches in diameter, cutting into timber 1 foot 9 inches square. The mean elevation of this upland forest was 4000 feet above the level of the sea.

We had a long ride through this dark and monotonous forest, and it became after sunset dreary and difficult; the roads being uneven and strewn with logs of wood, or blocked up by fallen trees. During the latter part of the journey we were followed by a troop of jackalls, who ever and anon burst from the covert, as if to attack us, and then went running and howling away, chasing one another as if in play.

At length we arrived at a village in the forest, called Kavvashah Tekiyyeh, being, as its name indicates, a place for retired dervishes, of whom there are four out of the inhabitants of about fifteen cottages. A room in an empty log-house was given to us, after we had with some difficulty roused the inhabitants, and we soon forgot our fatigues, sleeping before a roasting fire.

We started early the next morning, and, after travelling two hours, partly through forest and partly through open country, we came upon the valley of the Blue River, which here presented a very picturesque appearance, from the acclivities of the surrounding hills being deeply furrowed by ravines, which presented a curious succession of different-coloured indentations. The vale below, immediately after the river left the mountains, became as crowded with villages, as it was above the pass.

A little more than an hour's ride over hills, clad with juniper and prickly oak, brought us to a steep descent, leading to the small town of Boïabad, between which and us was a rivulet, issuing from a rocky ravine, on the opposite side of which, andon a lofty and nearly isolated rock, were the remains of a rather extensive castle.

The town itself, like the generality in Asia Minor, presented from without a cleanly and inviting appearance, and its situation was eminently picuresque. The governor assigned us an apartment which had no windows, so that we were obliged to write our notes by candle-light, but we had the compensatory advantage of being left to ourselves, and were not intruded upon by any visitors.

The next day was spent, the greater part in astronomical observations, as we wanted to regulate the chronometers; the remainder in exploring the town and castle, and laying down a plan of the latter.

Boïabad contains about 300 houses, in which the population is said to consist of 1000 females, and 800 males. There are many jamis and mesjids, three khans, and two baths. The houses are rather scattered, and stretch up the valley called Kaz Derehsi, or that of Geese; this valley to its junction with that of the Blue River, is occupied by luxuriant gardens, full of fine fruit-trees overrun by vines.

The castle contains within its walls about thirty dwelling houses, which are said to have been deserted only about eight years ago, when its lord was a certain Hussein, who is called by the natives the last of the Sipahis. When we visited this feudal castle there was not a human being within its walls, and the houses, still good, although built of wood, looked as if deserted only a few days before; the path was overgrown with viper's bugloss, and the whole had an almost painful aspect of sudden desolation, but the inhabitants below spoke of the thing in a manner highly characteristic of the utilitarian feeling now gaining ground throughout Asiatic Turkey: "Of what use is it to live secluded in yonder mountain? Is it not better to dwell among gardens and vineyards?"

November 10*th*. This day we continued our journey along the valley of the Blue River; a greyhound, of the Turkoman breed, followed us out of the town, and was immediately admitted of the party as a general favourite. We travelled four hours by the banks of the river, passing villages almost every mile and a half, when we turned to the right about a mile to the village of Ali Pasha Shali, and where, for want of accommodation on the road, we had to pass the night, and that in a room, similar to what we had in Boïabad, without a window, and dark as a dungeon.

The valley of the Blue River averaged to-day a width of from one-half to one mile; and from its numerous windings, wooded hills, and rocks, its general luxuriance of vegetation, and its corn and rice fields, furnished a continuous succession of picturesque and varied landscape.

November 11*th*. Quitting the valley of Ali Pasha Shali, we again entered upon that of the Blue River, and passing Tahiran, formerly a small Mohammedan town, but now a poor village, we found the valley to be narrowed and nearly shut up by dykes of volcanic rocks, which advanced in wooded precipices or rocky promontories upon the bed of the river.

A little farther we came to the junction of Gök Irmak, with the Halys, which occurs at a more open spot, but where there are no habitations.

It was our intention to have proceeded hence up the banks of the Kizil Irmak to Hajji Hamsa, and notwithstanding the many representations made to us of the impracticability of that route, which were set down as Oriental exaggerations, we determined to judge by our own eyes. We therefore travelled up the banks of the river till we came to a village called Beg Keuy, beyond which were perpendicular rocks hemming in the stream, and allowing no further passage. So we were obliged to retrace our steps.

We forded the river near its junction with the Halys; the greyhound, disliking water, was carried over, and we then advanced through the pass called the Kara Dereh (Black Valley). The river here ran through a narrow gorge in the mountains, having on the south side a pillar of rock nearly two hundred feet high, islanded in the waters, while the cliffs rose as a bold and rugged rampart, nearly a thousand feet above the stream: the acclivities were strewn with huge masses of stone, amid which, here and there, a rude pine or cypress spread its dark fronds, while the summits terminated in steep terraces and cliffs, or broke into fantastic pinnacles.

This pass, which constitutes the sole entrance into Paphlagonia from the west, if we except that of Hajji Hamsa, which does not lead into Paphlagonia proper, is undoubtedly the same as that described by Hecatonymus, one of the ambassadors from Sinope to Xenophon, and who said that Paphlagonia must of necessity be entered by one pass, and that lay between two points of a rock exceedingly high.

The same defile has, in modern times, obtained notoriety from the frequency of the robberies committed in a neighbourhood so well adapted for such exploits, and under so weak a government; but a guard-house has at length been built for its safety, and we found it tenanted by two worn-out veterans, who, however, kindly gave us shelter for the night; and so warm was it in this low and secluded vale, that we slept most agreeably on an open platform in front of the house, surrounded by wild and beautiful scenery.

Travelling the next day along the pleasant banks of the Halys, we were ferried across that river, at a distance of nine miles from the guard-house. Our greyhound was nearly worried here by some dogs belonging to travelling Turkomans, while we were measuring the width of the river.

We now entered Pontus, by what Strabo calls the fertile Gadilonitide, but which at first was uncultivated and covered with low shrubs, but became productive and tilled as we approached the town of Vizir Kupri, which we did not reach till night set in, when we had much difficulty in obtaining quarters; these, however, were ultimately assigned to us in the house of a Mohammedan.

The next day we explored the town, which contains 1000 Mohammedan families, 50 Armenian, and 20 Greek, each of which latter persuasions has a place of worship. The town is divided into quarters, which are in some places separated by walls, and the market is partitioned in the same manner, each portion having gates for its protection. There is also a bezestan, or covered market, for silks and fine goods, which is a good-looking and well-kept edifice, and has four domes of tiles.

At each of the two gateways of this latter building, a tombstone is dovetailed into the wall. One of these contains a mutilated inscription, and the sculptured insignia of a Greek priest; the other bears the following inscription, turned upside down: "*Honourably, and having lived respectably forty years, Cyrilla, daughter of Syrtus, who bore children to him. In memory*" [*of him, erected this monument*]. The name of the deceased was wanting.

We did not remark any ancient buildings of importance in the precincts of the present town, but remnants of such are common. Fragments of columns are not infrequent, and many hewn stones are met with belonging to ancient days. Although now called the "Vizir's Bridge," the town was, till within a short time back, designated by the Turks as Ghedakara, which was a mere corruption of its old name, Gadilon.

At an altitude of 800 feet above the sea, mulberry trees are cultivated in the neighbourhood, and storks' nests abound in the chimnies.

November 15th. Quitting Vizir Kupri, we travelled over a well-cultivated country, with occasional villages, for fifteen miles, when we arrived at the foot of the Tavshan Tagh (Hare Mountains). There were the ruins of an ancient castle, upon a rocky peak belonging to this chain, which advanced upon the plain several miles to the eastward of our road. It also was called Tavshan Kalehsi (Hare's Castle).

We commenced our ascent amidst forests of shrubby

and deciduous oak, gradually becoming trees, and towards the summit of the hills, interspersed with beech and pine. On the crest, the trees grew so close together, that most were unhealthy, and covered with lichens and mosses, while the intervals between were almost filled up with fallen timber. The elevation was here 3690 feet above the sea, and the ascent took us two hours and a half.

We did not descend far on the opposite side of the hill, before we came to a village in a ravine called Kosajah, inhabited by charcoal burners attached to the mines of Hajji Keuy. Our arrival here was not the less agreeable, as night was coming on, and the road was very bad. Our accommodations here were, however, of the worst description; the only room we could get was full of chopped straw and vermin, and at this elevation it was too cold to sleep out of doors. There were no cooking utensils to be found (which was not so great a loss, as there was nothing to cook); and these charcoal burners received us with most malicious grins, and more than suspicious looks. They crowded, in the most unpleasant manner, into our small apartment, and laid their hands upon everything, so that we had enough to do to keep a sharp look-out; at length our temper could brook it no longer, and we turned them all out by positive pushing.

Next morning, on packing up, we found that a pistol, a shot-belt, and several small things had been taken away, which, however, we did not claim, or say anything about, till the mules were loaded and ourselves mounted and prepared for any emergency. We then requested to see the sheik of the village, who had also been with us the preceding evening. He came out with only one or two attendants, when Mr. Rassam immediately told him that he must consider himself our prisoner, and must go along with us to Osmanjik, there to be handed over to the mutesellim, unless the lost things were given up. At first an attempt was made to deny positively any knowledge of the theft, but finding that we were resolute, and even began driving their chief before us, the missing objects were produced, and we rode away, leaving the charcoal burners to their cogitations upon the folly of robbing *gawur* travellers.

We kept descending all the early part of our journey, and about nine miles from Kosajah we fell into the great Constantinopolitan road at a place called Hajji Hasan (Pilgrim Hasan). From this to Osmanjik was a further ride of four hours, by a road which two of the party had travelled on a former journey, when they lodged at the governor's house. On this occasion we were happy in obtaining an untenanted house for our repose, and were thus less disturbed by visitors.

CHAPTER VII.

Town of Osmanjik.

Town of Osmanjik. Thermal Spring. Monument of Icesius. Town and Castle of Churum. Passage of the Halys. Town of Eskilub. Reception by the Governor. Sepulchral Monuments. Castle of Blucium. Celtic Fort. Baptismal Font. Interior of a Cottage. Salt Mine. Arrival at Changri.

Osmanjik is a small town, but a place of interest on several accounts. It is the only town in Asiatic Turkey that bears the name of an Osmanli sultan; originally the Otresa of the Greeks, it received its present appellation from the founder of the Osmanli dynasty. It was garrisoned and fortified with an additional castle in the time of Bajazet, in order to keep in check Kutrum, the paralytic and yet rebellious Prince of Kastamuni. The same sultan also constructed the noble bridge which still affords a passage over the Halys at this place. It consists of 13 arches, and is 283 yards long, and 8 wide.

The modern town is a bustling little post town, with 300 houses, five mesjids, a khan, and baths; but what gives it its greatest peculiarity are the cones of rock which rise out of it, bearing the ruins of two different castles, with loopholed and casemated ramparts following a zig-zag direction along their precipitous sides, while another rock is caverned with variously formed recesses and sepulchral grots, and there are other smaller and more pointed obelisk-like summits, which are distinguished by bearing on their peaks the great nests of storks.

November 17*th*. We left the great road at Osmanjik, and proceeded along the banks of the river for a distance of ten miles, when we were turned aside by ranges of wooded mountains, through which the river forced its way by a narrow and pathless gorge.

The Kizil Irmak is in every respect a fine river here, as well as at Ada Teppeh, and preserves its character as such above the pass, even as far south as the district of Sivas; but it does not equal what would *à priori* be expected from a river of such a long course. An exaggerated idea of its magnitude has obtained credit in Europe, from the vague reports of travellers, who have not adopted the test of actual measurement. It is certainly hardly navigable, except by steam vessels, and that only at intervals.

We turned from the river into the valley of Hammam Gozi (Warm Bath's Eye), so called from thermal springs situated at its head, in the Karchak Tagh, and not far from the mines of Hajji Keuy.

This valley contained two villages of Turkomans, at one of which, called Mujteli, we stopped for the night, as we wished to explore the environs. Mr. Rassam was much annoyed in his search for quarters, by the gratuitous insults of a showily dressed young Turkoman, whose spear we afterwards found in the apartment assigned to us; this explained the cause of his ill-humour, and we refused to give up the weapon to him till he had made an ample apology for the barbarian language which he had used.

It appears that these baths were formerly much frequented, for we found in the neighbourhood many fragments of Byzantine buildings, columns, hewn stones, &c. At the side of a fountain there was a tombstone, with scallop-shell, pilgrim's crook, and a deacon's badge, such as are still used in the Greek church. There is still this neighbourhood a Greek village called Rum Keuy.

November 18th. We approached the Kirk Delim hills by a narrow pass, flanked by nearly perpendicular cliffs, wooded at the base and the summits, the naked sides of which displayed occasionally small sepulchral grots, but on entering a narrow part of the pass, we were struck with the appearance of a tomb, of much more than ordinary dimensions, and reminding us at once, in style and appearance, of the tombs of the kings of Pontus at Amasiyeh.

This huge relic of human labour was at a height of about a hundred feet above the valley, and cut into the side of a precipice. It consisted of a hollow stone mass, hewn out of the solid rock, with which it was still connected at top and bottom, but separated at the sides by a passage four feet nine inches in width, and thirty-one feet deep. The total height was thirty-two feet, and the total width forty-four feet nine inches.

The tomb was ornamented with two lateral pilasters in bas-relief, and could only be entered by a small aperture, about four feet high, and fifteen feet from the ground. Above the aperture was inscribed in colossal letters,

ΙΚΕΣΙΟΝ,

"of Icesius." Besides this, there were some rudely painted letters and a red cross, evidently the work of later hands, and for which the monument may be indebted to some modern Greeks,

Our ascent of the Kirk Delim took us exactly an hour, when we attained an elevation of 3090 feet, and from this point the country extended as a bare, elevated upland, with a small lake in the centre, otherwise generally cultivated,—a different space each year, and not different crops in rotation. In other respects, without wood, village, or house, the aspect of the upland was dreary.

In the evening we arrived at Churum, situated on the same upland, at a rather lower elevation, and had to wait some time in the streets before the governor, who was at his siesta, could be seen, to order us accommodation. This was ultimately given to us in a Mohammedan's house.

The next day we explored the town, in which the number of houses amounts to 1800, but as they are generally of one story, the population can scarcely be estimated at more than 7600. There are four khans, and as many baths, and we counted sixteen menarehs. There are but few Christian families, and these not resident, but engaged as tile-makers and potters. Much wheat is sold in the market.

The castle, which is a modern building constructed of ancient materials, is nearly square, walled round, with towers at the angles, and two square towers between these on each side. The interior is occupied by dwelling-houses; the walls are of various dates, and have often been rebuilt, the original plan of the building having probably been preserved. A number of white marble columns have been worked into the walls, besides many Greek tombstones, with crosses, and sculptures, and numerous inscriptions. What we copied did not, however, throw any light upon the history of the place.

If Churum is not Tavium, with which its name has certainly a remote relation, it is difficult to decide upon its ancient appellation. According to Strabo, there were in Trocmian Galatia two other castles besides

Tavium, one called Mithridatium, the other Danala. The latter is the place where Pompey and Lucullus met together, and where, according to Plutarch, they addressed each other with much politeness and mutual compliments on their great success. It is, however, described as a mere village.

Mr. Hamilton, in his travels in this region, in 1836, heard that the Greek Christian remains came from other places, but this did not agree with what we learned from the natives. On the contrary, we heard of a large stone with inscriptions having been carried away from hence by the Christians. Mr. H. errs also in supposing himself the first Frank who had visited this town, as Colonel Chesney had been there before him There is no doubt, however, that there is a very strong Mohammedan feeling in it. It is indeed chiefly a Turkoman city, and the unconcealed scowls and frowns which the traveller has to put up with, on visiting any little frequented Asiatic town or village, were not wanting on the occasion of our visit any more than on his.

On leaving Churum we crossed the plain and passed over the range called Koseh Tagh, which separates the watershed of the Halys from that of the Iris. On our descent, which was deep and very abrupt, we passed a guard-house, and then entered upon a low undulating country with wide grassy plains, occupied by nomadic tribes of Turkomans, who in summer time lead their flocks to the heights of the neighbouring mountains.

On arriving at the banks of the Halys, we found several parties waiting to be ferried over, as there was but one small raft on skins that could only take two persons, or one and his luggage, at a time; so to avoid a lengthened delay, we were obliged to bribe the boatman to carry us over first, each with his saddle, and the horse swimming behind.

We travelled some distance over marshy and grassy lands before we reached the foot of the hills of Eskilub. We here entered a small valley, the acclivities of which were covered with vineyards. Advancing by a winding road we came to where a vegetation of trees and shrubs, and richly productive gardens, gave promise of the neighbourhood of human habitations, when suddenly on turning an angle of the road, a city and a castle burst upon our view ; the latter was perched upon a singularly bold and naked-looking rock, in front of which was an almost perfectly conical hill with a smooth and slippery surface. Below, menareh after menareh, and houses crowding from the deep valley up the rocky sides of the hills, gradually opened upon us, till they were seen sweeping circularly round the castle as far as the eye could reach.

The governor of this secluded town gave us but a sorry welcome, perusing our firman, and then inquiring what brought us thither; our answer "motives of curiosity, and to visit the antiquities of the place" only made matters worse and the Turks more suspicious. "And of what use," he added, pointing to a cavalry sword which Mr. Rassam wore, almost as long as himself, "do you think those arms would be to you, did we wish you any harm?" curling his lip in contempt. The worthy Chaldean was non-plussed, while encouraged by his master's rudeness, another added, "Eh ! and still less use I think on the mountains, if we chose."

We were at length led to a room in the house of a

poor Mohammedan, who was nearly blinded by a chronic complaint in his eyes. The inhospitality of the authorities did not prevent us doing all in our power for the old man, and the remedial measures pursued succeeded so well, that we afterwards left the town with blessings which we had entered under scarcely suppressed curses.

I think I am not wrong in saying, that we certainly were the first Europeans who have, in modern times, visited the ancient town of Eskilub, formerly Blucium. At all events, the inhabitants had no memory of a Frank's visit. Rayahs or Christian subjects were allowed to trade in the town, and dwell in the Kerwanserai, but none were privileged to make it their place of residence, or bring their wives and families there.

The next day we commenced our explorations, and found the town to contain 1500 houses in round numbers, chiefly of two stories with tiled roofs. The number of menarehs was considerable, and the khans, good commodious buildings. At the foot of the castle hill, we visited, in some private gardens, several sepulchral caverns of greater beauty and elegance than are generally met with. Two of these are particularly remarkable for their pillars of handsome proportions, although indistinct order, and were ornamented with sculptures much mutilated. The subject of one of these bas reliefs was two angels advancing towards each other, the one bearing a cup in her hand, the other a branch.

The castle, or hill-fort, was an old structure of irregular form and very much dilapidated. The remains of towers at the different angles, is now almost all that is to be seen. The gateway and most of the walls have, however, been repaired within half a century, but not in more modern times. There are about thirty houses in the interior of the castle, and the female portion of the community hooted us sadly while we were taking a few admeasurements. They seemed to consider it as one great harem.

The castle of Blucium is mentioned by Strabo as being one of the royal castles of Deiotarus, the last of the Paphlagonian kings. The country around is all volcanic, and this, which gives their peculiar conical form and dark rugged aspect to the hills around, at the same time imparts to the soil of the valley an exuberant fertility.

November 22nd. We quitted Eskilub in a dense fog, and soon leaving the hills entered upon the cold upland of gypsum, having the river in a deep hollow to our left, and a hilly range to our right, the inner portions of which were thinly clad with pine trees.

After a journey of about eighteen miles, we came to the valley of Bayad, in which there were four villages, in one of which, called Nahadan, we obtained quarters for the night in the house of the mollah, who, strange to say, was a liberal-minded man, conversational, and even hospitable.

On the summit of a hill, close to the village, and commanding the valley below, are the ruins of a rude rock fort, the foundations of which were formed of huge stones irregularly piled one upon another. This ruin certainly appeared to be of Celtic origin, and I never met with any other like it, except in Galatia, near the Ishik Tagh.

There was also close to the mesjid of Nahadan a large and handsome Christian baptismal font hewn out of a mass of pitchstone porphyry; and the bridge over the rivulet of Bayad had also the appearance of great antiquity.

November 23rd. Our route lay over a country nearly similar to that of the previous day. In the valleys to the right we observed, occasionally, villages of pastoral Turkomans. A little beyond this, we passed a guard-house, which, by a very common process of transformation, had become also a coffee-house, and the "water of life," as they designate it on their doorways, was handed to us without our dismounting, when the customary small bakshish was contributed.

This vale was succeeded by dreary uplands, which at length terminated at the village of Olajúk, round which there was some cultivation. Here we found a resting-place for the night in a cottage, which, in the style of most Anatolian cottages, had loop-holes for windows, a fire-place in the rear, and the two sides of the room, the floor of which was of clay, raised about two inches to put the divan or mattrass and cushions on; the mattrass was composed of a bed of hay, with a carpet on it, and cotton prints stuffed with the same cheap material served for cushions, the whole well replete with vermin. A small space that has no raised portion is railed off at the lower portion of the room, for the attendants to stand in, and here in a recess in the wall is generally a copper basin with a sieve that supports the soap, also a ewer to pour the water out of, so that as a person washes himself the water that is used flows through the sieve out of sight.

In this case, as in many others, when hay was the foundation of the divan, we set the villagers to work to carry it all out of the room, a little water was then thrown down, the place swept out, and we then spread our carpets upon the bare ground. This was our only chance of procuring sleep, but it did not always answer the purpose, as the fleas came out of the mud walls in myriads.

November 24th. Our road to-day lay still over these same continuous uplands, with scarcely a shrub or a stone upon them for a bird to rest on; when such does occur—a single stone in the traveller's pathway—it was sure to be occupied by a hawk or some other raptorial bird, and if examined would be found whitened with dung, so long had it been that bird's customary point of repose.

After a ride of about two hours we came to a spring, where we parted with the seruji, whom we sent on with the baggage to Changri, while we ourselves turned down towards the village of Beli Bagh, to inquire after the salt mine which we had heard was in the vicinity. The direction was pointed out, but as it was raining hard, and had been doing so all the morning, we could not get one of the peasants to accompany us as a guide, so that we were a long time in finding out the mine, the entrance to which was small, and up a cross valley.

On entering, the aperture soon began to widen, and we became aware of the presence of lights, and of business going on. We had not gone far before we met a loaded mule, and a little further on, the passage still widening, we came to a kind of hall, where a number of men were at work, stripped, although it was quite cold in the open air, and labouring away at a solid bed of salt, with small hammers having thin flexible handles. The people who come for salt have to dig for themselves, and there is a superintendent who receives from one to one and a-half piastres per load, or sixpence for every 250 pounds of salt.

Quitting the mines, a couple of hours' ride, over the same upland, brought us in sight of the castle of Changri, situated on a barren-looking promontory, which advances between two fertile valleys, each watered by its rivulet, while the great mass of variously formed buildings, houses, khans, and jamis with their tall whitewashed menarehs, stretch far away round the promontory, up the acclivities, and into the most southerly of the two valleys, where it extends to both sides of the rivulet, which is crossed by decent bridges.

Eskilub—Blucium.

CHAPTER VIII.

Kalahjik—Peium.

Town of Changri. Its Christian Inhabitants. Politics of the old Families of Turks. Guard-house of Tunai. Continuous Fog. Kalahjik (the Little Castle). Local Rebellion. Shock of an Earthquake. Are joined by suspicious Characters. Impaled Kurd. Ruins at Hasan Oghlan.

Changri being a large town, with a Christian quarter, we were handed over, on application at the Serai for lodgings, to the kyaya of the Christians, who led us by narrow streets and steep ascents, till at length he came to a house which he pointed out as fitting for us. We were quite agreeable to any arrangement, but the inmates not at all so, for they carefully barred the doors, and heeded not the reiterated knocks and repeated threats of their nominal chief. At length some among the crowd that collected, mentioned that there was a small house belonging to an absent tailor, in the neighbourhood; thither accordingly we proceeded, and the key having been found, took tranquil possession of a tolerable room with a terrace in front, well adapted for observations, and commanding a pleasing view of the town and valley below.

We spent the greater part of the night observing, and the next day, I being rather unwell, Mr. Russell proceeded with Mr. Rassam to explore the antiquities of the town. They first directed their steps to a curious Mohammedan monument, designated as the Mejid Tash (the Glorious Stone). There were several tombs and open coffins within this building, which was also tenanted by some of those dervishes who are always found near tombs that are objects of pilgrimage, or of donations, or to which are attached some lucrative foundation. These dervishes pointed out the tombs as those of Mohammedan saints, but a Christian who accompanied the party, kept whispering, "Don't believe a word he says: they are Christian relics, stolen from us by the Mohammedans." The same dervishes asserted that this tubbeh, or ornamental tomb, was built in the time of Harun al Rashid, while an Arabic inscription on the porch dated its erection about the time of John Lascaris at Constantinople, and not long before the overthrow of the Khalifate by the Moghuls.

The castle is a mere ruin, the vestiges only of the ancient walls existing; there are some curious passages like slanting wells, the purposes of which we could not even guess at, and the interior is as usual filled with habitations.

The town itself contains about 3000 houses, and a population of 18,000 or 20,000 souls. Out of these there are thirty-three Greek families and sixteen Armenian. The Greeks have a church dedicated to St. Obadias; the Armenians have no place of worship. The Mohammedans, who are chiefly Turkomans, have eight jamis and several mesjids; there are six khans and four public baths. The chief trade is in salt and wool; yellow berries are an article of export, and the Christians bring European manufactured goods. Like Kastamuni, it is a place the trade of which is completely neglected by Europeans.

During our short stay here, we became very friendly with many Christians, from whom we received and returned visits; but we did not obtain any thing very new from our conversations. On religious subjects their ignorance was so great as to debar us even from any discussions on the matter; they scarcely knew the difference between the Greek and Armenian churches, and they were equally void of all traditionary lore or local reminiscences.

Strabo remarks of Gangra, that it was the residence of Deiotarus, the son of Castor and surnamed Philadelphus, who reigned over the kingdom of Morzes, (king of Paphlagonia in the time of Antiochus the Great).

Under the Byzantine empire, Gangra, or Gangaris, was an episcopate, and it ranks in the ecclesiastical notices, in the first place, as a metropolis. Bosporius, bishop of Gangra, attended the council of Ephesus, and, according to a passage in Sozomenes, (lib. iv., cap. 14,) there was also a synod held in Gangra itself.

The site chosen for the retirement of the ancient kings of Paphlagonia, as the advance of the successors of Alexander drove them out of their legitimate country, and comprising the three royal castles of Blucium (Eskilub), Gangra (Changri), and Peium (Kalahjik), is an open country, having few or no pretensions to beauty, being almost totally void of wood, and the soil generally saline, parched, and dry, but it is quite a secluded district, a portion of the valley of the Halys that is hemmed in all sides, and shut up at both extremities, by ranges of mountains and narrow and impassable ravines.

At the earlier period of the Osmanli history, Gangra held out for a long time under the first families of Turks against the encroaching power of the family of Osman. The Isfindabergs, being driven out of Kastamuni, sought refuge here; and to the present day, this district has little adhesion to the sultan of the Osmanlis, and what little did ever exist, has been still farther weakened by the favour shewn by the Sultan to reforms, which the older families of Turks look upon as inconsistent with the supremacy of Islamism and the all-conquering character of the nation.

The eventful life of Chapwan Oghlu shews how strong is still the feeling of clanship among the old Turkoman families, and if, as may be one day anticipated, (unless the Hatti Scheriff is rescinded at the Porte itself,) a revolt against reform should declare itself, all the great pashaliks of Peninsular Asia would be opposed to the present unfortunate vicegerent of the Prophet, who is forced to reform by the pressure from without, at the same time in dread of the rising supremacy of his numerous intelligent and industrious Christian subjects at home, and yet impeded and threatened by the prejudices of his own Mohammedan followers. It would really appear, that the last chance of the Sultan, if not delayed too long, when Armenia shall be restored to its kings, and St. Sophia be again a Greek church, would be to establish a truly Turkish empire in central Anatolia, which might vie in barbarous splendour and oriental pageantry, jealousy and abstraction, with the court of the Khalifs, or that of the chief of Ghiznee or Grenada.

December 3rd. We quitted the city by the new barracks, goodly edifices, but built in low marshy ground, and much exposed to malaria, and after following the valley of the river of Changri, about six miles, we turned over the same continuous uplands, alternating with occasional valleys with their brackish rivulets.

We were much hurt, on passing a village called Akghoran, at seeing some travelling Rayahs scoffed at and assailed with the most contemptuous language, by a parcel of boys and children, whom, however, we soon dispersed.

A little beyond this we came to the valley of the Tunai river, which flows from the hills of Yaprakli, where an annual fair is held which is celebrated all over Asia Minor; it begins on the 17th of September, and lasts seven days, and is generally attended by the Pasha of Angora. The Christians say, that there is a tomb of the Prophet Elias at this spot.

Travelling about two hours up the valley, we came to the village of Tunai, inhabited by guards, who are required for the protection of travellers in the time of the fair, and who received us hospitably. One of these men, who had the marks of several sabre cuts on his face, said he had killed six Kurd robbers in his lifetime.

During the whole of this day's journey we had

travelled in a dense fog. At times, when on the high uplands, we rose above it, and it was seen to occupy chiefly the valley of the Halys. As we approached Tunai, near sunset, the sun's beams partly penetrated the mist, and there was a decomposition of the least refrangible rays, which gave to the cliffs above the village a beautiful and remarkable appearance. At day-break next morning, the sky was clear, the ground covered with hoar frost, and the summits of the neighbouring hills tinged with the first rays of the rising sun; but a dense bank of mist lay along the valley, and in a few minutes the diffusion of vapour became general, and every thing was again wrapped in fog, which continued more or less all day, clearing up at intervals, but never leaving the sky cloudless.

Our progress the same morning through the fog, was cheerless enough, and it lay over the same kind of upland as before, till we came to a country broken up by volcanic rocks, where was cultivation and a large village called Chandur, while in one of the valleys lay a herd of camels, ruminating with their heads, by an unfailing instinct, turned to where the sun ought to have been.

From hence we crossed a more level country, having the high rock with the castle of Kalahjik upon its summit always in view, although the town itself was hid. On our arrival at this small town we had to wait some time in the Bazar till the kyaya of the Christians was found, but we were afterwards kindly received in the house that was assigned to us.

The town itself is built around the base of an isolated and nearly conical hill, upon the summit of which is the proud-looking castle filled with dwelling-houses, which in some places, assist in forming part of the walls. From the precipitous character of the rocks on all sides, and its own strength, Peium, which was the Gazophylacium, or place where the royal rolls and treasure were kept, must have been, in ancient warfare, a redoubtable stronghold.

Kalahjik was sacked at the time that Ibrahim Pasha came to Angora, in 1832, and is now in a state of great poverty and partial ruin. It contains 800 houses of Mohammedans, and 60 houses of Armenians, but the Christian population is very crowded. The Armenians have a well-kept church, dedicated to St. John the Baptist, and there are the remains of an old monastery in the neighbourhood. The circumstance which led to its partial destruction in 1832, was a local rebellion against the governor, Hajji Ahmed Bey, on the occasion of his levying an oppressive tax. The governor was besieged in his own house, and an old rusty gun was brought down from the castle, but nobody was found who could persuade it to go off; at length—a great resource among rebels of all countries—the serai was set on fire, and the governor was ultimately killed by the populace, who appear to have had no regard for his sanctity as a pilgrim. The Kalahjikiyans then placed themselves under the protection of Ibrahim Pasha, who sent thither troops under a certain Yardachi, but the brother of the late governor ruled at Changri, and, having raised a body of men sufficiently strong to overthrow the Egyptians, he re-captured the town, and exercised the most severe retribution upon its unfortunate inhabitants.

The morning after our arrival, at a little after two

o'clock, we were roused by a severe shock of an earthquake, which threatened to tumble the house about our ears. The movement was in undulations, and not irregular, and the house rolled like a ship at sea. The sensation was anything but agreeable, and the mortar falling from the rafters, and the loosened dirt down the chimney, added to the strain which the building underwent, gave a momentary feeling of alarm, but nothing fell near us, and there were only two houses thrown down in the whole town.

When we got up to examine the state of the barometer, the scene on the terrace was rather picturesque. Dogs barking, lights moving from window to window, and persons rushing upon the terraces with very incomplete toilettes. The first shock was followed shortly afterwards by a second, but which was very feeble. At half past two, P.M., we had another shock, rather circularly undulatory. At eight and ten o'clock the next day, we had other irregular rumbling shocks. At midday the weather cleared up a little, and we could distinguish the castle over our heads, the first time since we had been at the town.

Mr. Rassam, although a native of the East, was much affected by these repeated shocks. We were boiling some eggs for breakfast when the first shock occurred on the second morning at eight o'clock. Mr. Russell and myself ran to watch the indications of a basin of treacle, left on the terrace for that purpose, requesting Mr. Rassam to be so kind as to mind the eggs: "You know, Rassam, how long they take to boil." "Yes, yes," was the answer, "half an hour, half an hour, I know."

The morning of the 7th, at 35 minutes past 2,

we had another sharp shock. The fog had continued, with slight intermissions, pretty nearly the same during the continuance of the shocks; there was no wind, and there was only upon one occasion a distant rumbling noise that accompanied the shock. The effect upon the soil was imperceptible, nor could we hear of it affecting any of the springs. The electrical condition of the atmosphere must have been, from the previously described state of the weather, subjected to great tension and great extremes. The direction of the undulations coincided with the direction in which the igneous rocks of the country have extended the line of their upheaving force, and is the same as the direction (not the dip) of the beds or strata of the superincumbent sedimentary formations. The castle hill of Kalahjik is trachytic.

December 7th. However interesting it might be to watch the phenomena of earthquakes, we were not at all sorry at leaving this unstable and rocking place, on which, at the morning of our departure the fog still lay as thick as ever; but when we ascended the hills, we found that it only occupied the valley of the Halys, and spread from thence over the adjacent cold uplands of gypsum.

On our left we had a mountain range (Edris Tagh), the summits of which were now clad with snow. As this part of the country had been described to us at Kalahjik as very unsafe and infested with robbers, we were not at all pleased, when about twelve miles from the town, at the appearance of two well-armed Kurds, who came down upon us from the hills, and who, after indulging in a series of scrutinizing scowls, trudged on, as if belonging to our party.

As we were the strongest in numbers, being three, besides an unarmed seruji, we consulted in a few brief words, and then positively insisted upon our new companions either dropping behind or passing on before, as the odds of numbers might at any moment have been rendered null by a surprise; besides which, the constant attention requisite to the movements of such persons was extremely irksome.

Our wishes, although communicated in the most decided manner, were only received with disdainful sneers, whereupon we stopped short to enforce them. The Kurds then dismounted, while we proceeded on our journey.

Scarcely a mile beyond where we parted from our visitors, we met with a cause for the turn for brigandage in this district, in an example of severe justice, which, in a country so constituted, serves rather to keep up than to allay evil propensities, by inoculating predatory habits with a spirit of revengeful retribution. This was the impaled body of a Kurd, suspended by iron spikes, one of which passed through both legs, another through the abdomen, and the third was passed through the head, immediately below the ears. He had been a fine tall man; one arm lay upon his bosom, the other hung pendant below, and the body was wrapt in a cloth bound round the waist by a band.

Our attention was soon diverted from this sad sight by the presence of numerous partridges, which we proceeded to chase, as we descended a rocky ravine, at the head of which was a village where the Kurds who rendered the district so insecure were said to dwell.

The country after this began to improve, some cultivation showed itself, and we arrived towards sunset at the large village of Hasan Oghlan, inhabited by peaceful Turkomans, whose women were busily employed in making those carpets for the production of which their race is so celebrated.

Hasan Oghlan has evidently been an antique site or station, for we found numerous fragments of ruins scattered all over the village, including wrought stones, columns, and capitals, but no inscriptions.

The distance from Hasan Oghlan to Angora is about sixteen miles, and we arrived at that city the next day, (*December 8th*,) after a pleasant ride of three hours and a half, over low cultivated hills, feeding here and there flocks of the beautiful Angora goat.

CHAPTER IX.

Basaltic Pass.

A French Instructor of Cavalry. Visit to Izzet Mehemet Pasha. A Swiss Renegade. Severity of Winter. Start for the Mines of Ishik Tagh. Fort of the Galatians. Mule buried in the Snow. Thermal Baths. Remarkable Basaltic Pass. Pine Forest in Winter. The Mines of Ishik Tagh. A Sacrifice to Pluto. Quit the Mines. City of Angora. Its Ruins. Temple of Jupiter. Christian Churches. Angora Goats. Trade and Commerce.

Our arrival at Angora was characterised by a ridiculous circumstance, the mention of which, however, may serve to put travellers on their guard. Among the resident Europeans, who came to visit us, was a certain Captain Müller, a Frenchman, in the service of Izzet Mehemet Pasha, then mushir, or governor of the sanják of Angora, and with whom Mr. Pulsford had left, on his passage through the town, a letter for us. This person earnestly requested our company to dinner the next day, when we were introduced to his lady. When the cloth was removed, the gallant captain asked, with an air of much earnestness, if we had heard the news? upon our acknowledging what was very true, a profound ignorance of all political movements for some time back, he informed us, with anxious condolence, that war had broken out between England and the Sublime Porte, and that it was the pasha's intention not to allow us to leave Angora; or, if we did, that he certainly would have us destroyed, his resolution and cruelty being both equally familiar to every one. He then asked if we had yet waited upon the pasha, a point of etiquette which we were forced to allow, we had as yet neglected to perform. He then proposed that this should be done instantly, and that he would introduce us, in order to propitiate his Excellency. Such hasty movements, accompanied by such improbable statements, had not failed, however, by this time, to awaken our suspicions that all was not right, so I positively declined his proffered service, and declared my intention of waiting upon the pasha next morning, when I should be accompanied by Mr. Rassam, who was all I could possibly want on the occasion. The Cavalry Instructor had, however, buckled on his sword, and lifted up his stock in martial trim, and it was a difficult matter to get rid of him; but bowing away, we gradually got out of the yard, and felicitated ourselves on our escape.

The ensuing day we waited on this mushir, so renowned for his inflexible wrath and savage cruelties, and his appearance did not belie his reputation. He was winding up a number of watches at the moment of our introduction, and only looked up after the lapse of a few moments, and, when he did so, it was with the look of a very intelligent tiger—a mixture of sagacity and cruelty, for the time being lit up by a willingness to be civil.

In a short time, after the usual compliments on our part and inquiries on his, the conversation became more general. He asked for our firman, and when he observed among the reasons why we had insisted in that document for post horses and accommodations off the great road, and in every part of the Sultan's dominions, that we intended exploring the mines of the country, he said he had already heard of us; that we had been to the mines of Bakir Kurehsi; and he then proceeded to detail our journey, step by step, in his province, taking pride in showing us how well-informed he had been, with regard to our movements. He next asked us if we would examine certain mines situate in the Ishik Tagh, also in his sanjak; when, as we wished to propitiate him, in order to obtain his assistance in visiting the Kurdish and central district of Haimaneh, we proffered our services. We then mentioned the result of our meeting with his cavalry instructor the previous evening, and insisted in gentle but plain words that if our lives were not in danger under his protection,—and it was quite ridiculous to suppose the contrary—that the man who had ventured to surmise such a thing of his Excellency, should be dismissed his service. The Pasha, after a moment's silence, reflected upon the captain's conduct in language that has become an apophthegm in the Turkish, but is not fit for ears polite, although it may be represented by the saying, "He has eat his words." We left the pasha, with a promise to dine with him the next day, and in a short time afterwards Captain Müller was dismissed to Constantinople.

He did not, however, cease his hostility to our party. Soon after our arrival at Angora a Swiss renegade one morning made his appearance in our room, for whom I at first entertained a great abhorrence, on account of his apostasy, but when I upbraided him for the fact, he answered so piteously, that it was *une affaire de cœur*, that I could not help commiserating the man. He was a medical man, attached to the person of the pasha, and the object of his visit was (for, as a renegade, he was denied the privilege of corresponding with his Christian friends,) to get me to forward a letter for him, as we intended sending a parcel hence, for Constantinople, by private hands, and not by the pasha's tatars, which might have been fatal to its safety. This I consented to do, and, in gratitude, he brought me, some time afterwards, a letter from M. Müller, from Constantinople, again denouncing us as spies to the pasha, from what he said was the very best authority.

A few days after our arrival at Angora a heavy fall of snow came on, and continued without intermission for six days. This was followed by a sharp clear frost, which gradually increased in intensity, till it attained a severity quite unknown in these climates, and not to be expected in such southerly parallels as Asia Minor, if we did not take into consideration the elevation of the great central uplands, only broken up by groups and ranges of mountains, which constitute all save the extreme littoral portions of that peninsula, and are seldom below 3000 feet in elevation; the plain of Angora, which is among the lowest, averaging exactly 3000 feet, and in the month of January the thermometer frequently fell to + 5° of Fahrenheit, or 27° below freezing point.

In such a severe frost the swiftest rivers were sheeted with ice, and the mountain torrents seemed as if arrested in their fall. The bazaar dogs perished in numbers in the markets, and many were the sad tales of benighted travellers, or of whole caravans, lost in the snow, that reached the town.

Under such circumstances, it was an absurdity to think of continuing our journey. Could we have traversed the central plateau of the Haimaneh or trudged along the valley of the Halys, our observations could have been of no use to physical geography or to geology. A few points might have been brought to bear upon one another, some might have been astronomically fixed, and there our utility would have ended. But, had we been willing to go, we should not have found a muleteer to accompany us, the post had long broken up, communication even with near villages had almost ceased, and, in this case, necessity, as well as our consciences, determined the choice, when none, in reality, remained to us.

The pasha had not, however, forgotten our promise about the mines, and he sent for us, one morning, to converse upon the subject, and inquire if we would start. We represented the impossibility of getting into the mountains while the snow was so deep; he said he would obviate this, if it required a hundred men to clear the way. We then said that if there were no physical impossibilities to overcome, we were willing and ready to start at a moment's notice. He turned round to his followers and said, with a triumphant air, "Look at these Franks! they will travel in the frost and snow, while you sit shivering by the fire-side."

We accordingly started about mid-day of the 8th of January, accompanied by an officer of the household, who was to see us provided for on our route and at the mines, his suite, and two Greek miners.

Our road lay over the plain, which was covered with from two to three feet of snow, towards the foot of the Baulos Tagh (Hills of St. Paul's), on arriving at the outskirts of which, we fell in with a flock of the largest vultures of the country,—lammergeyers of the Taurus—that were feeding upon a poor donkey, which had starved on the road. We were quartered this night at Yuya, a village at the foot of the hills, our expenses being charged upon the peasants' taxes.

The ensuing day our road lay over the side of the hills, when our difficulties first commenced. The horses got on with great labour over the even slopes, but each time that we came to a rut or ravine we were sure to have many tumbles, and the horses, sinking deeper in the snow-drifts though their plunging efforts to release themselves, were often with difficulty extricated from their perilous situations.

During the day's ride we passed Miranos, a village where there are ruins of a castle, and the name of which, mis-pronounced by the Turks, appears to have some relation to that of Minizus of the Itineraries, but it is a few miles off the present great road from Angora to Constantinople.

On our way we observed several foxes, prowling about, the severe frost having driven them out in quest of food. Besides these, a few snow-buntings and stone-chats were the only things visible. We passed a river coming down from the St. Paul's hills on the ice, and were quartered for the night at Al Kahun, a village in the fertile vale of the Tcher Su, where there is an abundant spring, which, from its preserving its mean annual temperature, had the appearance of smoking in the frost.

January 10*th*. We left Al Kahun at half-past six, in a dense snow-storm, so dark that we could but just distinguish the different members of the party. We only travelled up the same valley, as far as the village of Jighiler, where we stopped, as our officer, who was not accustomed to cold, had become very unwell.

Mr. Russell and I, however, started on foot, to visit a ruin about three miles off, called Kara Weran (the Black Ruin). It was a rude and primitive structure, consisting of a single wall, built of huge stones, put together without mortar, and inclosing a space of 127 feet in diameter. Not far distant, upon a neck of rock below, was a smaller fort of a similar description. As I never met with similar ruins in any other part of Asia Minor, except in Galatia, as at Bayad, I am inclined to look upon these remains as Celtic, and probably erected by the Galatians. On our return, we came through the village of Ak Weran (White Ruin), where we found another party of Greek miners, under an officer, who were coming to join us and assist at the mines, and to whom we paid a visit.

January 11*th*. We travelled, our party now much increased in numbers, over hill and vale, to Bazar Keuy, a village with a jami. It was market-day, which, notwithstanding frost and snow, was held in open air. The objects exposed for sale were goats, sheep, corn, geese, wood, hare-skins, horse-shoes, and nails.

Our ride hence was a most dreary one, winding among low hills, occasionally slightly wooded, a few bright-coloured jays flitting about on the desolate-looking branches. On this waste we met with a poor man, whose mule had got entangled in the snow, so that he was not able to extricate it. Our Osmanli companions laughed at the traveller's predicament; but, much to their dissatisfaction, for they wanted to push on, we dismounted, and lending a hand to the work, got the mule into the right road again.

This long upland terminated in a sudden and precipitous ravine, which led us into the valley of the Beybazar River, which a little further up we passed on the ice, arriving a little beyond at the village of Upper Jighiler, where we halted for the night; the pasha's officer and attendants having one apartment, ourselves another, and the Greek miners being billeted about.

January 12*th*. We ascended the hills to our right, and, crossing over them, came to the upper valley of the Beybazar River, which opened upon us in considerable beauty, notwithstanding the cheerlessness of winter. The mountain heights on both sides were well wooded, and the dark pines were canopied in snow, till they sometimes resembled Esquimaux huts. The river flowed in some places between precipices, which remained naked from their perpendicularity, wild and fantastic needles of rock also jutted from out of the general white expanse, while the river itself appeared as if arrested in its course by the icy arm of winter. After a journey of seven miles up this valley, we turned off, to the thermal waters of Sey Hammam, formerly visited by Pococke. We found the waters issuing in a very copious stream from a curious siliceous rock. The water was pure and colourless, but deposited iron. The temperature 107° Fahrenheit, or 41½° Cent.

The remains of an old building which adorned these waters, and which, from the few remnants yet extant, evidently possessed some claims to architectural beauty, had been used in the construction of a modern mesjid, which, with a stable for horses and a modern bath-house, constituted all the edifices in the neighbourhood. The actual baths are divided into two; one for the men, the other for the women.

The rivulet formed by the spring was not frozen for some distance below, and the intervening free space was, from its higher temperature, so sought for at this season of the year by fish, that they could be caught with the hand, and seemed to delight to swim up to where the water was quite warm.

About two miles beyond where it is joined by the rivulet of the thermal springs, the *now* rivulet of Bey-bazar flows through a pass in the mountains, which is a great natural curiosity.

The base of the hills on both sides is formed of an immense number of prisms of basalt, of great regularity of form, some vertically, others horizontally disposed, and others striking out at various angles of inclination, succeeding one another in steps, or grouped together in figures resembling those produced by a kaleidoscope. Above these, polyhedral masses of similar characters tower up in rocky pinnacles of fantastic shape, in which the colossal prisms are variously disposed, giving origin to much contrasted effect, sometimes constituting a wall of pillars, horizontally placed one upon another, at other times sweeping round in prolonged curves, and then again standing out at various angles of inclination, but straight and unbroken. This motley distribution of basaltic prisms surpassed anything to be seen at the Causeway, Fairhead, or the Cave of Fingal, and most resembled sketches that have been published of the volcanic senery of the islands of St. Helena and Ascension.

Beyond this remarkable pass, the valley widened, and became full of villages, in one of which, called by distinction Sahlun (the Place of Taxes), we were quartered for the night.

January 13th. This day we again commenced the ascent of the mountains, up which we toiled above an hour before we reached the verge of the pine forests. These fine trees seemed in their native element when shrouded with snow: their strong spreading branches bearing vast accumulations, that sometimes weighed them down to the ground; while others rose above these, fringing the mountain sides with a lace of leafy white, or climbed up the mountain heights, till lost in cloud or mist; at other times they gracefully swept down the long acclivities, till suddenly stopped by some vertical cliff, from crevices in which isolated trees would still start here and there, in bold relief, amid rock, ice, and snow.

After travelling about an hour through these forests, and teazing our poor shivering Osmanlis by shaking the heavily-laden branches upon them, we came to a little open space in the forest, where were four or five wooden houses, which had a most desolate aspect. These we found were attached to the mines, and one of them, containing a single apartment, was assigned to us, while the officer quartered himself in another.

The first few days after our arrival we spent in the examination of the shafts and galleries sunk in the neighbourhood, with a view to drawing up a general plan of the works, ascertaining the probable distribution of the metalliferous veins, and the promise held out to future labours, more especially by the present or other works. This was a work of no small toil, as the veins had often, through inadvertence, been left behind by the miner, while he followed another route, in pursuit of some vision or fancy of his own, and at other times had never been reached at all. We had thus to spend the greater part of several days, candle in hand, examining the walls, floors, and roofs of the ancient and modern galleries.

While I had been engaged in this work, Mr. Russell had been industriously making the admeasurements necessary for a plan of the district. This accomplished, he superintended certain necessary alterations in the furnaces, which being completed, enabled us to commence smelting; when, although the selection of ores which we had procured did not give us all the results anticipated from blow-pipe analysis, still they were quite satisfactory as to the general produce of the metalliferous veins.

We now prepared to take our departure; but this, from the depth to which the snow had accumulated, was found impossible, even although we set thirty men to work to clear us a passage as far as Sahlun.

The winter had been desolate enough in such a place, even when occupation robbed it of part of its dreariness; but our labours completed, it became doubly so. During the period of our residence we had several snow storms, which increased the depth of the accumulated mass, and finally cut off all communication with the villages. Provisions, under these circumstances, became exceedingly scanty, and this increased till the treat of an onion to flavour our daily repast of bread was a great desideratum.

One morning in the midst of this scarcity, we were surprised to find a cock, newly killed, yet not eaten, in front of the houses. Upon our inquiring, the Greeks said they had killed it, in order to propitiate the genius of the mines, and a sacrifice must not be eaten. This is a remnant of a very old superstition, for cocks were sacrificed to Pluto by the ancients in a similar manner.

At length, on the 25th of January, the thermometer rose, and the weather became perceptibly milder. Crows and magpies for the first time visited us; and traces of deer were observed in the snow. The dogs now went out of the houses, and made themselves beds in the snow. On February 1 we made an attempt at departure, and had some trees cut down, to make a temporary bridge for the horses over a deep snow-drift; and the next day we succeeded in effecting the pass. The descent of the mountains was comparatively easy; and in the evening, to our infinite joy, we found ourselves at Sahlun.

As the mild weather had already influenced the lower country to a much greater degree than in the mountains, our journey next day presented no great difficulties, but we were detained a day at Jighiler, by the swelling of the Beybazar River. It was in vain that various attempts were made to ford it; we had to stay till early the ensuing morning, when the night frost had diminished the waters, and when we all of us got over in safety.

From Lower Jighiler we struck across the mountains of St. Paul's, fording the river of Kara Bazar with some difficulty. Our Osmanli and Greek friends we had left long behind us. On arriving at the Chibuk Su (Pipe or Strait River), or River of Angora, Mr. Russell took the water at a deep place, when both rider and horse were soon carried away, and only extricated on coming to a shallower spot. With this slight mishap, we arrived the same evening at Angora, and the next day reported ourselves to the pasha, who scarcely thanked us for the labour we had been at on his account.

Before quitting Angora, we may be permitted one or two observations on this metropolitan town. The population appears to consist of 10,000 Mohammedans, 5000 Christians, and 200 Jews. A large portion of the town is built within the castle, where are some of the best houses. The streets are narrow and irregular; the houses, as usual, poor and unsubstantial. The remains of antiquity are numerous; but as these have been described by so many travellers, we will not weary the reader with reiterated details.

Pococke and Tournefort have described the remains of Roman architecture, among which stands foremost a temple in honour of Augustus, on which a separate memoir has been published in this country. It is a most valuable historical monument, and is so considered by Heeren. In later times, Mr. W. J. Hamilton has copied a portion of the inscription previously neglected.

Several massive but irregular ruins of temples, guard-houses, or other public buildings, besides numerous inscriptions in the castle, and some rather rudely-sculptured lions, belong probably to the Roman era, if they do not also illustrate partly the state of arts among the Galatians; but of that period few, if any, well-authenticated remains appear to have been found.

Remains of Byzantine architecture are by far the most frequent: a column of little pretensions to beauty, and which tradition has dedicated to Licinius, the conqueror of Maximin, numerous sculptures in the walls of the castle and of the town, some inscriptions, and various tombs and monuments, illustrate this period.

Amid ruins of a more modern date, are the castle as it now exists, a church of doubtful antiquity, and a subterranean viaduct or aqueduct of some extent; and in a small castle which occupies the highest part of the castle rock, are some old coats of mail.

Tournefort's Temple of Jupiter presents nothing but the vestiges of an oblong building constructed of large stones, on the summit of the Khedrelez, where is a modern ziyaret. This name of the hill is, according to the Foreign Secretary of the Royal Geographical Society, a colloquial corruption of Khidr Iliyas, the name of a Turkish saint and hero, confounded by the Christians with St. George and the prophet Elias. This is a tolerably extensive field for misreadings and misinterpretations.

The Armenians of Angora had formerly seven churches, of which only those of the Holy Cross and Sergius (St. George), are now used. The Schismatic or Romish Armenians have no church of their own. The Greeks have two churches, St. George and the Trinity.

During our stay here we made several excursions in the neighbourhood, more especially to the Chibuk Owahsi, traditionally the field of the combat between Tamerlane and Bajazet; to Hosein Ghazi, a volcanic mountain, with a dervishes' monastery on its summit, to which is attached a tradition that we shall relate afterwards; and to Chal Tagh, a mountain which bears indisputable evidence of having been one of those fire beacons which are described by the Byzantine historians, as crossing the whole peninsula.

Although the extreme climate of the upland of Angora, that is to say, its great summer heats and severe winters, constitutes the main cause of the peculiarity in fleece of the goats, sheep, cats, and dogs of Angora, still it cannot be the sole origin of the peculiar race of the former; or whence their local circumscription, while spots with nearly similar extremes of climate are met with on the Asiatic peninsula, yet without the breed of Angora goats? It is one of those cases of a peculiarity having in the first instance a relation to climate, yet afterwards propagated as a permanent variety that remains constant and undeviating for generations, as we see in races of dogs, and, as Dr. Pritchard has so ably shown, also in races of men.

The quantity of wool now annually exported amounts to 500,000 okahs of $2\frac{3}{4}$ pounds each; but of this only 200,000 okahs, or about 500,000 pounds, are of the more valuable fleece. The other articles of commerce are yellow berries, of which the amount of produce is said to be 25,000 pounds. The roots of madder, gum-mastic, gum-tragacanth, wax, and honey also form articles of commerce. But the chief trade is in wool, merino twist, and goats' hides. The demand for British goods and manufactures was generally admitted to be considerable.

The older European commerce of Angora was always great. The tombstones in the burial-ground of the monastery of St. Paul's attest how many of our countrymen must have been engaged in it*. It is difficult to account for its decline, unless from unwillingness on the part of merchants to open communication with a place where consular protection has been abrogated for a period of now eighteen years. Abandoned by both English and French, who have now only a few native Christian agents in the place, the Armenians have had the courage to establish a house of their own in London. When the benefits to be derived from the new privileges granted to commerce and industry, by the Hatti Scheriff, and the commercial treaty, become more effectively insured (if ever they are destined to be put in force at all), there may be still some chance of the revival of commerce, and communications with the interior will undoubtedly obtain new activity as its resources become more generally known and better appreciated.

* A learned medicus of Angora told us he had discovered near that city the tomb of Edward the Black Prince. We went to see this great curiosity, and found it to be the tomb of one Edward Black Mercator Anglus.

CHAPTER X.

View at Angora.

Quit Angora. Epidemic among Cattle. Istanos and its Caves Ascent of the Goklu Tagh. Mountain Cave. Castle and hot springs of Germesh. Robbers' Cave. Junction of two Rivers. Upland of the Haimaneh. Warm Baths of Yanina. Distrust of the Kurds. Red Castle. Plague in the Villages. Monastic Caves.

We quitted Angora on the 19th of March, and were accompanied by a khawass bashi and two khawasses, sent by Izzet Pasha, as a guard through the Kurdish districts of Haimaneh. Frequent discharges of guns and pistols, loud shouts from the khawasses, who were galloping in every direction, testified to the satisfaction which we felt, and which reflected itself upon all the party, at our liberation from long imprisonment.

This first day we merely made a short journey, stopping at the village of Emir Yaman, about four hours, or fifteen miles, from Angora. There had been lately a severe

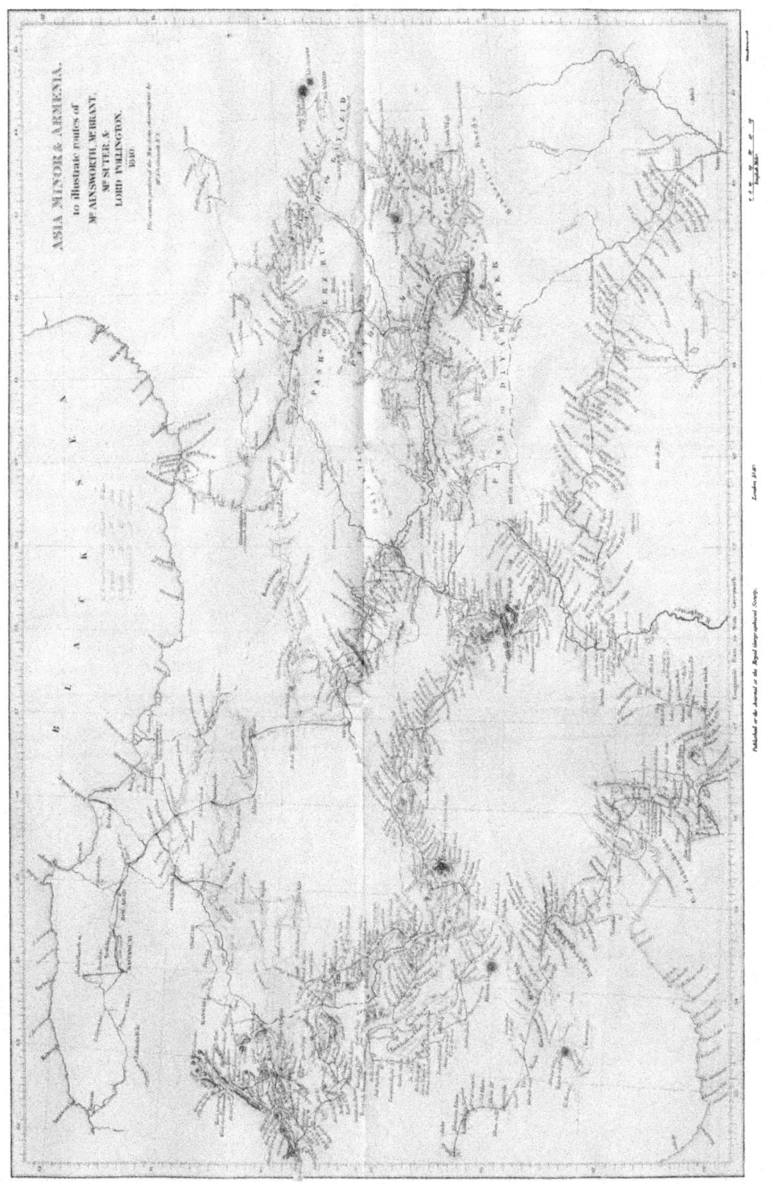

The material originally positioned here is too large for reproduction in this reissue. A PDF can be downloaded from the web address given on page ivof this book, by clicking on 'Resources Available'.

epidemic among the cattle at this place, and in the open space before the houses, the yards, and all around the village, bodies of dead animals were left to putrefy. I could never ascertain whether this singularly filthy and unwholesome practice originated from slothfulness solely, or from religious superstition. I am inclined to think both feelings are concerned, and that there really exists a prejudice against removing the bodies of domestic animals, from the threshold where they died; be this as it may, it is one of the common causes of the origin of endemic plague in the rural districts of Asia Minor.

The next day our ride was diversified, by endeavouring to get at some wild fowl, which were observed in great numbers on the surface of two small lakes that occurred on the road. Beyond this, we came down upon the open and fertile valley of the Tcher Su, which at this, its southerly end, is shut up by a ridge of trachytic rocks. We entered this ridge by a narrow pass, through which the river forced its way, and arrived shortly afterwards at the small town of Istanos, picturesquely situated on the banks of the river, and backed by bold and precipitous cliffs, which break off into fantastic peaks and pinnacles, the latter as well as the cliffs themselves, being burrowed by numerous caverns.

The town itself contains about 400 houses, 50 of which belong to Mohammedans and the rest to Armenians; it occupies the right bank of the river, and being confined by the rocks, forms a long narrow street well built up on the river, which has thus the aspect of a quay, and adds to the general appearance of comfort and cleanliness.

The opposite side of the river is occupied by gardens

and a new church—an edifice that redounds to the credit of the industrious Christians of the place, who are chiefly engaged in the manufacture of camlets, merinos, and twist.

A remarkable rock, almost insulated from the cliff, advances over the lower part of the town. It is crowned by ruins of former times, covered with storks' nests and burrowed by cavernous passages, which are extremely difficult to reach.

Another series of caverns, also approached with difficulty, stretched along the face of the rock in the rear. The first chamber of these was reached by a gallery, and from it another gallery ascended, partly hewn out in stairs, and a little protection given, by a rotten wooden rail. A long series of chambers are then entered, some having reservoirs for water, and most of them fire-places. The whole extent was 145 paces; the chambers seven in number, the galleries four, but many of the chambers were again divided, so as to contain two or three families. There were no monuments or inscriptions of antiquity discovered by our research, and all that can be said is that the caves appear to have been retreats for security and defence, and not improbably, places of refuge from religious persecution.

Nearly all the male part of the population of Istanos had gathered together to watch our progress, but none even of the boys, attempted to follow us up the side of the cliff.

Mr. Russell and I, accompanied by one of the khawasses and a seruji, rode out early the next morning to ascend the Goklu Tagh (Mount of the Sky), the culminating point of this part of the country, which towers conspicuously on every side over the plain of Angora.

After a sharp ride of two hours, over a barren, hilly country, during which we passed a ruin having somewhat of a Pelasgian character, we arrived at the village of Goklu, situated not far from the base of the hill, and where we obtained a guide.

We began our ascent under unfavourable circumstances, the wind being high and snow falling so densely, that objects could not be discerned even at a short distance. This, however, added at times to the mysterious picturesqueness of our road: we had several glaciers to pass over; and the steep depths below being filled up with mist, combined with the obscurity above and around, which prevented us seeing terra firma, conveyed the momentary impression of ourselves being buoyed up upon the bosom of a cloud.

About an hour's ride brought us to the entrance of a large cave, which is celebrated throughout the adjacent country, being visible at a great distance. It is situate on the exposed face of a cliff, which rises almost perpendicularly to the summit of the mountain. The cave was fronted with a wall of stones, and from formerly being a place of refuge and defence, had now become a retreat for cattle, when led to their summer pasturage on the mountain.

We did not ascend any further, but made the best of our way back, partly, after reaching the more level country, at a canter, and partly at a galloping pace. The fullest speed was, however, put forth on our entrance into the town, through the streets of which we rode, clatter and dash, the seruji first, the khawass second, shouting and flogging the first onward, and lastly, Russell and I, all ungallantly throwing an enormous quantity of mud upon the Armenian ladies, who lined the streets to see the procession go by.

The next day we parted from our Angora landlord, who had accompanied us as far as Istanos, and who showed much kindly feeling on the occasion. I made a brief visit to the junction of the Angora River and the Tcher Su, which takes place among caverned cliffs with wood at their base. On my way back I met Russell shooting field-fares, and together, we soon overtook the remainder of the party.

We travelled fifteen miles through a bleak miserable country, but cultivated in some places, and not without many flocks and herds sprinkling the barren-looking hills. During our ride we passed through two or three villages in a very ruinous condition, and containing very few inhabited houses. On our left was a remarkable peninsulated hill, called Ada Teppeh.

We were quartered for the night at a farm belonging to a brother of the then pasha of Erzrum, and called Kara Koyunli (the Black Sheep), containing about twenty houses, inclosed in a square like an Arab or a Persian fort.

Russell and I rode out early next morning to visit the castle and hot springs of Germesh (Germa or Thermæ?), fording the Angora river with some difficulty, although in summer it is said to be nearly absorbed by the surrounding friable and saline soil.

The thermal waters were on the acclivity of this hill, with but a medium temperature (84° Fahr.), and covered by a semicircular dome, apparently of the

Mohammedan era, although ascribed by the natives to the former possessors of the soil, under the common designation of Genoese.

The ruins of the castle occupied the summit of the hill, which is of plutonic origin. It is most remarkable for having huge masses of stone built into its walls, and consisted of an interior portion, bounded on one side by a precipice, and defended on the other by an outer wall or curtain.

On our return, we found that Rassam had started with the baggage, but we soon overtook him, as the road lay over a level plain, till blocked up by a ridge of hills, through which the river flows by a winding and picturesque pass.

Within this, we found another abundant thermal spring, and traces of an ancient hewn road, but what most excited our curiosity was an old building, the ruins of which stood within a large natural cavern, situated high up on the side of the cliffs. The peasants knew nothing about it, "except," they said, "that it had been formerly a robbers' hold," but to our frequent inquiries, we only got the usual reply, not very civilly communicated, "Who should know any thing about it?"

Beyond the pass, we came upon an open plain bounded by low hills of gypsum, and travelling over this, still in the valley of the river, we arrived in the evening, at the large village of Sarrubas, where we were to change horses. We followed our usual plan here, of claiming a room for ourselves and quartering the khawasses in another, for the rude and boisterous manner of these irregular troopers rendered them any thing but desirable companions in a room.

In the morning we had to obtain a change of horses, which caused some delay. We then separated into two parties: Mr. Rassam to go with the baggage, guarded by two khawasses, directly across the plain, to the village of Mislu, while Russell and I, accompanied by a khawass, rode to the junction of the Angora river with the Sakkariyeh.

On this ride, we passed a flock of sheep of the Angora race, that were suffering fearfully from the epidemic; their carcasses were strewed all around, and many were lying down at that moment perishing. The shepherds had as much as they could do to separate the dead from the living, and numerous vultures had so glutted themselves as to be too lazy to move.

The point of junction of the two rivers was viewed from an eminence, on granite rocks, amidst deep defiles of which the two streams fought their way to unite a short distance below.

We had a long ride across a dreary plain to Mislu, but being unincumbered with baggage horses it was accomplished in a short time. This village, from its ruins around, was evidently once flourishing, but its old walled-in gardens are now neglected, and its houses falling to decay. As Rassam had obtained quarters, and had had dinner prepared, we finished in time to go out with our guns before dark, there being both ducks and partridges in the neighbourhood.

Mislu is in a pass of the Germesh mountains. Leaving this, next day we crossed a valley with large village, and commenced the ascent of the Shabanuse hills. The prospect from the crest of these was extensive, and embraced the undulating district of Haimaneh, the valley of the Sakkariyeh and Angora rivers, and the Goklu mountains, with the distant chains of the Idris Tagh, the Elma Tagh, and the Sevrihisar hills.

We descended these hills by the summer quarters, called the Father of Rain, and passing some small caves with hewn arches, reached a fine cultivated plain abounding with the large partridges which build in the boundless pastures of the interior, and which we found more easily approachable when feeding on cultivated lands than on their own plains, but never to be approached within any thing like the distance of the rock, or the red-legged, or the common partridge. The natives call them taoke, or fowls.

We this day reached Kargah-li (Spear Town), the residence of one of the vaivodahs of Haimaneh. It was a large and flourishing village of agricultural Turkomans, whose antique pride still exhibited itself in their herds of camels, their gaudy dresses, their haughty manners, and numerous black slaves. There were several Christians here with long rows of mules, bartering for corn; and here we first learnt that the plague was raging in the Haimaneh, and that we should come to it after two hours' ride, the next day.

The rich agricultural land around Kargah-li does not extend far; we did not travel an hour the next day (the 26th,) before we found ourselves upon a high undulating upland, without wood or cultivation, and with but little variety of vegetation, which was, indeed, almost entirely composed of grasses and wormwood.

After travelling about sixteen miles without any thing to interest us, we came to a valley, which was divided into two parts by a range of hills, through which the rivulet had to find its way by a narrow and precipitous pass. This valley was generally cultivated and contained several villages, at one of which, called Alif, (the first letter of the alphabet), we found numerous tombs, columns, and other fragments, evidently of Byzantine origin, and indicating an ancient site.

We halted in another and smaller vale beyond, at the village of Kadi Keuy (Judge Ville), formerly the seat of government of the whole of the Haimaneh, but now only containing about forty houses built on the acclivity of a rocky hill. We heard nothing here of the anticipated plague, and amused ourselves after our usual observations, with the children of the village, several of whom had joined us while sitting at the door of our cottage, and entered playfully and willingly into conversation, examining with great delight and wonder, every thing that was European.

The baggage horses, accompanied by Mr. Rassam and two khawasses, started early next morning for the village of Juluk, while Russell and I, with one of the khawasses, went in another direction to visit some warm baths, celebrated throughout the Haimaneh, and where there were said to be several remnants of antiquity.

After a short ride, we found a large and abundant hot spring, strangely situated upon the top of a hill, and within ruins of some interest and considerable extent. The bath itself is inclosed in the usual Mohammedan building, domed and with horse-shoe arch, separated for the different sexes, but one of these divisions has been rent in two by an earthquake. The supply of water, which is pure, is very abundant, the temperature 125° Fahrenheit.

These baths are inclosed within a space surrounded by an old wall which was defended by bastions, the dressed stones of which may, in some cases, be more modern than the wall itself. Within the inclosure, besides the baths, there are the ruins of dwelling-houses, and a burial-ground, in which are numerous Byzantine tombstones, cornices, pillars, and other fragments. There is also a modern mesjid, constructed chiefly with the stones of a former Greek temple, but this is tumbling in ruin. Outside the inclosed space there appeared also to have been formerly gardens and good houses, but the neighbourhood is now as deserted as the interior, and not a being is to be seen at or near these silent attesttations of a place of much former resort. The natives call the place Yanina, or Yapak Hammam.

We ascended hence by a flowery vale, the Ardij Tagh (Juniper Hills), from the crest of which, at an altitude of 3590 feet, the view was extensive and monotonous. We then descended a long hour's trot to Kizil Keuy (the Red Village). Independently of the peculiarity of dress, many other points shewed to us at once that this large village was inhabited by Turkomans; such particularly were the numerous camels browsing or ruminating at the thresholds, while the women carrying on their domestic avocations with uncovered faces, and the children playing about, made the traveller feel at home; so as it was a fine day we did not go into the Sheik's, (for we had to obtain a change of horses here,) but sat down outside his door, to the great delight of the villagers who congregated around to see us.

We lost two hours before the horses were ready, when we mounted, accompanied by a guide, and proceeded at a rapid pace up a long valley, and then over naked grassy uplands to the mountain of Gokcheh Bunar (or Heaven-Gate Spring). We found that the Kurds had already arrived here, on their spring migration northward.

On turning into the recess occupied by their encampment at a canter, the men ran to arm themselves, and such as had not time to do so, picked up stones for weapons; but when they found that we paid no attention to them, nor came to exact or extort any thing from them, all symptoms of hostility ceased.

At the extremity of the upland of Heaven-Gate Spring we found ourselves above a long valley, stretching north to the foot of the Karajah Tagh, a vast cone of trachytes, now only a few miles from us. Between us and the monntain was a rude rock, with an almost equally rude stone fort on the summit. We were much disappointed to hear that this was Kuzilja Kaleh (the Red Castle), which we were in search of, and still more so, that after various efforts to that effect, the guide and khawass persisted in not venturing nearer, as the plague was raging in the village close to it.

We accordingly retrograded to a certain extent, till we reached the large Turkoman village of Chaltis, where for the first time we perceived symptoms of plague in persons lying sick in the street. This did not prevent us partaking of the hospitality of the sheik of the village, who presented us with sour milk and bread on the roof of his house, which was crowded with as many people as it could hold.

We crossed hence another range of hills, on the crest of which some graves were pointed out as belonging to rayahs, who had been killed by the Kurds. It was dark before we terminated our long ride, and arrived at Chuluk, where we found Mr. Rassam in a state of considerable agitation at the ravages which the plague was said to be making in the village.

Chuluk is a posting village, on the great road from Angora to Koniyeh, and although it scarcely contained twenty houses, two persons died that night and were carried to their graves before day-break, just as we were preparing to start.

The next day our road lay at first over a plain. After a short time Russell and I left the remainder of the party to enter some hills to the right, where there were said to be some monastic ruins. We first passed some hewn-out sepulchral grots, and then a Kurd village, the inhabitants of which received us with the same open hostility as at Heaven-Gate Spring, and where there were also some grottoes; beyond this, we came to a narrow glen, on one side of which were several artificial caves arranged in tiers. The lower story contained a few large chambers, one of which was supported by square pillars and had sepulchral recesses. This was evidently the burial department.

Above this was a central chamber, nineteen yards deep, with an arch in the centre, apparently hall, refectory, and dormitory all in one; to the right was the chapel, seven yards long by five in width; and to the left, a long narrow gallery, scarcely admitting a person to walk upright, led circuitously to a lateral chamber, just large enough for one person to sit and turn himself in, with an aperture opening to day, large enough to put the nose through. As the monastery in the rock would have held from four to six ascetics, this was evidently the spot for retirement for he whose duty it was in rotation to minister spiritual comfort and grace to the others. But what an extraordinary self-devotion must have characterized those men who could thus immolate themselves, and live and be buried, in the same rocky tomb!

We dashed from this monastic relic, glad to think that such practices were now discarded at least by our own church, first across hills and then down Kara Gedik (the Black Fissure), a narrow ravine, by which we descended upon the plain and gained a village, where we rejoined the remainder of the party. "Well," said Mr. Rassam, inquiringly, "did you see them?" "Oh! yes," was the answer. "Thirteen?" said Mr. R. "Oh! no, only two that were of any magnitude, but real tombs for the living." "Why, do you think," quoth Mr. Rassam, "that they were buried alive?" "Who?" "Why, the plague patients to be sure." It now turned out that while our thoughts were revolving upon the monastic relics, Mr. R.'s were filled with the vision of thirteen graves, which he had seen in the village mezar (burial-ground), and which had been filled up within this day or two.

We rode the same afternoon fifteen miles further over a dreary, monotonous, and uncultivated plain to Banam, a large village situated between the two mountain ranges called the Elma Tagh (Apple Mount) and the Ura Tagh (Fire Mount), and where the sound of a drum beating cadences in slow time, announced that a connubial ceremony was on the *tapis*.

CHAPTER XI.

Mevelevi Dervishes.

Deserted Mines and Foxes. Khawasses part from us. Bridge of the King's Taster. District of the Short-Lance Tribe. The Silver and Lead Mines of Denek. Wild-goose Chase. Independent Turkomans. Castle of the Black-Eye. Rude Turkoman. Tradition of Jemalah Castle. Hosein Ghazi. Valley of the Sword River. Town of Kirshehr. Numerous Dervishes. Artificial Mound. Thermal Spring.

The ensuing morning the sheik of the village, accompanied by one of his followers, rode out with us to visit the deserted mines of the Ura Tagh. We ascended the mountains, the acclivities of which were shingly, but wooded, and travelled a short distance along the crest before we came to the object of our researches. There were several shafts sunk in the mountain; and, having struck a light, Russell and I prepared to explore them; but here a new difficulty presented itself. I had not penetrated far, with a bit of burning pine-wood in my hand, before I became aware of something running away before me, and, descending a well, and holding the light above my head, perceived a fox couched in one corner, and another in another, and the dung of the animals strewed all around. We had now to return for our arms, to drive out these four-legged tenants, which, it can be easily imagined, where there was but a narrow passage for them to pass between our legs, was not accomplished without difficulty, nor did the khawasses or any of the Turks offer to assist us.

We descended the opposite side of the mountains, amid forests of pine and oak, in which the snow still lay very deep. We arrived at the foot of the hills at Karghahli (Spear Town), a village of about forty houses, near which is the refuse of copper furnaces, formerly wrought here.

In the evening we walked out to visit an abundant spring in gypsum, near the village, and strolled about its wooded but neglected gardens. Nothing can exceed the quiet and beauty of these Asiatic villages, when the peasants will leave one alone to enjoy them.

An extensive, slightly-undulating plain was spread before us now, to the south stretching from the Ura Tagh to the Kurah Tagh, a distance of about ten miles. This plain, covered with a rich natural crop of cereal grasses and berry-bearing shrubs, abounded with bustards both of the large and smaller species, and with the heavy-winged taoke of the plains. As some of the party trudged on the beaten road, with the baggage horses, others of us traversed a large extent of plain, at one moment in the pursuit of game, at others in the vain attempt to get to the windward of the wary flocks. Our labours were not altogether fruitless, but the peasants complained sadly of their horses being employed to hunt down bustards.

During our passage of the Kurah Tagh, in the afternoon, we were overtaken by a storm of wind and rain, through which we had yet to travel some distance. We descended amid low hills and ravines, till, as evening was coming on, we came to low cliffs that overhung, by some two hundred feet, the large village of Karagiler. Here we got a room, which was full of hay, and so crowded with vermin, that none of us found a moment's repose, even after our long day's ride and evening wetting. The weather at the same time continued so bad, that we could not sleep out of doors.

Our khawasses had a quarrel in the morning with the surly villagers of Karagiler, who had given us such despicable shelter, and who were with difficulty prevailed upon to furnish horses to go as far as Kupri Keuy (Bridge Village), distant only two miles and a half, as the territories of the Pasha of Angora terminated at the Halys.

The transport, however, having been arranged, our khawasses, after riding with us a short distance, and receiving a present for their services, bade us farewell, while we proceeded, for the fourth time, to traverse the Red River of the Turks.

The Halys is crossed here by the celebrated bridge of Chasnigir, commonly called Cheshni (the King's Taster).· This bridge occurs at a remarkable spot, where the river leaves an open valley, to enter a bold rocky pass, amid granite rocks. It has one large and four lesser arches at the water level, one high upon a rock, and some other smaller ones below. It has no parapet, and is twelve yards high, the river being thirty-one yards wide.

While the horses were collecting at Kupri Keuy we were engaged in making observations, attended by the ayyan and a crowd of the curious, attracted by the glitter of brass instruments, and equally curious to examine our European arms.

On leaving this village, we commenced the ascent of Begrek Tagh, a rude granitic mountain, on the sunny exposure of which the dwarf almond was already in flower. On the ascent one of the baggage horses got loose, and galloped back to the village, which occasioned us some delay.

The prospect from the summit presented to us an extended and remarkable granitic district, composed of low, rounded, whitish, and bare hills, which appeared like so many hillocks at our feet, but which, when we entered upon them, were found to be broken up by deep rocky ravines with rivulets, but having a very scanty covering of vegetation. This singular district was inhabited by Turkomans of the Jerid (the Short-Lance) tribe.

After a ride of about four hours, we found ourselves on the other side of this district, and on a level cultivated plain. Our usual bad luck overtook us here, and we had to terminate our ride to Denek Maden, a distance of seven miles, in a pitiless rain. Much discussion ensued on our arrival at the mines, as to where we were to be quartered. The governor of the mines was unfortunately absent, having gone to Constantinople to plead his cause against Izzet Pasha, who was anxious to get the mines under his jurisdiction. Some Greek miners, one of whom we recognised as an old acquaintance who had wrought with us in the Ishik Tagh, wished to obtain a room in the absent governor's house for us, but this the Turks refused, and we at length got a small, but tolerably cleanly room near the furnaces.

In the evening, among the visitors, the Greek priest made his appearance. We paid every respect, as was our wont, to the sacerdotal character of the old man, a reception which he appeared so little prepared for, that, in the fulness of his heart, he produced an evidently much valued bottle of communion wine—a not unacceptable present in our drenched condition.

Under the circumstances, of the governor of the mines being at the moment under the persecution of Izzet Pasha, and that we were known to have been already engaged by that pasha in the examination of other mining districts, our arrival here occasioned many suspicions, and much personal distrust; and we found so many difficulties put in our way, and such evident disinclination not only to serve us or to give us information, but even to be seen in our company, that on the next day, April 1st, we thought it best to continue our journey.

The present produce of the mines, when in full work, is equal to a thousand okahs, of $2\frac{3}{4}$ pounds each, weekly, of galena, which quantity yields $2\frac{1}{2}$ okahs of silver. The village itself was in better order than any establishment of the kind I had previously seen in Turkey: the charcoal was kept in a wooden inclosure, while a handsome fountain poured its waters into the washing pond, which was further surrounded with trees.

There were fourteen roasting furnaces, two smelting furnaces, and one open one for the oxidization of lead and the reduction of silver. The mines have a large jurisdiction that includes seven kaziliks or governments, from which both men and fuel are obtained, and the produce of the taxes is also devoted to the mines. This is the usual practice in Turkey.

The bey, governor of the mines, had, like a mushir, command over the lives of these under him, and there was a scaffold for impaling culprits erected near the village. If the Hatti Scheriff was not a dead letter, such a remote and unchecked responsibility could not be in existence.

We turned southward from Denek Maden, and on reaching a village of the Jerid Turkomans, called Jinal Oghlu, our seruji wanted to obtain a change of horses, and endeavoured, without having previously warned us, to get over the peasants on his side, as an ill-treated man. He did not, however, succeed in entailing upon us this delay, which would have cost us the loss of the day, for we persisted in driving on the baggage horses, and he was ultimately obliged to follow.

In the course of our ride we passed several encampments of the Jerid Turkomans, and two rivers, one of which, issuing from a lake not far beyond, we had some difficulty in fording. On this plain, we found a flock of wild geese, which made complete April fools of Russell and I, who having descended from our horses in their pursuit, watched them down to a distant eminence, which we slowly encompassed without our hats, and in almost breathless anxiety, stealing up the long acclivity step by step, fully expecting to get upon them unawares;

when, upon gaining the summit, not a goose was to be seen, except our two selves.

We arrived in the evening at the Turkoman village of Ahmed, where they appeared to have no government nor authority. One of the leading men visited us in the evening, and proclaimed his titles, as descended from the most warlike and most noble of all the Turkoman families, than whom for war or for power there were none equal. This, to us rather interesting preamble, for we liked to see the old spirit of the Turkomans still abroad, being closed, he asked for araki, and as we had none, the illusion of friendship was broken, and he departed sulky, and without doing anything for us. Next came an old gentleman, who, in answer to demands for food for man and horse and for horses next day, said we could have some burghule (boiled wheat); but as for horses there were none. He was accordingly dismissed with some polite Turkish expressions, at which he grew very irate; but Rassam was now roused, and he and our Greek servant scoured the village in search of provisions, and we and our steeds got some supper at last.

The next morning, after much wrangling, we were obliged to put up, with arabahs or carts drawn by oxen, for the luggage, and it was with difficulty that we could obtain from these independent Turkomans, who laughed at the Sultan's firman, horses for ourselves. So while the waggons ascended leizurely the Kara Goz (Black-eyed Mountain), Russell and I made a little excursion, up one of the culminating points of the hills, to explore an old castle, but of which we only found the foundations and ruinous walls, now divided into cells for sheep and goats. As the valley of the Halys is shut up by mountains, this castle commanded, in former times, the great road to Gadasena and Cæsarea from Tavium and Ancyra.

After waiting to see our baggage safe through the pass, for we had now no khawasses, we descended to a large village called Isa Kojahli, where we were overtaken by a Turkoman, who seized my horse by the bridle, holding at the same time his stick up in the air, and threatening to strike. This, however, was prevented by Mr. Russell, who caught hold of it in a moment, and the poor fellow only got bastinadoed for his undue excitement upon the occasion; so he was soon glad to follow on foot, till the next change of horses would release to him his much-loved steed, to obtain which he had been so willing to run the chances of war.

We crossed hence a nearly level plain, generally cultivated, till we arrived at Sighir (Buffalo Village), where we were to obtain horses, but of which there were none forthcoming, so we had to spend the evening and night there. It was, however, a pleasant, peaceful village, facts pre-eminently testified by the storks' nests, which these truly domestic birds had built on walls within the reach of every little urchin of the village, and yet in undisturbed security. The Turkoman women also came where we were observing, and looked on and chatted with us as if we had been in an European village. During the night, at an elevation of 3320 feet, we had a sharp frost. The mountains around were still covered with snow.

April 3rd. We crossed the plain early this morning, a most delightful day, to visit some ancient marble quarries, called Tash Kasmah. At the south-western extremity of the plain the valley of the Kolitchi Chaye (the Sword River), and the river of Kirshehr, opened before us, but we turned aside to enter a rocky ravine, where was the large village of Jemalah, and upon an isolated mount of granite close by, the castle of the same name.

While Mr. Rassam kindly undertook to fight the battle of getting our arabahs and their slow-paced oxen changed for horses at this village, Russell and I ascended the mount to explore this castle. We found an edifice of various ages, having been in more remote times constructed of large hewn stones of granite, repaired and modified by the Mohammedans in their flourishing eras, and again put together, in a more slovenly manner, in modern days. It appears to have been battered and breached at various times, and also to have suffered from earthquakes; it is now consequently in a state of complete ruin.

I am indebted to Mr. Russell's note-book for the following tradition concerning this old castle, which derives the more interest from its being associated with the remarkable hill, with its superimposed monastery of dervishes, near Angora, and called after the hero of the tradition. Hosein Ghazi was a Mohammedan general, whose brother was serasker of Malatiyeh. Hosein besieged Ancyra, the Rum or Greek inhabitants of which made a sally, and cut off his head: whereupon he indignantly caught it up, and like St. Denis walked away with it under his arm, to a cave in the mountain that still bears his name, and where, strange to say, he died; a monastery being subsequently erected there to his memory. Shortly after, an eagle winged its way to that cave, and there laid an egg. The Greeks, fearful that this was ominous of Hosein's resurrection, blocked up the cavern with stones.

The Prophet, however, had other ways of working good for the cause of the faithful: for Hosein had left behind him a son then eleven years of age, and who resolved to revenge his father's death. He, with his uncle's consent, took upon himself the command of the army of Malatiyeh, and marched to Ancyra, on a visit to the governor, who politely invited him to his house, and treated him, pressing the son of Hosein, whose name was Jaffa, to drink araki. Jaffa, however, declined this, but kept encouraging the Greek in his libations; after the feast he requested from the governor permission to visit the castle with him, to which the Greek having staggered acquiescence, Jaffa there stabbed him and the friends who accompanied him, in due succession, giving at the same time the signal to his followers to assault the town, which then fell into the power of the Turkomans, from whom it was taken by the Osmanlis, under Murad or Amurath I., in the year 1360.

Jaffa, after sending the heads of Christians innumerable to his uncle at Malatiyeh, marched against the castle of Jemalah, and demanded of its governor Shamas, what he did there? Shamas replied, that he held the castle for the Emperor; whereupon the brave Turkoman, who could not take the fort, challenged any of the Greeks to single combat. I am ashamed to say how many of these unfortunate Christians fell in this kind of warfare by the ruthless sword of Jaffa. Shamas himself was at length obliged to go forth and meet the antagonist, before whom, one after another, the whole garrison was falling. Now Shamas was a mighty warrior, and Jaffa was still very young; but though the Greek succeeded in getting at Jaffa's windpipe, he might as well have cut at a gun-barrel, for the Prophet had made his skin sword-proof, and would have made it bullet-proof, but that there were no fire-arms at that time. Soon it became Jaffa's turn to strike, which he did with a stick and that with such execution that Shamas was bastinadoed out of his religion into Mohammedanism, in which holy belief he lived and died, always in great amity with his juvenile conqueror.

From Jemalah we began to descend the valley of Kirshehr; a pile of stones, marking the site of a castle designated as Gekchi Kalah (She-Goat Castle), occupied the summit of a bold mountain to the left. Four miles down the valley, at the village of Kizilja Keuy, the beautiful and renowned gardens of the once flourishing town of Kirshehr commence, and extend not only to the town itself, a distance of five miles, but also far beyond.

On our arrival at the town, quarters were assigned to us in a coffee-house, in the most populous part of the town, which was rather inconvenient, as we had to sit almost in public, and were obliged to make our astronomical and magnetic observations in the burial-yard of the most frequented jami of the town, and upon the tombstones, a proceeding which the faithful at first did not appear to relish much, and one or two more bigoted dervishes endeavoured to oppose, and to get up a party in the town against us, by extravagant tales of our bringing down the sun—the evil eye—and other vile necromancies; but in this they failed signally, and the merchants in the bazaar, to whom they chiefly addressed themselves, growing every day in intelligence, only laughed at them.

Kirshehr is a sad example of a town ruined by former religious fanaticism. It never was probably over populous or rich, but, with gardens of unbounded fertility, possessed most of the necessaries and many of the luxuries of life. Its tranquil comforts brought around it, however, a host of all the various orders of dervishes—of people who do nothing, but live upon the industry of others—in the empire; and to these, religious zeal bequeathed various edifices, while others planted themselves as guardians to the tombs of their early benefactors, and which they consecrated as holy, and holy tombs rose up one beyond the other, and the frequent houses of the dervishes around them, till in the present day there are seven quarters or suburbs of the town inhabited solely by the Mevelevi, or spinners, the Kadri, or yellers and emaciators, and the Bektashi orders, while the streets themselves are full of the Seyahs, or wandering and begging tribes.

The Mevelevi, or spinning dervishes, are to be seen here in full perfection, performing their extraordinary devotional exercises, an idea of which, and their exact costume, is to be obtained from the engraving accompanying this chapter; and as for the howling dervishes, we were rendered painfully sensible of their numbers by the hostility which they exhibit to the repose of their peaceful and somniferous neighbours.

These various orders of religious devotees have drained and exhausted the resources of the town to the very last; what houses still remain are mud hovels of the lowest description, the only jami is ruinous, and its menareh broken in half, three khans are abandoned, and the bezestein, which is a goodly building, shut up and untenanted.

There are six mesjids in the town, and the population amounts to from 3500 to 4000 souls. There is only one Christian resident, who stated himself to be employed in the manufacture of gunpowder, but his real employment is the manufacture of araki, to which most of the howling and spinning dervishes are very partial, as well as to opium.

In the centre of the town is a high artificial mound, indicating an ancient site. On this mound are now some religious edifices and sepulchral chapels of some beauty. At a short distance west of the town, and beyond its extensive mezar, or burial-ground, there is a hot-spring, amidst some rocks of contorted appearance, which have been deposited by the hot waters of the spring, and which contain lime, iron, and other earthy matters in solution. This spring is protected by a wall, and its waters fall into a small bath; the temperature is 113° Fahr.

At this season of the year we got nothing of the produce of the gardens but dibbs, or the saccharine juice of grapes, and a few preserved pears; of vegetables, potherbs or salads, which we should most have relished, we found none.

CHAPTER XII.

Utch Ayak.

Utch Ayak (the Three Arches). Rock Forts of Buffalo Plain. The Castle of the Lake. Mujur—Mocissus. Haji Bektash, the Founder of the Janissaries. Evils of the religious and social condition of the Turks. Noble Prospect in the Valley of the Halys. Caves of Osiana. Fantastic forms in the Rock.

We ascertained upon inquiry at Kirshehr, that the ruins of Utch Ayak, to which our attention had been called in our instructions, had been passed on our way. Accordingly the day after our arrival, Russell and I, having procured a guide from the governor, mounted our horses and retraced our steps up the banks of the Sword River, as far as Jemaleh, where we turned off to the right to Juhun, a large village, for the sheikh of which the governor had given us a letter, in order to procure a guide for further on.

Our road hence led over the side of a huge granite

mountain called Boz-uk, and in an hour's time we gained the crest, from whence we could perceive an extensive district stretching before us, with here and there the sombre tents of the Turkomans like moles on the face of the plain, while immediately below us, was a ruinous and rather lofty structure isolated at the foot of the hills, and without any adjacent building or ruin.

Upon closer examination, this ruin was found to be built of red tiles, with joints three inches thick, and cemented by a deep mortar bond; as many as six arches, four of which had upheld a semi-circular dome, remained entire, but this having fallen in, had left the arches to stand forth in nakedness, whence the modern name (the Three Arches or Legs), given to the place.

In these parts was situated, in olden times, a temple of Jupiter, which, according to Strabo, had an establishment that rivalled that of Commana, there being 3000 persons employed in the service of this seat of hierarchal pomp. As Haji Bektash is a holy place among the Mohammedans, Rennell was inclined to identify this temple of Gadasena with it, simply on the ground, that celebrated seats of devotion, while preserving their locality, so often change the object or the mode of worship, a fact, which is, indeed, frequently observed in the East, but Rennell was unacquainted with the existence of ecclesiastical ruins in Morimena, as is here shewn to be the case, while at Haji Bektash, besides the tomb of that celebrated man, there is only a mound, the probable site of a castle defending the road, and we found no other ruins.

It is not at all improbable, on the same grounds as those assumed by the before-mentioned able critic and geographer, of the perpetuity of places of worship, that the temple of Jupiter was succeeded by a Christian church and monastery. To our great regret, we learnt afterwards at Nev Shehr, that, notwithstanding the assertions of the sheik of Juhun to the contrary, there existed further and extensive ruins an hour beyond these.

On our return over the mountain to Juhun, situated at the bottom of the plain of the Buffalo, we found a repast prepared for us by the hospitality of the sheik, and which we partook of in his company, that of the seruji, and of a host of visitors, whose alertness with their fingers left us but very little chance.

This Buffalo plain, as it is now called, is remarkable for the state of defence in which it appears once to have been placed. To the north is the castle of the Black-Eye; to the south, that of the She-Goat; within the mountain recesses, the stronghold of Jemaleh; while the lofty summits of the Boz-uk and Baranli mountains have also their rock forts.

We returned to Kirshehr by night fall. The Hasan Tagh, with its bold and sharp two-headed summit, reflecting the gleams of the setting sun from its perpetual snows, was an object of admiration during our ride. From the mountain of Boz-uk we could perceive both this mountain and the Arjish Tagh, the two loftiest peaks of peninsular Asia, at the same time.

As the night was clear, we repaired shortly after our arrival to the court of the jami, to observe, much to the surprise of the mollah, who was proclaiming evening prayer time from the top of two stones, piled to do duty as a menareh.

April 7th. We started from Kirshehr the next day. Our road lay over a mixed grassy and pebbly plain, that stretched from a low range of hills on the left, down to the valley of the Halys on our right.

Three miles from the town we passed an early circular mound of earth, which was surrounded by the ruins of a wall. The traces of six lateral towers are also to be observed; close by there is a spring, the waters of which flow into a pond covered with aquatic plants. These are, evidently, the remains of an ancient fort or guard-house which defended the road, and was situated for convenience sake near a spring. It is in the present day called Göl Hisar (the Castle of the Lake).

The plain itself abounded with golden plover, which not only afforded capital amusement, but replenished our larder considerably, for we sometimes brought down as many as seven with one shot.

After a ride of three hours from Kirshehr, and passing a valley with villages called the Dry Lake, we arrived at Mujur, the ancient Mocissus. This place is distinguished as a cassabah, which literally signifies a place where butchers' meat is sold, but is applied colloquially to all such places as are smaller than towns and larger than villages.

Mujur is built upon a soft rock, that is easily quarried and wrought; hence most of the houses are subterraneous, and many mere caverns. There are gardens around, and a little higher up the valley is an artificial mound, the site probably of an ancient castle.

We took the bits out of the horses' mouths and sat down on the grass, while our seruji and servant went in quest of sour milk and eggs, our customary breakfast.

From Mujur we had four hours' ride, partly over the same kind of dry plain, and partly by a gentle ascent, passing two villages of Troglodytes, to Haji Bektash; on approaching which by the deep hollow of a rivulet, our baggage horses stuck in the mud, and were with some difficulty extricated.

On ascending the opposite side of the hill, we learnt the way to the ayyan's house, in front of which a very fine old shaggy male camel was chained. A tolerably clean room was assigned to us, which was the more agreeable, as not being anticipated, the general aspect of the town being that of great poverty and filth.

Close to the town is the usual mound of ruins, surrounded by a moat or ditch, but in this case only semi-artificial. It is called Kara Kavuh (Black Bonnet).

The celebrated Mohammedan enthusiast, Haji Bektash, was, according to local tradition, born at this place, where he is also said to be buried, and a sepulchral chapel, or imam, is built over his remains; but the jami of Beshik Tash, near Stambol, also claims this last distinction.

Haji Bektash was the founder of the order of dervishes that bears his name, but he is still better known as the founder of the Janissaries (yeni cheri), who became to the Osmanli dynasty what the Prætorian guards were to the Roman Cæsars, and the Turkomans to the Khalifs of Bagdad.

When this corps had become numerous, Murad I., then Sultan of the Osmanlis, sent to Bektash, praying him to consecrate them by a name and a banner. The holy man tore off a fold of his garment, and placing it on the head of one of them, said, "Let their name be Yeni cheri, 'the new soldiers; their countenances noble and proud, their swords sharp, and their lances always ready to strike the head of their enemies."

Local tradition also assigns to Haji Bektash the discovery of the salt-mines of Tuz Keuy, which are hence sometimes called after his name, and pay a small annual tribute to the support of his tomb and sanctuary.

The town called after this religious enthusiast is a remarkable case, to be adduced against the constant complaints of the natives, that taxation is the sole cause of poverty, and of the present ruinous condition of villages and towns in Lesser Asia, and is a proof that this state of things is rather connected with a bad social condition and the evil influences of a false religion uniting to produce both mental and physical degradation of the people*. Kirshehr, which, with its luxuriant soil, abundant water, and warm sheltered situation, might be made a mart for the production of silk, we have seen, is, by the fatal incubus of dervishes, but a wreck. When asked why the town was so fallen and prostrate, the ready answer of the natives was, "Excessive taxation." At Haji Bektash no one complained; on the contrary, the inhabitants boasted of their privileges and immunities. The holy memory of the dervish has saved the place from the saliyaneh, or any other tax, save a small annual

* Mr. Consul Brant, in his notes of a journey through part of Kurdistan, in 1838, (*Journal of Royal Geographical Society*, vol. x., part iii.,) gives some remarkable examples of how low the saliyaneh, or taxes levied for the expenses of the public administration, are even under the supposed extortionate pashas.

contribution towards the support of the tomb, and of the resident dervishes connected with it; this, indeed, is merely nominal, as, besides several foundations of pious persons bequeathed for this purpose, the tax upon the salt-mines would alone cover these expenses.

Yet notwithstanding these advantages, almost every other house is a ruin. The ayyan has built himself, the only stone mansion in the place; scarcely a thing was to be obtained, a fowl was out of the question, a few eggs with great difficulty; the inhabitants having little to pay, work still less, but sit in listless groups sunning themselves, and smoking through a day's existence. The whole appearance of the place is that of unproductiveness and idleness. The tomb itself, which ought as a matter of proper appropriation of funds, to be in a good state of repair, is crumbling into ruins.

April 8th. Our road to-day lay over hills, one of which was remarkable for its sugar-loaf form, and of similar geological structure to its compeer in Ireland bearing that name.

The view on crossing this range of mountains was especially grand; the low, wide, tortuous valley of the Halys, backed by rugged volcanic hills, from whence dark floods of lava had descended to the river's brink; sandy cliffs, ungladdened by any vegetation and burrowed by innumerable caverns; Osmanli and Turkoman villages embosomed among trees; the Sierra-like summits of the granitic heights of Garsaura in the rear; and beyond, the snowy summits of Mount Argæus and the Hasan Tagh.

About an hour and a half from where we descended to the river's bank, we came to a ferry opposite to the cassabah of Yarapason. We, as usual, had to cross over in detail, and swim the horses, an operation of some time, including the unloading and unsaddling, saddling and reloading. This accomplished, we rode off a short distance along the banks of the river to a grove, under the shade of which the governor was feasting a party of friends; a fact which he had sent a khawass to announce to us, and at the same time to invite us to join them. We sat down in form and accepted pipes, the conversation soon became friendly, and we found our host had been formerly kyaha, or deputy, to Izzet Pasha*. Fragments of the repast were then laid before us, and we did honour to the good things; for we had come that morning from a higher and colder country. The ayyan at our departure pressed us to stay the night at Yarapason, an act of self-inspired hospitality and kindness, that occurred for the first time, on this journey. After many compliments, we mounted again, the baggage proceeding along the river side, Russell and I starting inland to examine the caves and grottoes of Yarapason, the ancient Osiana, which are almost innumerable.

Yarapason at present contains 300 houses, partly caverns, and all more or less subterraneous, built on the side of a cliff that stretches thence nearly a mile in distance up the river, and is burrowed throughout that extent by numerous caves and grottoes. Sometimes the

* The governor told us, in answer to our inquiries to that effect, that in summer time the river Halys had very little water in it, and was quite salt to the taste. We had observed that it was now brackish, and that there were frequent efflorescences of salt on its banks.

cliff is intersected by a ravine or cleft, at other times portions are broken off from the mother rock. The same repetition of caverns occurs in these, and even if only a small fragment rises, obelisk-like, from the plain, separated from all others, it has its cave, or tiers of caves. We were quite astounded and perplexed at the variety and number of those presented to our view. Our baggage horses, with Mr. Rassam, were getting on far a-head, still our enthusiasm was too much excited to be quickly contented; at one moment we clambered up to examine some design rudely carved in bas-relief; at another, lateral columns of fair proportions would arrest our attention. No doubt some of these caves had been sepulchral, while others had also evidently, from their extent and ornate character, served as places of worship, but the generality were manifestly dwelling-places.

We galloped away scarcely half satisfied, after the rest of the party, but only to be stopped by new and still more astounding curiosities. Turning up a glen which led from the river inland, we found ourselves suddenly lost in a forest of cones and pillars of rock, that rose around us in interminable confusion, like the ruins of some great and ancient city. At times these rude pinnacles of rock balanced huge unformed masses upon their pointed summits, but still more frequently the same strangely supported masses assumed fantastic shapes and forms—at one moment suggesting the idea of a lion, at another of a bird, and then again of a crocodile or a fish.

These marvels of Garsaura long ago excited the wonder of old Paul Lucas, and have also been noticed in the more subdued and polished lukewarmness of modern travelling, and there is certainly one thing remarkable in these productions, that no two persons, as was exhibited in our own case, can agree as to whether they are natural or artificial. The fact is, that if natural they have decomposed into forms that have become rude representatives of animals; if artificial, they have been shorn, by time and the operation of the elements, of all proportion and beauty; or a middle line might be taken, that nature commenced the work, and a rude and fantastic art fashioned these forms upon it. Tradition cuts the gordian knot, and proclaims them the work of the genii*.

An hour's ride from this remarkable vale, over a higher and more level country, brought us to some rocky hills, at the entrance to which was the town of Nev Shehr (the New Town, *par excellence*), and which we were delighted to find was more cleanly, more promising, and altogether more substantial, than any town we had yet seen, and rivalling, in these attributes, the pleasant town of Tokat. Mr. Rassam was kind enough to go on first, to obtain quarters, and after some little delay we advanced with the baggage to the governor's serai, when a domestic was sent with us to the Christian quarter, where a room had been assigned to us, and which they attempted to prove was the cellar, but we

---

* According to Oriental mythology the genii governed the world long before the creation of Adam. They were famous for their architectural skill. The Koran relates that they were employed by Solomon in the erection of his Temple—(chap. xxxiv). The Pyramids of Egypt were ascribed to them, and the author of *Vathek* alludes to a fortress in Spain having a similar origin.

taught them better, and preferred a boarded room on the first floor, the more especially as Mr. Russell was unwell, and I intended stopping here a day or two to put him under medical treatment.

The master of the house, his sons and visitors, came in the evening to eat, and afterwards to sleep with us, in this small apartment, a proceeding which, with the greatest delicacy possible, we begged to object to, but, as was always the case, it required more than delicate insinuations to get rid of them.

Excavated Stones at Osiana.

CHAPTER XIII.

Rocking Stones.

Christians of Nev Shehr. Conversation with the Priests. Attempted Deception and Extortion. Rocking Stones. Salt Mines. Tradition of Haji Bektash. Subterranean Chapel. Curious Missal. Difficulties with the Turkomans. Place of Sipahis. Vale of Parnassus. Pass of Kazi Uyuk. First view of the Great Salt Lake.

THE town of Nev Shehr is built on the acclivity of a bold ravine, darkly backed by high cliffs of basalt. It contains 200 houses of Mohammedans, 800 houses of Greeks, and 60 houses of Armenians, having a population of about 15,000 souls.

The Cappadocian Greeks, who constitute so large a portion of the community, appear to have congregated into the "new city" from all the numerous troglodyte villages in the neighbourhood, which are now for the most part bereft of their original inhabitants. They have certainly made a change for the better, and it is difficult to imagine the reason which made them once dwell in caves, as was so much the case throughout Garsaura.

In a commercial point of view, also, this town is, when compared with others in Asia Minor, in a very flourishing condition.

We were much pleased with the Christian inhabitants; we visited their church and schools, and attended divine service. We had also frequent and long conversations with the priests, who were of far less domineering dispositions than those of Angora. One of them giving reason for the faith that was in him, said confession was a divine institution, being first used by Adam, who confessed his own and Eve's transgressions to God himself. We took this opportunity of informing him that confession of that description, or spiritual confession, was much approved of and indeed insisted upon by our Church, but that this differed very much from confessing to a man. He next quoted the confession that Lot made to Abraham. The ordinary authority from James, was then quoted by ourselves and commented upon, that "one to another" did not mean privity of confession, and we further admitted, that confession was not avoided but rather enjoined by our Church, explaining the cases and their application.

On the subject of baptism, the priests objected to the sprinkling of water, but we explained from Matthew, that the sign was the principal matter, and consecration in the Holy Spirit, true baptism; that there was no positive objection to immersion, but that it is unnecessary.

The holy sacrament of the Lord's Supper appeared

to be but imperfectly understood by them; "Why," they asked us, "do you go to that ordinance after breakfast?" to which it was answered, because the historical fulfilment would be a mere ceremony of passing the bread and wine about after supper. In spirit, the elements of the Eucharist, might be dispensed in the ordinary state of man's habits and feelings, if his mind and spirit were prepared—but that in England, many worthy persons considered it advisable (without the injunction of priests) to take that holy sacrament fasting.

As regards the marriage of priests, they did not hesitate to acknowledge St. Paul's injunction to Timothy (I. Tim. iii. 12) as an interdiction to a priest's being the husband of more than one wife at a time, and not as forbidding second nuptials, after the decease of the first wife, as is maintained by many Oriental Churches.

In justification of councils and legends, they asserted that Our Lord left his religion imperfect at first, like a piece of rough wood or timber, and that the fashioning and polishing of this was reserved for the workmen—the apostles and the early patriarchs—the fathers of the Church.

The dress of these Cappadocian Greeks had much originality about it, and still more particularly so in the females, who dressed showily, and enjoyed a great degree of freedom, exhibiting themselves openly and with uncovered faces, and even at times entering into conversation.

The day after our arrival at Nev Shehr, Mr. Russell being unwell, I had intended riding myself to Uch Hisar and Urgub, to see the remarkable caves and rocks of those places, as described by Mr. Hamilton, but I was prevented by a dense storm of snow, which came on that night, and continued all day. We therefore busied ourselves effecting a new arrangement of our baggage, by which we could send off part to Kaiseriyah, while we only took the necessary instruments, and should start as lightly equipped and as unencumbered as possible, for the Salt Lake of Koch Hisar, which it was our next object to visit.

Previous to our departure, however, we were destined to experience a draw-back to the general good impressions we had received of the intelligence and morality, and the advancing social condition of the Christians of Nev Shehr, in the misconduct of our host, who, though a respectable merchant, yet condescended to enter into a petty conspiracy with the shehr kyayasi, or deputy of the governor, in order, under the pretence that Mr. Russell was sick of the plague, to force from us the sum of 400 piastres, or four pounds sterling, for the use of our single apartment for three days, also requiring two piastres per hour for horses, the ordinary post price being then one piastre, and, what was worse than all, that horses should only be given to us for one road, viz., that of Nigdeh by Ak Serai.

Upon this we immediately started off to the governor, a strange and eccentric old man, generally designated as "Black Beard," and who to the statements which Mr. Rassam made to him, answered at the tip of his voice; but after asserting his authority, by telling us (notwithstanding the clause in our firman to that effect,) that he would not let us go which way we pleased, on account of the usual bug-bear, the Kurds, he finished by yielding all that we desired, viz., horses as far as Saramas, on the road to Koch Hisar, and leaving the remuneration of our exorbitant host to our own generosity.

April 12th. We started from Nev Shehr this day,

for the salt mines of Tuz Keuy, situated on the banks of Kizil Irmak. Our road lay over a plain of volcanic sand, and in a little less than an hour we came to a naked cliff of soft rock of the same description, with numerous excavations and caves, and designated as Teppeh Weran (the Hill of Ruins).

Beyond this were four different hills, a hard kind of rock at the top of which, formed cliffs with caves; while a softer material below, broke off in gentle acclivities. At other times the softer material was of sufficiently firm texture to disintegrate in cones, upon the point of which there rested huge masses of the harder rock, poised in such a manner (as shown in the engraving at the head of this chapter) as to appear at first sight, truly extraordinary; but are not so much so, when it is considered that this phenomenon is the result of gradual disintegration, and that the superincumbent mass itself at once determines, and causes to be preserved, the position of the pivot on which it rests.

An hour hence we came to a stream of lava, which it took us five minutes to ride across. We passed, after this, three other streams, having cliffs of volcanic rock to our left, at the foot of which was Agri Keuy (Poor Village). Turning hence, by Weran Burnu (the Ruined Cape), (for these oriental names serve to describe a country as well as the most minute details,) we arrived at Tuz Keuy (the Village of Salt), containing about eighty houses, part of each of which was hewn out of the solid rock, and fronted again with the same material.

We were received in one of these dens, which was soon filled with individuals curious to know the object of our visit, when, leaving Mr. Rassam to explain particulars, Russell and I rode out with a guide to the salt mines, which were about a mile distant from the village.

Passing over some low hills, we found ourselves suddenly upon the borders of a great pit, which might be about five hundred feet in circumference, and two hundred feet deep; the sides formed of crumbling and sliding clay and mud, and perforated here and there by apertures, which led to as many different galleries, or descents by steps, by which the salt bed was approached, There were about seven of these now open, and one, strange to say, at the bottom of the pit. It had consequently long ago become the grand receptacle for all the water that flowed into it. Many others had also fallen in, from the extreme looseness of the clayey beds and want of support within.

The salt occurs in a powerful bed about forty feet below the surface. The galleries are carried down at high angles of inclination, and the salt is quarried and taken out in baskets, up stairs cut in the clay.

While we were examining these mines, there came on a severe thunder-storm, and torrents of water began to pour, in a few minutes, from all the adjacent heights into the pit; the soft clay gave way in masses, several slips occurred in the sides, and so great was the danger of being overwhelmed in the shafts, that we preferred ascending to the brink—which was not done without some difficulty—and remaining exposed to the rain, than to run the chance of such an insecure shelter.

The quantity of salt excavated annually is estimated at from 300 to 400 camel loads, and as part of the profits have to go to the idle villagers of Haji Bektash, and part to government, the miners say that less than 300 returns them no profit. The tradition of Haji Bektash's discovery of these mines relates, that this holy man stopped in the neighbourhood to request food, whereupon a dish of eggs was laid before him, but the hospitable hostess forgot the salt, and he did not, even after several requisitions, obtain this condiment so essential to the digestion of eggs. The dervish, reduced to perform a miracle, vowed that the village should never again be in want of salt; so, putting his staff into the ground, he opened the subterranean store which lay buried there.

Our route, the next day, lay up the valley of the Tuz Keuy rivulet. Passing Ahmid Teppeh, an artificial mound, said to be a ruin, we came to "Red Village," consisting entirely of caves, of which there are about thirty inhabited. A bit of rag swung from a pole to serve as a flag announced that there had been a troglodyte marriage. A short distance beyond we came to Tatlar (that which belongs to Tatars), a cassabah, or large village, situated in a fissure in the rock.

The houses were, as usual, caves, fronted with one or two arches of basalt, and which supported the fire-place and chimney. The cliffs above were perforated with caves, which had so weakened the mass, that in several places slips or falls had ensued, entailing, at the time of their occurrence, the destruction of the dwelling-houses below.

We breakfasted here, and rode afterwards to visit the caves noticed by Mr. W. J. Hamilton, as containing a book, and concerning which we had heard much importance attached to the tradition, that whenever it should be removed, it would find its way back again. This manuscript is preserved in a subterraneous chapel, which has only two entrances, one by a perpendicular well, about seven feet deep, the other a narrow passage, through which the intruder must creep on all fours. It is quite evident from this, that it had been an object to perform religious rites, when these caves were inhabited, in secresy, and this, with other considerations connected with the very nature of their dwelling-houses, tends to show that they were retreats of Cappadocian Greeks, from the persecution of the Turkomans, and afterwards of the Turks, who have, however, to a certain extent, emancipated them. The chapel itself was adorned with fresco paintings of our Saviour and his apostles, the colours of which were still bright and in good keeping. The book itself was a missal of the Greek Church, lying on the altar, and torn and thrown about. Determined to try the efficacy of the tradition, Mr. Rassam took away some of the pages, but compunctions coming over him afterwards, more especially from our quizzing him for the act, he gave them over to my charge, and as they were lost with the rest of my luggage at Nizib, they may by this time have found their way back to the cave again.

From Tatlar our route lay over undulating downs to the westward. Passing Chular, a Turkoman village situated on an obtusely conical hill, we entered a rocky pass, among sienitic hills, called Tash Tellah, and which, from their serrated, or saw-like, form of crest, had been long remarkable objects to us from the vale of the Halys. From hence we travelled over a granitic plain, with a scanty herbage fed on by many scores of camels.

A little beyond, a valley opened upon us to the left, containing the village of Dursanli, chiefly of caves, and near to it a ziyaret, built upon other ruins, which appear to be at the site of the Nitazas of antiquity. Beyond this valley was the lofty mountain of Akajik, the central mountain district of Garsaura, and corresponding to the ancient Argustana. It is, by mistake, in the map placed to the north of Sari Karaman. This district contains several lakes, and is tenanted by Kurds.

In the evening we arrived at Sari Karaman, a large village, where we were to obtain a change of horses. It is the seat of a Turkoman vaivodeh, who rules over the surrounding district. We were shown into a dirty room full of hay and its minute inhabitants, which we had much difficulty in getting the peasants to clean out for us. The dogs of these shepherd people were extremely fierce; they absolutely deprived us of the opportunity of making the slightest observation, as they never for a moment ceased their daring hostility, and none of the villagers offered to drive them away. Mr. Rassam, having ventured out after dark, had a large portion of his coat torn off in a moment, and was glad to regain our apartment.

April 15th.—Descending from Sari Karaman, we crossed the rivulet of Akajuk, which must, from the number of tributary streams that flow into it, attain some size before it joins the Halys, and is the chief branch of that river in this district. We ascended hence to a rocky terrace with caves, constituting the village of Buz Khur. There was a ruined khan by the side of the road, and a fine cultivated valley beyond. We traversed this, passed Dormanli, a Turkoman village, entered upon a grassy hilly country with protruding granitic rocks, and then descended into the village and gardens of Chamurli (the Place of Mud), where the burial-ground was ornamented with fragments of columns and other remains. Half an hour's further ride brought us to Jamli, another Turkoman village, and the seat of an ayyan.

This day, and the day before, we had a continued strong wind from the west, which brought with it a dense fog. This afternoon the wind abated, and it began to rain; the wind then veered north-west, and this was followed, at first by hail, and then by a dense continuous fall of snow which lasted all night, and by the morning these lofty uplands and cold hills had put on a most wintry and uninviting appearance.

Two of the steeds that had been contributed by the Turkomans of Sari Karaman were mares, and were accompanied by their young foals; and their owners refused, in the morning, to allow of their proceeding any further in such unfavourable weather: while the villagers of Jamli, without being willing themselves to supply two others, took part with them, and heaped all kinds of abusive and insulting epithets upon us, among which "cruel infidels" was by far the most modest. Our cruelty was, however, imposed upon us by sad necessity, as we could not willingly consent either to remain ourselves or to leave our baggage in these rude and inhospitable districts; so amidst a shower of stones and ill-words we forced the horses onwards as far as the village of Sipahiler, only eight miles distant.

It was snowing hard, as we thus left Jamli, in a double storm. Half an hour to the right were some ruins, which, under other circumstances, we would have visited, as they appear from their position to represent the ancient Ozzala. The natives call the place Kilisa (the Church). Our road lay over an undulating granitic district, and, after a short ride, we arrived at Sipahiler (the Place of Sipahis), the ayyan of which kindly promised us a change of horses if we would stop with them that evening, so as to give him time to collect them. We accordingly accepted a room, and the visits of the villagers at the same time, who were kindly disposed,—a thing the more sensibly felt, as contrasting with the violence of the Turkomans of Jamli.

The mountain range of Kojah Tagh rose behind this village, and contained, on its summit, the ruins of no less than three rock forts, two of which we visited in the evening.

Our next morning's ride was over a beautiful country, at the head of the vale of Parnassus. The magnificent Halys extended beneath our feet, from the red rocks of Osiana up to the fastnesses of Chasnighir Kupri; and our wanderings of many days, including the towns of Kirshehr, Mujur, and Haji Bektash, lay before us like a map, backed, however, by soaring and snow-clad heights, that reared themselves up in all the reality of mountain grandeur.

Our contemplation of this splendid distant panorama, and softer but pleasing scenery closer to us, was interrupted by the arrival of some strangers, who attempted to be very enterprising till they found the odds were against them. Their spite at this was not, however, at all concealed. "Ah!" they said, "times have changed now; a short time back Gawurs could not have travelled with impunity in these districts." This, however, was only a repetition of what was cast in our teeth at Jamli.

"How proud these Gawurs are," they again repeated, as we eyed them with contempt; "it would be easy to cut them off." They knew, however, that this was a task beyond their power to perform; and we proceeded on, glad to get rid of their ferocious scowls and taunting words.

At Demir Keuy (the Place of Iron), a village we came to a few hours beyond this, was a curious globular mass of granite, which had detached itself in such regular slices as to have become an object of superstition with the villagers, who supposed that it had been cleft by the sword of a hero, as that of Roland accomplished a breach in the Pyrenees.

Beyond this we turned in a south-westerly direction to cross the Kojah Tagh, the pass over which is commanded, but at some distance, by a hill fort situated on a granite peak, and called Toklu Kaleh. Our progress now began to be much delayed by one of our baggage horses, which kept continually falling, on each of which occurrences we had the trouble of reloading him.

It was with difficulty, and only after several hours travelling from the mountains, that we reached the pass of Kazi Uyuk, which carries the traveller through a range of low hills that border the Salt Lake to the east, nearly its whole length. At the head of this pass is a semi-artificial mound, evidently the site of a former defensive castle, and there was a curious upright stone upon a hill to the left.

At our exit from the pass, the Great Salt Lake itself opened before us in all its magnitude and splendour. The view, although perhaps wanting wood, was beautiful from its vastness. Narrow at the north, where it was backed by low hills, the lake subsequently expanded almost beyond the reach of the eye, was then lost for a moment behind the hills which rise upon the plain beyond Koch Hisar, and re-appeared to the south as a wide expanse of water backed by lofty snow-clad mountains. The memory of our troubles of the few days past vanished before this magnificent prospect;—we felt ourselves braced for new researches, anxious to tread the circumference of this great inland lake, and grateful to the Society which had thus given us the opportunity of exploring what had possessed a just celebrity from a remote antiquity, yet which but a few years back it was hardly known where to place on the map.

CHAPTER XIV.

Sultan's Khan.

Koch Hisar (Ram's Castle). Legend of a Mohammedan Girl. Kurd Migrations. Saline marshes and lakes. The Rock Pass. Peace Mount—Ruins of Congusta. Mohammedan Theological Students. Ruins of Perta. The Sultan's Khan. Seljukiyan Sultans. Broken-down Tatar. The Great Salt Lake. Extent, Characters, and Animals. Ak Serai (the White Palace). Saracenic Architecture.

Koch Hisar (Ram's Castle) is a ruin which occupies the top of a hill, nearly isolated from the remainder of the range in which it occurs, and which commanded, in former times, the entrance to the pass of Kazi Uyuk, and defended the town or village which is now called after the castle itself. In the present day only the foundations of the castle remain, with a few stones heaped together, as a refuge for sheep and goats.

This village contains 130 houses, and a population of

about 1800 Mohammedans, almost entirely Turkomans. The inhabitants spoke much of the visit of Mr. W. J. Hamilton to this place, and it was evidently owing to the favourable impressions left by that gentleman that we were mainly indebted for the hospitable reception we met with.

The lake is distant about three miles from Koch Hisar, between which and it is a low level grassy plain, in part covered with saline plants. A little north of the same parallel, the lake narrows considerably, forming an elbow, which stretches north a little of east. At this point are the remains of a causeway, which tradition assigns to one of the Seljukiyan sultans of Koniyeh. It is said to be still used in the dry parts of summer.

We started hence by early dawn on the morning of April 19th, in order if possible to gain the north end of the lake before mid-day, by which we should save a day's time, as we had to fix its latitude. Our road lay along a level plain, bounded by low naked hills on one side, the silent, desert-like expanse of waters, on the other. Although we saw no birds on the lake we fell in with a flock of large bustards, which afforded us some amusement, and by riding on a few miles a-head of the baggage, we got in time to effect the wished-for observation at the head of the lake.

Passing by Arghun Keuy, a deserted village, we observed a large upright stone, sixteen feet high by four feet wide, and two in thickness, concerning which it was related to us by our Koch Hisar guide, that a jami being about to be erected in that neighbourhood many of the faithful voluntarily engaged themselves in transporting materials. Among the rest was a young girl whose faith enabled her to carry this stone so far, when she was encountered by a young man who asked her her intentions. She had no sooner explained them than he rejoined, "Allah has accepted of your service, and is well pleased," upon which the damsel immediately gave up the ghost, and was buried beneath the same stone, which remains there to the present day in testimony of the fact.

However unworthy of credit, as a tradition, this may be, still it is not without its interest, as showing that all Mohammedans do not reject the idea of women being received among the faithful in the next world. We had been talking with a white-bearded Turkoman the very evening before upon this subject, and among other things this very tolerant Mohammedan related how a learned mollah once argued very sagely, but very savagely, against the sex, and how the Grand Vizier introduced him to a learned lady, and that this fair and witty person argued the mollah out of his favourite tenets.

We travelled hence over hills which only afforded a scanty pasture to large herds of camels, and food for flocks of bustards. We passed afterwards a lake to the left, and some Kurdish encampments to the right, then came to cultivated ground, and finally arrived, after a ride of twelve hours, at Kulu Keuy, a large village, not far from the Karajah Tagh, which we had approached a few weeks previously, on the side of the "Red Castle," in the Haimaneh district.

We had great difficulty in getting provisions here, as the village had been lately occupied by the cavalry of Haji Ali Pacha of Koniyeh, who had been in pursuit of Kurds, who, on their summer migration to the north, had taken with them sheep, and cattle, and horses that belonged to other people. On occasions of this kind, when the troops overtake the tribes, they often not only secure the missing property, but also avail themselves of the opportunity of making prizes on their own account. The consequence is, that on their winter migration back the Kurds indemnify themselves by other robberies, repeating the same systematic plunder in the pashaliks of Angora and Koniyeh alternately, each government seeking for an opportunity for reprisals within their own province, but neither pasha ever attacking the Kurds in the other's territories; and thus a mutual system of plunder and reprisals is carried on from year to year, the strongest party being always in the right.

From Kulu Keuy we turned in a more southerly direction, keeping along the shores of the lake, and after an hour's journey we came to an artificial mound, with a moat, and evidently a station of antiquity. It is recognised as the site of a fort by the natives, who call it Ba'lchah Hisar.

The country around undulated gently, and having many springs, was covered with grass, in consequence of which the tents of the nomadic Kurds were scattered about in every direction. Out of this district arose a circumscribed hilly range, of volcanic origin, called Tavshan Tagh (Hare Mount). Beyond these we passed a small salt lake, called Kupek Göl (Dog Lake); the soil here became covered with saline plants, only intermingled with the wormwood of the plains. We passed several saline marshes of this kind, which appear to be flooded at certain seasons of the year; and in the afternoon reached In-Awi, a large village, situated at a point where the plain is traversed by a stream of fresh water, leaving behind it a cultivated valley, about half a mile in width.

To the south of this valley the uniformity of the plain is broken up by some remarkable conical and isolated volcanic hills. One of these is called Boz Tagh (Ice Mount). Upon another, called Kara Teppeh (the Black Hill), there were said to be some ruins.

We got a change of horses at In-Awi, and continued our route next day (April 21st) down the valley of the rivulet, which was full of aquatic birds, ducks, and teal, with large flocks of herons. At a distance of about six miles from the village, we turned again over the plain till we came to a salt lake, called Murad Su Göl (Murad River Lake), a dreary expanse of water, without trees, but with slightly-elevated banks, a rare thing with the Great Salt Lake.

The plain here became more varied and covered with flowers. Animal life was, in consequence, more abundant; and we obtained during our ride two species of gerboa and a beautiful phalarope. We soon arrived at the Murad Su, which presented the peculiarity of pouring part of its waters into the Great Salt Lake, while part overflowed into the Murad Su Göl. It was, in fact, one great marsh, with a narrow tongue of land dividing the two lakes.

The same point is characterized by a ruin of olden time, which appears to have been used as an aqueduct, the masonry of which is completely hid by a thick incrustation of travertine, deposited, as on the aqueduct near Antioch, by the waters trickling down from the channel above. This pass is called by the natives, from the existence of the ruin, the Kaya Boghaz (the Rock Mouth or Pass).

We continued from hence across an almost perfectly level plain, having always to our left an impenetrable marsh that flanked the south end of the Great Salt Lake. The extreme monotony of such a ride was only occasionally relieved by the distant reed huts and inclosures in which the wandering herdsman assembles his flock at night, to shelter them from the wolves. After a ride of nine miles, we arrived at a large artificial mound on the plain, which apparently once supported an edifice. The ruins of what appears to have been a town of some size are also circularly disposed around this mound. These ruins are, however, now, with the exception of a few upright shafts of columns, level with the ground; nothing but foundations and scattered fragments are met with; so that after riding over and among them for some time, we discovered nothing of interest, nor any inscriptions. This place is now called Tusun Uyuk (Peace Mount), and appears to be the site of the ancient Congusta.

On leaving this place, our serujis seemed to be at fault as to which way to go, so we thought it best to ride off to one of the previously described herdman's reed-huts, which was just discernible on the verge of the level horizon. This answered two good purposes; for we got indications as to our route, and at the same time a bowl of delicious goat's milk.

Our route now lay again across a marsh, the road over which was in part prolonged by an artificial causeway; but it is difficult to say which was most fatiguing to the poor worn-out and jaded horses, the rugged irregular stones of the causeway, or the slippery mud or deep bog of the marsh. At length we arrived late in the evening, amid heavy rain, at Iskil, a large village of Turkomans, which presented the peculiarity of having wide streets, probably for the convenience of the cattle and sheep which are brought in in winter time.

The odah, or public room, of Iskil, to which we repaired to dry ourselves, was deserted by all but two young men, educating for the Mohammedan priesthood, one of whom had been a tinker at Churum, and had wandered hither on his way to Koniyeh, where he intended to pursue his studies at one of the madresehs, or colleges, of that place. They complained bitterly that the peasants gave them little food, sour milk and bread at mid-day, and the same diet again at night; so as we were rousting up the villagers to produce firing and food, we invited the poor students to supper with us.

The ensuing day we made but a short journey, still over the same great plain, to Sultan Khan (the Sultan's Khan), which is a posting station on the road from Ak Serai to Koniyeh, and where we were to obtain a change of horses.

On our road, we passed some interesting ruins, consisting of a high artificial mound, having many fragments and portions of buildings apparently belonging to the Byzantine era, with numerous grottoes around. A Mohammedan mesjid, built of the hewn stones of former edifices, had succeeded to older ruins, but was itself also now falling into decay. These ruins extended over a considerable space, and had been formerly surrounded by a wall. This place is now called Uyuk Bowat, and appears to have been the ancient Perta.

Close by the town there flowed a fine stream of

water, which loses itself in marshes immediately beyond. These marshes limited the easterly range of road in ancient times as well as modern; hence the physical necessities of the soil have caused the same line to be preserved; but these marshes are said at this point to be so far dried up in summer, as to allow of a cross road nearly direct from Iskil to Ak Serai.

Sultan Khan derives its name from a splendid khan or kerwan-serai, which rises with remarkable effect from out of the uniformity of the surrounding plain, and when seen from a distance, contorted by the waving lights of the mirage, as it generally is, puzzles the traveller, by the fantastic forms that it assumes, and its apparent magnitude.

We had some difficulty in obtaining permission to examine the interior of this khan, as a poor but proud Bey lived in it with his Harem. Luckily, however, we heard that he was sick, and accordingly we sent in our compliments, that we should be happy to do anything in our power to alleviate his sufferings. We were accordingly soon admitted to an interview, which took place on a terrace on the top of the khan, and after giving the old gentleman some suitable medicine, we were allowed to roam about the ruins at our leisure, followed by the curious eyes of the Harem below.

We found the building to be divided into two parts; the most easterly not very lofty but wide, and ornamented by a gateway of rich Saracenic workmanship. The interior was also richly ornamented. The westerly part was in the best state of repair, and consisted of a large covered space, supported by lofty columns and arches. It is altogether one of the handsomest khans to be met with in Lesser Asia. Over the gateway was an Arabic inscription, which was thus translated by Mr. Rassam:—

"The exalted Sultan Alau-d-din, great King of Kings, Master of the necks of Nations, Lord of the Kings of Arabia and Persia, Sultan of the territories of God, Guardian of the Servants of God, Alau-dunya Wa-d-din, Abu-l-Fat-h, Commander of the Faithful, ordered the building of this blessed khan, in the month of Rejeb, in the year 662" (A.D. 1264).

This remarkable specimen of the vain glory and pompous pride of Oriental kings, appertained, as Mr. Renouard has remarked, not to one of the Khalifs, but to one of the Seljukiyan Sultans of the small kingdom of Rum, whose capital was Koniyeh. The princes of that dynasty probably assumed the title of Commanders of the Faithful, on the murder of Mostasim bi-Uah, by order of Hulaku, A.H. 656, A.D. 1258; so that according to the date given on the inscription above, could we trust the historian Ahmed el Dimeshki, quoted by Adler, (p. 74,) the prince here named was eldest son and successor of Ghayyathu-d-din, the tenth Sultan of Koniyeh, who died A.H. 654, although historians give no such successor to that sultan. Few parts of Asiatic history are, indeed, more in want of elucidation than the chronology of the Seljukiyan Sultans of Rum.

We had another claimant for medical advice this evening, in the person of a broken-down tatar, who shared the odah with us, and whose illness being the result of his professional exertions, peculiarly demanded repose as well as medical aid. The old man's spirit was not gone by, however, and when this was represented to him,

"Oh!" he said, "that was impossible." He was an Osmanli, and could not live off his horse; "on and off," he repeated, as if proud of his wild rattling occupation, although his physical capabilities were nearly all gone, and would by his malady, no doubt, have a speedy end put to them. He rode on with us next day part of the way to Ak Serai, but he made a poor attempt of it, stopping at each ruined khan to sit upon the flowery greensward, while his servant lit him a pipe; so we soon left him behind.

In pursuing our road from Sultan Khan to Ak Serai, we had at starting to go round the sources of a rivulet, that rose from six different springs, and thence continued our progress over marshy land, on which were the remains of a causeway. There were also several ruined khans by the road side, besides numerous wells, the descent to which was effected by covered steps. They were only from six to eight feet in perpendicular depth, and the water not good. Three and a half miles from Ak Serai we passed the river of Ulur Irmak, by a stone bridge; this river flows into the Bayaz Su (White River), a little beyond the town, and the fertile and shaded gardens of which we entered immediately after crossing the river.

As we here left the Great Salt Lake, which we had been so many days in encompassing, it may be as well to repeat briefly what we noticed as most interesting concerning it.

It appears when the waters are high to be about forty-five English miles in length by eighteen in extreme width. It is not deep, and is said to dry up to a very considerable extent in summer, leaving in places nothing but a salt desert. So saturated are its waters, that even at the present season, the bottom of the lake was occupied by a deposit of salt, which, evidently, if the waters were not saturated would be re-dissolved.

It is called by those residing in the neighbourhood Tuz Goli, or the Salt Lake, sometimes also Tuz Choli, or Salt Desert; Aji Goli, Bitter Lake; Koch Hisar Goli, lake of Koch Hisar; and simply Tuzlah, or Saltern. The latter appears to be the favourite name among the Turkomans. In some maps it is marked as Memlehah and Mellalah; the first, incorrectly, as being the Arabic for salt cellar; the second corresponds to the Turkish Tuzlah, a saltern.

The eastern banks of the lake are tenanted by pastoral Turkomans of quiet habits; but the western side is rather travelled over than inhabited by Kurds, who are constantly giving trouble to government by their predatory habits. It was most likely on this account, that Mr. W. J. Hamilton could not find any one to take him to the lake on that side from Ak Shehr, Ilghun, or Koniyeh.

To the north, where the lake receives no large tributaries, its limits are well defined; but to the south, where it is joined by several large streams of fresh water, and the plain is low and level, these tributary waters spread themselves out, and convert the whole land into extensive marshes, so that it is difficult to determine the exact boundary of the lake, a difficulty that is increased by the fresh water giving origin to a prolific vegetation, that is not met with on the arid and salt shores of its northern extremity.

The lake is said to contain no fish, nor did we find

any molluscous or conchiferous animals; its waters and its banks are, therefore, frequented by few aquatic birds. Although constantly on the look-out, we cannot say that we ever saw a bird on its bosom, though the story of birds being unable to rise if their wings are once dipped in the water, as related by Mr. W. J. Hamilton, is evidently fabulous, as we saw many Turkomans, women, and children, lading their buffaloes in the water, upon whom the saline substances would have crystallized as soon as upon a bird, if such a state of supersaturation could have existed.

A series of barometrical observations gave, for the mean height of the lake above the sea, 2500 feet.

The revenue derived from taxes levied on those who take salt from the lake goes chiefly to the mushir or pasha of Koniyeh, who deputes the superintendence to the mutesellim or governor of Ak Serai. The representatives of the late Turkoman chieftain Chapwan Oghlu, claim also a portion of this revenue, so, as the whole is said to amount to only 200*l.* sterling per annum, the division leaves but a small revenue.

On our arrival at Ak Serai (the White Palace,) we found that the Christian inhabitants had all gone to celebrate a festival in a neighbouring village, so that we had to remain two hours in the streets exposed to the gaze of the Turkomans, before we could be accommodated with a room.

This town derives great interest, not only from its beautiful position at the foot of hills, watered by a clear bounding stream, and surrounded by fertile gardens, but also from its numerous remains of Mohammedan buildings, chiefly in a rich style of Saracenic architecture.

Some of these monuments are still very perfect, and of great beauty. There is every reason to believe that they belong to the same period as the causeway and its numerous khans, extending from this place to Koniyeh, and that the White Palace was the summer resort of the Sultans of Iconium, in the times of their greatest power and opulence.

It is also identified in more ancient times with Archelais Colonia, a colony of the Emperor Claudius, which is placed by Pliny upon the Southern Halys; yet there does not appear to be any reason to believe, that the White River had ever any outlet into the valley of the Halys.

We did not get a room till Rassam had quarrelled with the khawass, who, upon being asked to give us a Mohammedan one, generally the most cleanly, answered that, "Gawurs always went to Gawurs." Now this term Gawur was always extremely unpleasant to our companion's ear, and derogatory to his dignity, as not being a Rayah or Christian subject; so he resented the insult by belabouring the Turk with his whip, explaining to him at the same time that he was the infidel and not us.

We were abstracted from the amusement afforded by contemplating this public discussion as to infidelity in religion, by the arrival of an Armenian seraf or banker, who led us to his house and received us in a kindly and homely manner; these Eski (Old) Armenians being much more tolerant and hospitable than the Romish Armenians.

In the evening we were visited by some other Christians, among whom was a Greek, who became very disputatious. Mr. Rassam had been mentioning the number of languages into which the New Testament had been translated and printed in England, to which the Greek vouchsafed an uncalled-for and unnecessary denial. Mr. R. retorted upon him, by asking him, why they burned the copies with which they had been supplied? "Because," he anwered, "they were not correct translations, inasmuch as you had introduced things against fasting, &c." This we promptly refuted, and explained to him and to the Armenians our views on this subject, but not to the satisfaction of the Greek, who upon matters of commerce also showed the same hostility to everything that was English.

CHAPTER XV.

Castle of Sevri Hisar.

Iron Village. Ravines with Grottoes. Garsabora, a town of Caves. Castle of Sevri Hisar. Secluded Greek Church. Lose our Way. Monastery of St. James. Kaiser Keuy—Dio Cæsarea. Valley of Soandum. Numerous Caves. Greek Festival for the Dead. Castle of Zingibar—Nora and Cybistra. Plain of Kara Hisar. Fortified Khan. Town of Injeh Su (Narrow Water). General Conclusions. Cappadocian Greeks. Natural Features. Hasan Tagh. Contrasted Configuration. Various Rock Architecture.

As we were leaving Ak Serai, the next morning, the wife of our seruji came to beg that we would not beat him, as she acknowledged that he was rather stupid. We, however, quieted the poor woman's alarms, by saying that we hoped he was acquainted with the road, or he should get no bakshish, but that he certainly would not be beat by us.

We entered hence upon a hilly country, a great

change after our long wanderings on the level plain of Koch Hisar. The variety was also great, level uplands terminating in abrupt cliffs over deep ravines, with shingly and sandy declivities, and which were generally covered with the ruins of rocks, fallen from above.

Eleven miles from Ak Serai we came to Demirchi Keuy (Iron Village), built at the base and ascending the acclivities of a bare hill, which was overhung by rocky cliffs. So many masses of rock, and some of considerable magnitude, had fallen into the village, that it appeared as if overwhelmed, and it was difficult to distinguish rocks from houses. The White River flowed in its front.

Three miles higher up the same valley was the village of Salmadder, remarkable for its numerous grottoes. From hence our route lay over plains and uplands, till we approached the Sevri Hisar hills, when we turned to the right, and entered deep and rocky ravines, at the foot of an outlying spur of the Hasan Tagh. The first we entered contained a few grottoes and caves, which kept increasing in number as we progressed, till we came to what had evidently been a very populous site, and where, superadded to the caves, were ruins of dwelling-houses, arches of stonework, &c., still standing in the valley. This place is called by the Greeks of the present day, Belistermeh.

Ravines of the same character, almost without interruption to the succession of grottoes, many of which were rudely ornamented in front, led us to Gelvedery, where we were equally surprised and delighted to find a large colony of Greeks living in these caves, mostly built up in front, and occupying not only the acclivities of the hills, but also the face of the precipice to its very top, and stretching up a narrow ravine, which, towards its upper part became choked with these semi-subterranean dwellings.

We had now the pleasure of contemplating what one of these cave villages or towns was when inhabited; and were all anxiety to get into one of the houses, but this anxiety on our part was not at all met by the natives, who were disinclined to receive us, or to hold communication with us. At length we got into a house, where was a caverned odah, but it was full of khawasses; so Mr. Rassam repaired to the house of a priest, who acted kindly, and allowed us a room for the night.

These Greeks, although thus secluded from the world, were not poor, and had a goodly stone church in the vale. From what conversation we had with the priests, it appears that they claim a high antiquity to the site of Gelvedery, which there is every reason to believe corresponds to Garsabora.

What interested us greatly, was to endeavour to trace the origin of Greek colonies, in such remote and sequestered spots, but upon this subject they could offer us no information; their fathers' fathers had lived in the same spot, but why it was chosen by them, and what advantages it had ever offered to them, appeared scarcely ever to have been a subject of a moment's thought. It is not many years since the Osmanli government, by a rather enlightened policy, dragged the Christians from the caves of Osiana, Tatlar, &c., and made them reside in the New City, and the troglodites of Gelvedery appear to have much horror of the same fate hanging over them; and thus our questions excited their suspicions, and awakened fears which all our expressions of kindly and brotherly feeling towards them scarcely sufficed to allay.

April 25th. Leaving Gelvedery, we ascended, in a storm of wind and rain, the rocky path, which led us to the crest of the hills of Sevri Hisar. The ascent occupied us upwards of an hour, and at the summit we found the ruins of a castle, upon a conical rock to our left, at the base of which were some curious grottoes. This appears to be the Comitanasse of the Theodosian or Peutingerian tables.

On our descent, the rocky cliffs to our left were burrowed by numerous caves and grottoes, and in the valley below we arrived at a small village of Greek Christians, which was surrounded by culture. Mountains, which extended from the Hasan Tagh to the eastward, constituted a long and impenetrable barrier to the south, and everywhere limited this rocky region in that direction; this village is thus exceedingly confined and hemmed in on all sides by volcanic rocks, as were also all the adjacent valleys, giving to each a wild and isolated character.

The ascent over the next low range of hills brought us to another of these secluded and rocky spots, but what surprised us not a little, was a rather elegantly built Greek church standing in its centre, but with no habitations near it, and gradually falling into ruins. So regular and handsome an edifice, isolated in the midst of such savage scenery, naturally interested our feelings very much, and we could not but sympathize with a religion, which in the hour of distress or persecution, whether on the rock or the desert, still sought refuge and found consolation in the house of prayer.

Our guide did not know his way through this district of alternate rocks and vales, and we were not long in losing our track; nor did we regain it, till, after wandering several hours amidst wood, glens, and marshes, we came upon some hilly heights, from whence we obtained a view of the great plain of Mar Yakub, or of the Monastery of St. James, fertile and cultivated, with numerous villages scattered here and there, and conical mountains rising like domes from the otherwise nearly uniform level.

I descended to this plain by a narrow glen, in which were numerous caves and grottoes, and at the entrance of which was the large village of Kayali. On emerging from this, it was some time before I could find out the party who had descended from the hills by another and less steep path.

As it was raining hard, Russell and I then rode on in search of the village of Mar Yakub, but after proceeding some distance, we found that Mr. Rassam, the seruji, and baggage horses were not coming on, and accordingly retraced our steps, but sought for them in vain. In this dilemma we perceived a peasant in the fields, and galloped after him for information; as might be naturally expected, the poor fellow took to his heels and ran away as fast as he could, so that it was with some difficulty, as the ground was heavy, that we came up with him; and highly delighted he was, to find that we only wanted to know our way to Mar Yakub. This was pointed out in a direction rather different from that which we had taken, so we rode on another hour and a half, when we arrived at the place—a goodly-looking, well-built, and in many respects, interesting Christian village. Rassam, we found, had not arrived, and we became rather anxious about him, but were fain to accept of an empty stable, without fire or food, and wait for him. At length, late in the evening, he made his appearance. He had taken refuge from the storm in a village near the entrance of the plain, and after refreshing himself, had rode on in the evening to Mar Yakub.

The houses of this village were built all upon the same plan, the frame-work being formed by three or four well-turned semicircular arches, and the interval filled up with rubble and masonry. The basement is always more or less excavated, and the building generally comprises one or two apartments that are subterraneous. This is the ancient style of building still persevered in, and the ruined arches that are to be seen in various parts of Garsaura, and also in deserted Christian towns in Syria and Mesopotamia, were built on a similar plan, and it is a style that appears to have had its origin in its adaptation to extreme climates, affording warmth in winter, and yet being cool in summer.

Mar Yakub, commonly called Malakob, is subject to great inconvenience in summer, being built upon a plain of volcanic sand, which is drifted about by the slightest breeze. In order to protect their cattle and fodder, the inhabitants have paved circular spaces in front of their houses.

There is also no running stream on the plain, and water is obtained only by considerable labour from deep wells, and these are surrounded by stone reservoirs, each family claiming its own; so that the labour of drawing may only be undergone in the cool hours of morning and evening.

There is attached to the same village, one modern church, in part built of the ruins of an older edifice, and dedicated to St. Theodore. It was embellished in the interior with the usual profusely gaudy taste of the Greek church, and, as may be imagined, the gaudiness was here unrelieved by taste or skill. Another church in ruins was dedicated to St. Michael, and there were also the ruins of a small chapel, beautifully constructed, and prettily disposed as a cross, and dedicated to All Souls.

There are also fragments of a monastery or church, where we copied from an altar-piece the only distinct and consecutive letters which had any appearance of antiquity. The inscription was from

"The Achæan Achatob
To his good (or brave) Father."

Mar Yakub altogether presents an appearance that reminds one of a remote antiquity, and of what one would always wish to see—a town of old times, preserving all its forms and customs. The houses of hewn stone with their lofty arches, the clean paved courts, the numerous wells with their white and massive troughs grouped around them; and, rising above all, the tall ruinous churches partook of the same primitive and antique simplicity. The dress of the inhabitants is also peculiar; we had an opportunity of seeing this to advantage, for the evening of our arrival a marriage procession paraded the streets. We could not help thinking, on contemplating such a scene, that perhaps such were the villages when St. Paul himself "went through Syria and Cilicia, confirming the churches."

After visiting the different ecclesiastical edifices in

the morning, we started across the plain towards a conical hill, called Chevri, on the top of which a festival is held by the Christians at Easter. Passing over a low range of rocky hills, we came to Kaiser Keuy, a small village with a ruined church and some other relics of ancient times, but now inhabited by but few Greeks. One of the most fierce and ill-looking men we had met with, for a long time, came to answer our inquiries. He examined us with a more than usual scrutinizing scowl, and it was certainly not for want of will, that he did not appropriate to himself some of our property. This place would appear by its name to connect itself with the Dio Cæsarea of antiquity, and may have be encalled Kaiser Keuy, as Cæsarea is now called Kaiseriyeh.

Our road now lay over a hilly country, having to the right a conical hill, bearing the ruins of a church, and called Chiring Kilisa (Bell Church). About five miles from Kaiser Keuy, we came to some ruins of a village, where, as at Mar Yakub, the houses had been arched and paved in front. There were also some grottoes and excavations around.

Immediately connected with these ruins was a narrow and deep hewn passage that led down a steep cliff into the beautiful and remarkable vale of Soandum, now called Sowanli Dereh*.

* This word is written by Mr. Renouard as Soghanli Dereh (Onion Valley), but Soghanli, *an onion*, is pronounced Soran, as Aghatsh, *wood*, is pronounced Aratsh; and we took particular care to obtain the correct name of the valley, which is Sowanli Dereh, and has no reference to the modern growth of onions, as far as we could learn.

The cliffs at the head of the valley were not very high, but became loftier as we proceeded downwards Already at this extremity the vertical portions were occupied by excavations of various forms and kinds. The middle of the vale was watered by a rivulet, the banks of which soon became verdant with trees, shrubs, and gardens. As the valley widened, and the cliffs rose higher, the caves became more numerous, often ascending in tiers, one set above the other, some open, others partly closed, and sometimes continuous for a distance, with little apertures for light dotting the line of their extent, and at an elevation, and on the front of precipices which the most daring troglodyte would scarcely be expected to scale. Ruins began also now to show themselves at the foot of the acclivities, and in the valley pathway. Modern habitations were also met with.

Our usual bad weather marred the pleasure which we otherwise should have derived from inspecting this remarkable valley and its caves, and we were obliged to hurry on to Orta Keuy (Middle Village), tenanted by Greeks, and where, arriving rather hastily and unexpectedly, we frightened the inhabitants, who, in their panic, shut themselves up in their houses, and would hold no communication with us, although it was pouring torrents. At length, after toiling up rocky streets, and knocking each of us at separate doors, till the very rocks re-echoed with the clamour, we got hold of a stray being, and having informed him that we were Christians and not robbers, we obtained a further hearing, when the villagers, now heartily ashamed of their cowardice and inhospitality, made amends by ushering us into a very cleanly and comfortable room attached to the church.

In the evening we attended divine service, previous to which a female came to us and offered for sale a manuscript, consisting of a few leaves stitched together, and containing a Greek prayer. Towards the conclusion of the service, a man entered the church with a basket containing some boiled wheat, in which a lighted candle was stuck. This was put down near the sanctuary, and the priest came out attended by two boys, one of whom carried a bundle of books, similar to that which we had been offered, and which he handed one by one to the priest, who mumbled over the contents with great industry and dispatch, and passed them to the boy on the other side; the chanters all the while hymning Kyrie Eleison at the top of their voices. At the conclusion of service the wheat was distributed to all present. Is this a remnant of the heathen custom of distributing lentils at funerals*? When we questioned the priest on the subject, he gravely assured us that it was a good thing for the dead in purgatory.

We were also told a ridiculous tradition here, which is not worth relating, as to how Soandum fell into the power of the Turks, through the treachery of a young Greek girl.

The ensuing day we continued our descent of the valley; branch glens began to open on both sides, exhibiting, although in less frequency, excavations similar to those of the main valley, and which are, in fact, prolonged from its head to the hill of Zingibar, a distance of about twelve miles. As we approached the

* See PLUTARCH'S *Life of Crassus.*

town of Devehli Kara Hisar (Black Camel Castle), the valley became filled with luxuriant gardens and shadowy groves. It was a fine clear noon, and we stopped a short time in these gardens to take a meridian observation, riding in afterwards to the town, where we were accommodated in the odah of the menzil-khan.

Immediately after our arrival, Russell and I started for the castle of Zingibar. This castle, one of the most remarkable ruins in these districts, stands on the loftiest of two cones, of a nearly isolated group of hills. It is a vast pile of building, composed of a great variety of parts, all difficult of access, from steep cliffs or artificial walls or slopes. The external castle is defended by walls and towers, and there are curtains in advance of the more exposed parts; within are numerous compartments irregularly huddled together. One portion is again inclosed within its own walls and forms a kind of capitol or castle of itself.

This castle has been identified with Cybistra, which is chiefly remarkable on account of its having been the military station of Cicero, while watching the motions of the Parthian army which threatened Cilicia and Cappadocia from the side of Syria.

The castle of Nora or Neroassus, celebrated as the stronghold of Eumenes, appears on a variety of grounds to be the same as Cybistra, and the descriptions left to us of that castle,—whether by Plutarch, who mentions the great inconvenience to the garrison, from the narrowness of the space in which they were confined, inclosed as it was with small houses, or by Diodorus,—agree very closely, both in character and in position, with the castle now called Zingibar.

The weather turned to rain in the afternoon, and it continued to pour all the time that we were making our examinations and admeasurements, a labour which occupied no small time, and as we had sent on our change of clothes from Nev Shehr to Kaiseriyeh, it was on our return to Kara Hisar, the fifth night in succession, that we had to sit, well drenched with wet, and without the means of changing our clothes.

28*th*. This morning we started over the plain of Kara Hisar, which extends from the foot of low hills to the west to the base of the Arjish Tagh (Mount Argæus) and the more southerly Ali Tagh in the east. The lower portions, especially near to Mount Argæus, were occupied by marshes and lakes, which present the remarkable phenomenon, of having, at an elevation of 3400 feet, no outlet.

The vegetation of the plain was monotonous, but the scenery, from the presence of the giant Argæus and the snow-clad Taurus, was varied and magnificent. While the pinnacle heights of these mountains rose up into the clouds, they had thrown from their acclivities long streams of lava, which advanced like dark claws of rock into the marsh and lake below.

On this plain we passed a ruinous khan, with an outer wall, having round towers at the angles, and in the interior, a quadrangular building, pierced with loopholes for defence. It is painful to think, what a state of insecurity these countries have been in from time immemorial, that a travelling caravan should have to seek even a night's rest in a fortified mansion.

Beyond this plain we came to some low cliffs of scoriaceous lava, one of the streams from Mount Argæus, the surface of which, uninviting as it appeared, was partitioned out for cultivation of the yellow berry by the industrious Christians of Injeh Su.

Shortly afterwards we arrived at the town so called, which is most remarkably situated in a ravine, built across at its entrance by a lofty and strong wall, which fronts at once a jami and a khan, and affords a passage by a well defended gateway into the rock-inclosed town.

The ravine is traversed by the rivulet that gives its name to the town, Injeh Su (Narrow Water), and expands at its upper part where it opens into another rocky valley. Both the declivities of the hills and the hollow of the valley are all occupied by dwelling houses, the Turks and Greeks having each about 750 houses, but the Christian population exceeds the Mohammedan. The houses are for the most part substantial and cleanly; there are also many grottoes.

Injeh Su is governed by a mutesellim, who is sent from Constantinople; the produce of the taxes being devoted to the maintenance of the Selatyn, or mosque, called Mahmudiyeh, in the Osmanli capital. It was indebted to a certain vizir, by name Kara Mustapha, for its khan and attached jami, which close up the entrance of the ravine so effectually.

At this place we quitted Garsauritis, to enter the district of Cæsarea, but the first-mentioned province of Cappadocia is so interesting, and has been hitherto so little explored, that it cannot be passed over without some remarks.

This ancient province is to be viewed as eminently a rocky country, remarkable for its wild and stony districts, and its secluded glens and ravines, with their picturesque outline; but it has also fertile plains and productive declivities: wood is generally wanting; it covers some portions of the hills, but dry dung and the roots of Astragalus are generally used for fuel.

Whether the Greeks of this part of Cappadocia willingly repaired to the ravines and fastnesses, with their subterranean dwellings, that belong to this singular country, by predilection for the morose seclusion and religious retirement which sprang from a young and devout, but ill-understood Christianity; whether they simply remained around the ancient abodes of their fathers, and thus escaped the dispersion and extermination that fell to the lot of the town dwellers; or whether, as is most likely, they sought refuge in those caverned fastnesses from the successive invasions of Persians, Syro-Circassians, Turkomans, and last of all Osmanlis, the present race can tell you nothing: yet certain it is, that these caverned dwellings, and chapels, and tombs, are as characteristic of the Christian Cappadocian Greeks, as stone dwellings and churches on the naked rocky plain, without culture or water, are of an early Syrian Christianity.

The present condition of the Cappadocian Greeks shews itself under a very favourable aspect. We have seen, that while in Gelvedery and Sowanli, they have remained buried in their caves, they have in other places issued from these, and congregated in now flourishing and cheerful towns, as Nev Shehr and Injeh Su. In these places there is an aspect of ease, freedom, and prosperity, which never belongs to Mohammedan towns. Children are playing about, flowers are trained up the house walls, females sit at their verandahs, and trade is bustling in the market; add to this, that the Cappadocian Greeks are, generally speaking, pleasing and unreserved in their manners, and their conversation indicated a very high degree of intelligence and civilization, where there are so few books, and so little education, and consequently, little learning.

In the villages, the men, marrying early, repair to Constantinople and Smyrna to trade, while to the women is left the care of the house, the flock and the vineyard; an evil follows from this, that the females become masculine and full of violent passions, and when the men return to their homes, they are often very far from finding an echo to the subdued tones and more polished manners which they had learnt to appreciate in the civilized world. The priests who remain at home might be supposed to have some connteracting influence, but they are often old, have rarely above moderate capacities, and are frequently disregarded and disrespected.

But apart from these minor considerations, these Cappadocian Greeks certainly constitute a tribe themselves, distinguished by their manners, their habits, and their independent prosperity and civilization, and not so much surpassing other Greeks in Asia Minor by their progressive civilization, as excelling them in having become less changed, and less humbled and prostrated, than other Greek communities are by four centuries of Osmanli tyranny.

The province also is remarkable from its natural features, its configuration and structure, as well as from its remains of art, its caves and ruins.

The north-eastern part is characterized by its great

upland of lava, broken down into cliffs, or denuded into round-topped ranges of hills, terminating in the marshy country at the north and western foot of Mount Argæus, but even more by its volcanic tuffas and sands, rent into deep and narrow glens, studded with cones and pinnacles, also the effect of disintegration, and often presenting an infinite variety of singular forms; and lastly by rocks and precipices, excavated almost wherever such present themselves, with vast multitudes of caves that have served or serve still, for dwellings, chapels, monasteries, and tombs, exhibiting forms and styles of rock architecture which vary with the locality of each series of excavations, and present a somewhat different system in places at little geographical distance from one another.

The north-west portion of Garsauritis derives its peculiar character, which is less remarkable and of a more inhospitable nature, from a long range of granitic mountains; rocky and picturesque in the Tash Tellah; undulating in the Sari Karaman; stony and wild again at Chamurli; bold and rocky, with castellated remains, in the Kojah Tagh; with abrupt and truncated cones at Toklu Kaleh; and, lastly, grouped and mountainous in the Sambulak Tagh, where the same range advances to meet the mountains of Galatia, only separated by the Halys, which flows through a deep and narrow valley between the two. This is the district, in the rocky portions of which are the sites of Nitazas and Ozzala; Nysia, on a fertile plain; and Parnassus, on the verdant slopes of the beautiful and mountain-inclosed vale of the Halys.

Central Garsauritis is characterised by the Akajuk

mountain, of a conical or saddle-backed form, clad with greensward, but not wooded, and from its loftiness visible from a large portion of Galatia and all Morimene. Connected with this mountain are many rocky offsets, in the deep valleys of which are the lakes called Devehli, Tursufu, and others. This district, corresponding to the ancient Argustana, is now tenanted by a tribe of Kurds, who are called after the mountain, the Akajuk Ashirat.

The Tattæa Palus or Great Salt Lake, and its accompanying plain, is acknowledged to have been in ancient Phrygia, and formed part of the kingdom made up by Antony for Amyntas.

The south-west quarter of the province is pre-eminently distinguished from the others by the lofty summit of Hasan Tagh, rising upwards of 8000 feet above the level of the sea. This mountain has a nearly conical form, and is said to preserve patches of snow throughout the year. Its western and north-western base is bounded by the plain of Perta; to the south, a low undulating rocky and volcanic country stretches to Kara Bunar, while a low level plain separates it from the Karajah Tagh. To the east, it is prolonged by one or two cones, and then a chain of mountains, not rising as high as the culminating point; these shut up Garsauritis to the south, but lowering towards the district of Sarima, or Saluberrima, allowed there of the passage of the great road from Tyana, Cæna, and Andabalis, which came round the mountains to join that of Archelais to Ancyra, or of Perta to Amorium.

Hasan Tagh, from wherever viewed, is a most picturesque and striking object, and is visible in almost every direction from a great distance. Like Arjish Tagh, it is eminently of volcanic origin, and it has spread over the whole country to the north-east, a vast deposit of effused and irrupted volcanic matters, which present great scenic as well as geological interest.

The nature of the rocks influences the configuration of the districts in which they occur, in a very material degree. The compact uniform products of effusion being spread in vast beds over the rocks of aggregation, give rise to plains and uplands, slightly undulating, with sometimes stair-like terraces; but where there is water, as along the course of rivers and rivulets, the subjacent rocks, generally of a friable nature, are carried away; while the more compact above are tumbled down, leaving vertical cliffs above and acclivities of sand below, with scattered masses of rock, with which the habitations of men are so intermingled, that it is some time before the traveller can distinguish them from the ruins of the cliff. The description of Demirchi Keuy gives but a faint idea of the profusion of this kind of scenery. The face of the rocks above, as well as the declivities of sand below, when not covered with fragments, are in many places studded with grottoes.

On approaching the foot of Hasan Tagh and the head of the waters, the tributary streams are more numerous, and the ravines, in consequence, more frequent; sometimes as many as three or four meet together within a short distance, and all crowded with excavations of the nest-like mansions of the living and the dead.

At other times, the volcanic rocks, of the sandy kind, are broken up and disrupted by basaltic lavas. The hills then become loftier and more rocky; the valleys are dark and infertile; there are few vertical cliffs or secluded ravines; but instead of these, long barren courses of black lava, and stony and pathless wildernesses. Such are the Sevri Hisar hills and the country immediately east of them, the district of Comitinasso. Isolated and fertile little basins occur in the midst of these naked districts, and here again are found the habitations of men and the ruins of stone churches built by their ancestors. The Cappadocian Greeks are not, however, confined to these wild spots, so difficult of access and so uninviting to the eye. The small town of Mar Yakub has been described as situated in the midst of a fertile plain abounding in villages, and Kaiser Keuy (Dio-Cæsarea) is at the head of the same district.

The south-east quarter of the province partakes of both features: of grassy uplands, with solitary hills, sometimes with old churches on their summits, as at Chiring Kilisa; and of cultivated plains, with little water or lakes without outlets, and out of which rise dome-shaped hills of volcanic origin, often the seat of superstition, as Chevri Tagh, or prouder and loftier summits, as the Argæus, but of similar nature. On the confines of this district we find again, at Sowanli Dereh, at Evdamasin, Injeh Su, and other places, the same deep-cut valleys, with the same repetition of cliff and cave scenery, and that variety of rock architecture which in these districts alone would supply the archæologist and the draughtsman with inexhaustible resources for his pen and pencil, and which awaken the traveller's interest and fix his attention at almost every step throughout the whole of this remarkable province of ancient Cappadocia.

CHAPTER XVI.

Mount Argæus.

Kaiseriyeh. Armenian Christians. Character of the City. Population and Antiquities. Mount Argæus—Arjish Tagh. Start from Kaiseriyeh. Group in a Market-Place. Armenians not Christians. Effects of the Bastinado. A fierce Ayyan. Enter Anti-Taurus.

Leaving Injeh Su for Kaiseriyeh, we turned round a great current of lava thrown out by Mount Argæus, and followed a line, between impassable marsh on the one side, and rocks on the other, the latter of which we were occasionally driven upon, by the encroachments of the water, when the path became rude, stony, and difficult. We observed, shortly after starting, a sepulchral chapel to the northward, beyond which were some more ancient ruins, now designated as Viran Shehr (the Ruined City), and probably the site of Odoga.

The Saslik (Marsh), which is composed of alternate marsh and lakes, aud occupies the plain at the northern foot of Mount Argæus, is chiefly supplied by the numerous springs that burst out from the foot of the mountain, in the same direction.

Beyond these basaltic lavas, with frequent springs, we came to a more open valley, everywhere covered with gardens, and making a short ascent over a mountain called Ulanli, we passed by what was, apparently, a subsidence in the rock, like the hollow of a crater. Hence we descended upon the plain of Kaiseriyeh, passing, before we reached the town, a long peninsulated hill called Besh Teppeh (Five Hills), at the extremity of which is a ruined castellated building, and upon which is said to have been built a portion of the ancient town of Cæsarea.

We were happy enough to obtain at Kaiseriyeh a good cleanly apartment, attached to the chief church of the Eski (old) Armenians, generally so called, to distinguish them from the Roman Catholic Armenians, but, who are Armenians, strictly speaking. We generally found these people more kindly-disposed and more communicative than the Greeks or the Romish Armenians, although both these sects look upon the others as scarcely Christians.

There was a daily school for boys in the same yard, and we took pleasure not only in visiting it, but in receiving as many pupils as chose to come in to us during play hours. We even got some of them to assist us during our night observations, and nothing struck them so much, as the great length of the astronomical calculations.

We had also frequent and long conversations with some of the priests and the schoolmaster, and, as we always attended divine service, this ultimately assumed a very friendly and communicative character, although they frequently alluded to the fact that several priests were at present confined in a neighbouring monastery, whither they had been removed from Smyrna and Constantinople, in consequence of their connexion with the American missionaries in those places.

The priest, whose duty it was to officiate the ensuing Sabbath, prepared himself by a week's seclusion and fasting. Thus there was always one of them, who dwelt in a lonely cell, close by the church door, and who, although he visited us sometimes, still appeared to spend the greater part of the day, as also the night, by the light of a flickering lamp, in religious contemplation or observances.

These Armenians are in the habit of practising nearly as many ceremonies as the Catholics and Greek Church, at least their mummery, in the eyes of a Protestant, appears much the same, yet the three sects mutually blame each others' rites. When we attended their service, they placed us between the railing and the altar, a place of honour, being among the priests and chanters. The officiating priest was very gaudily dressed, and bore a gilt crown on his head; the boys were also arrayed in bright coloured silks, with brocade or gilt fringes, but the other priests retained their sombre hues, and presented a strange contrast to the gaiety around; during the service the boys brought us consecrated bread to eat.

There are three Armenian monasteries in the environs of Kaiseriyeh, Surp Karabat, Surp Daniel, Surp Serkis (St. George), and Peri Karabat; the last, a ruin on the conical hill called Ali Tagh, between the city and Mount Argæus. The Greeks have two monasteries, Yamar Tash and Sinjah Dereh.

It is curious that, while within the city the Armenian population quadruples the Greek, the reverse is the case in the surrounding villages. In the jurisdiction of Kaiseriyeh, not including the city, the Greek population amounts to 5730 souls, the Armenian only to 287, monasteries not included; within the city there are 1100 Greeks, 5200 Armenians, and 12,176 Mohammedans. The system of hemi-subterranean dwellings is preserved in several of the neighbouring villages and rocky valleys.

Kaiseriyeh, like most other cities in Asia Minor, although encumbered with ruins, presents a picturesque appearance. Its central part is occupied by a castle with high walls and moat around it. Its market is extensive, and is well stocked with the usual articles of demand in these countries, including many of British manufacture. The commercial communication between this place and Smyrna is constantly kept up, and our commercial interests are now further ensured by the establishment of a Consular Agent at the same spot.

It is impossible, without encroaching too much upon our limits, to recapitulate the varied fortunes of this city. It appears, however, that the original population was Armenian, for their annals relate that Mishak, who is called Moshok by the Greek historians, founded a city here, surrounded it with stone walls, and gave to it the name of Mishak after himself, but the Cappadocians, unable to pronounce it corectly, called it Mazak, whence afterwards, when it became the Cæsarea of the Romans, it was distinguished as Cæsarea Mazaca; it was also called Eusebia.

The Persians ruled here, but probably brought few permanent residents; so with the Romans, whose general in the time of Shapur (Sapor I.) appears to have been a Cappadocian Greek*. The Syro-Circassian government was one of a licentious soldiery, which may have mingled its blood with, but did not characterize the population of the place. The passage of the Christian Crusaders was the most transient of all.

It was, probably, at the first contact of Mohammedans with the Armenians and Cappadocian Greeks, that the former in greater part withdrew to their own countries, and the latter began to retire to the caves and fastnesses of Garsauritis and the environs.

The population of the Turkomans, under the independent princes of the Seljukiyan dynasty, would under these circumstances soon become predominant, and it is not probable that subsequent Osmanli preeminence has ever much affected the latter engrafted population of the city.

The antiquities of Kaiseriyeh have not been yet fully explored, but as far as we could see were chiefly Mohammedan. We found several tombs with Greek and some with Latin inscriptions, but there are few monuments belonging to the same ages in the city itself.

---

* One of the Persian kings, according to Strabo, Ariarathe I., but more likely Ariarathe III., who was conquered and slain by Perdiccas, joined Cataonia to this satrapy. Under the Macedonians it was divided into ten prefectures, till Tiberius declared it to be a Roman province.

The number of Mohammedan structures, including imams, kumbets, ziyarets, tekiyyehs, &c. is very great, and they also rise out of the plain on every side around the city.

A tradition assigns the site of the ancient Mishak or Mazaca to the "Five Hills;" this will account for the paucity of ancient edifices.

The river of Sarimsak (Garlick) flows at a distance of 2960 yards from the town under a bridge and causeway, near which are some Mohammedan ruins. It is here eight yards in width, and is soon lost, like the rivulet of Kaiseriyeh, in the great Sazlik or Marsh, which again empties itself by the Boghaz Kupri (Pass of the Bridge) into the Kizil Irmak or Halys.

The vale of Kaiseriyeh, which is abundantly fertile and rich, is bounded to the north, by the low hills of Khidr Iliyas, so called from a village and church of that name; to the west, by the mountain of Ulanli and the marsh; to the east, by low hills at the head of the Sarimsak river; and to the south, by Argish Tagh, the ancient Mount Argæus, and its various offsets*.

---

* Our attention had been especially called by the Royal Geographical Society to the question, as to what river is the Melas of Strabo. The answer is very simple. Strabo, by inadvertence or otherwise, described two Melas'; for the river that sprang from the side of Mount Argæus, forty stadia or four geographical miles from Kaisariyeh, and which, by the bursting of the dykes overflowed the land of the Galatians, and which he calls the Melas, could not have been the Tokmah Su, as other travellers before us (particularly Mr. Hamilton and Captain Callier) have shewn that the rivulets around Kaisariyeh all flow into the Saslik or marsh, and empty themselves by the Kara Su into the Kizil Irmak or Halys. This little of bit of hydrography we examined more

The noble mountain of Argæus, called by the Turks Arjish Tagh, is the loftiest peak in Asia Minor. Almost perpetually involved in clouds during our stay at Kaiseriyeh, we had only an occasional glance, and that generally at sunrise, of its extreme summit and it being the season of the year in which the snow-line descends to within a few hundred feet of the plain, this circumstance put all attempts at an ascent out of the question.

The axis of the mountain appears, from a number of observations, to be about ten miles from its circumference, considering it for the moment to be isolated on every side, which it is not. This would give a mean area for the whole mountain of 300, and a circumference of 60 miles. Its elevation, as determined by Mr. Hamilton*, is 12,809 feet.

The tradition as given by Strabo, that both the Euxine and the Mediterranean may be descried from its its summit must be received with doubts, since its distance from the Black Sea is 170 British miles, and

---

carefully, and traced the largest tributary of this basin of the Sarimsak river to near its sources.

Strabo, however, in another place, describes the Melas as flowing through Armenia Minor into the Euphrates, and it is generally admitted, that the same river gave its name to the Cappadocian province and the town of Melitene; it was, indeed, from this circumstance, that both D'Anville and Rennell supposed the Melas to flow through the city of Malatiyeh. Thus, then, Strabo either adverts to the Melas as the river, that by bursting its boundaries overflowed the country of the Galatians, by inadvertence, or there were then two Melas' as there are now many dozen Kara Sus (Black Waters) in the same country.

* This gentleman has got the reputation in the country of remaining buried under the perpetual snows of the mountain.

from the Mediterranean 110 miles, with lofty ridges of mountains also intervening on both sides. There is also a tradition that the Romans had a castle on its summit where Tiberius Cæsar used to sit, but I suspect this belongs to some other hill in the neighbourhood.

The Armenians have preserved a written chronicle of the earthquake that ravaged the city of Kaiseriyeh in August, 1835, but it contains little of any interest to the philosophy of these destructive phenomena. It appears that it commenced two hours before sunrise, on the morning of Thursday, August the 1st, and was accompanied by a loud noise, the shocks being repeated at intervals for ten hours after that time. Many menarehs and lofty buildings were overthrown. The record says that there perished as many as 665 persons; the houses thrown down are mentioned, rather hyperbolically, as beyond enumeration.

Several of the neighbouring villages, especially such as were built in ravines, suffered severely. At Tagh-ler, seventeen houses were destroyed by the fall of a rock. At other villages, there was also considerable loss of life and property.

Having completed our astronomical labours at this city, we took our departure on Thursday, 9th of May, up the river of Sarimsak, passing first a Mohammedan ruin, and afterwards several Greek villages, in as many successive ravines, and so sparingly supplied with water, that their separate brooks dried up almost immediately beyond the habitations.

Passing a cliff of volcanic rock, the road thence wound among low hills, in the midst of which was a small lake, on which numerous bald coots were swimming amidst flowering crops of alisma. The birds were, however, wary enough not to allow us to come within shot of them.

After three hours' sharp riding from Kaiseriyeh, we came to Kuzuk, a large village, near which, and on the banks of the river, was an artificial mound nearly 700 yards long, with gardens around, growing on ruins of buildings. This, by distance from Cæsarea, corresponds to the Sorpara of the Peutingerian Tables, which was on the great road from that city to Sebaste.

Hence we entered a pass, from which we issued to join the banks of the river, where was a ruined jami and other Mohammedan remains. The valley of the Sarimsak now began to narrow much, and the stream had become a mere rivulet; we crossed it by a wooden bridge, the village of Sarimsak, whence it derives its name, being about two miles further up the same valley to our right.

At this point we commenced ascending grassy hills, from which we descended to a deep and nearly circular valley, the lower part of which was occupied by a lake, the remainder either marsh or cultivated, and dotted with villages.

This lake is salt. It was at the present season three miles in length by one in width, but is said to be nearly dry in summer. It is farmed for 40,000 piastres, or 400*l.*, annually, which would make it more valuable than the Great Salt Lake of Koch Hisar. Forty piastres (8*s.*) are paid for a cart-load of salt, and ten (2*s.*) for that of a camel or bullock.

On the south side of the valley is an old khan, called Sultan Khan, and the road at certain seasons of the year has to be carried in that direction. On the same line is Tuz Hisar (Salt Castle). We crossed, however, by the middle of the valley to the large village of Pallas, where we obtained accommodation for the night in a public odah.

May 10*th*. Crossing the lacustrine plain, we arrived at its extremity in less than an hour, and began the ascent of barren hills, only relieved by one fertile vale, with the village of Sari Oghlan. Beyond this, on some further bleak heights, was an artificial mound and ruins, another old station; passing this, we began to descend, and sweeping suddenly round, entered the posting town of Gelermek, which contains 200 houses of Armenians and 70 of Mohammedans.

It was scarcely noon, and the day fine, the odah of the menzil-khan (post-house) was crowded, and the lazy travelling khawasses who occupied it were smoking by a large fire, so that we preferred sitting at the door while horses were being got ready. This was a source of much gratification to the inhabitants and idlers in the market-place, who gathered round to examine us and our accoutrements; it was equally amusing to us, who found much in such a group to excite our interest. The market-place had a most wholesome aspect of business; there were numerous well-supplied shops, besides farriers, saddlers, &c., all in the hands of Armenians, who, as usual, constituted the industrious and productive class; there were also sitting with the Christian tradesman, haughty imperturbable Osmanli beys, as every man who holds a few acres of land is called, or equally proud mollahs were to be seen slowly pacing the streets; tatars and khawasses, with whip in hand, blustered about and ordered every one; while more particularly examining us were groups of Kurd peasants, their clothes in tatters, their hair long and dishevelled, a formidable stick in their hands, and a low sullen scowl on their countenances; here and there among them was a Kurd from the mountains, of a better class, with red turbaned kerchief, short jacket, his gun behind, powder-belt and cartridges before, and a haughty bearing, with at the same time a stronger and more active frame than the Osmanli.

At length the necessary horses came, with the exception of one, and that one was not forthcoming. After waiting some time, it was resolved that Russell and I should drive on the baggage-horses slowly, and Rassam offered kindly to wait with the seruji. We accordingly proceeded in advance, descending into a low marshy flat, which, while waiting for our companion, we beat in vain for game. We then ascended a more hilly country, which terminated to the south in a mountain range, having an Arabo-Turkish name, Khanzir Tagh (Wild Boar Mountain), the summits of which were still clad with snow. On our right were Sarichek Tagh (Yellowish Mountain) and Shemah Tagh (Candle Mountain).

Rassam and the seruji overtook us on the ascent, and we soon afterwards gained the Armenian village of Insanli, secluded in a ravine of snow-white gypsum.

The poor Armenians of Insanli, when we conversed with them in the evening, did not acknowledge themselves as Christians; to the leading question when put to them, they answered, "No,—Armeni." They were afraid to claim a title to themselves which is peculiarly arrogated by the schismatic papists of their own church, and by the Greeks, both of whom unite in denying the right of the old Armenians to designate themselves by the glorious epithet of followers of Christ.

May 11*th.* From Insanli, the ascent still continued for some distance, till, passing the crest of the hills, we descended by Kaya Bunar (Rock Spring) to an extensive level and fertile plain, crowded with villages, and watered by several rivulets, the largest and chief of which was the Yanak Chaye (Burnt River).

Passing marshes and rivulets, we came to the village of Chaushun, opposite to which, and at the south extremity of the plain, was the village of Kizil ja Kushla (Red Winter Quarters), having an artificial mound and ruins, and probably the site of the Armaza of the Itineraries.

Shortly afterwards, we arrived at Shehr Kishla (Town Winter Quarters), the residence of the ayyan of the district, and a posting village. On entering this village, and approaching the ayyan's house, we were somewhat startled by the loud and piteous moans of a lusty young man who was writhing on the ground, surrounded by men and women. Our first impression was that we had stumbled on a case of plague or cholera; the next that he was a maniac, which his struggles and contortions appeared to confirm; but we were wrong in both conjectures, for on inquiry it turned out to be a severe case of bastinado on the soles of the feet, which appears to be a very painful punishment.

It was our intention, at this point, to quit the great road to Sivas (Sebaste), and to enter the hilly country to the southward, in search of the ruins of Viran Shehr

(Ruined City), to which our attention had been called by the Society; but on visiting the ayyan, and expressing our wishes to that effect, we met with unexpected difficulties, and the most resolute opposition was made to our taking the horses out of the great road. Besides the direct opposition, openly expressed, all the difficulties which imagination could suggest and ill-will devise, were urged to deter us from our purpose. The incompatibility of some of these objections was quite amusing; at one moment it was all forest and marsh in our way; at another, dry plains, with no water to drink, or wood to make a fire with; but, above all, the country was infested by hungry Kurds, who would neither spare us, nor, what he cared much more for, his horses. We met his arguments for a time with good humour and submission, but gaining nothing by this, we asserted our rights as guaranteed by our firman, and said that we positively must have the horses, for we had taken care, being prepared for these difficulties, that a separate clause should be introduced into the firman authorizing horses off the great road, and in what direction we might be pleased to go. We should, however, perhaps have failed in this, with the inflexible old Turk, who was as fierce and as strong as a pasha in his own little jurisdiction, had it not been for an officer of Hafiz Pasha's army, who luckily happened to be present, and who, of a more intelligent and obedient disposition, represented that the Sultan's firman was entitled to respect. The wrangle being at length decided in our favour, the ayyan was polite enough to order us a dinner of sour milk, eggs, and cheese, which we preferred taking in the open air, and sitting not far from the poor fellow who had alarmed us by his moans, but who had now become quite calm, and was relating his past pains to the bystanders. He was, I believe, an Armenian, and was now connected by a strong chain to the manacles of a villainous-looking Kurd, whose neck was also encumbered with an iron collar. They had been robbing on the highway, or more properly, pathway.

It rained hard on leaving Shehr Kishla. Our road lay up the courses of the Yanak Chaye, and in little more than an hour's time we left the plain and entered upon low hills, at a point where the river divided into two streams, our party following the south-easterly tributary. We travelled three hours along the valley of the waters of this stream, which meandered very much; there were no habitations nor cultivation, but a superabundant growth of wild fennel.

Arrived at the springs forming the head waters of the river, we found there the village of Abasilli, situated at an elevation of 4680 feet, the hills around dotted with patches of snow. It is curious, that the head waters of the Yanak Chaye appear to have been regarded by Ptolemy as one of the sources of the Halys, probably because the range of Anti-Taurus, in which they are situated, divides the watershed of the Halys from that of the Sarus and Pyramus rivers.

The inhabitants of Abasilli were troublesome mountaineers and thievishly disposed. We found here that Viran Shehr was to the eastward, and out of our way, and the reports of the wildness and insecurity of the district were repeated with many evident exaggerations.

We therefore determined upon leaving the baggage at Abasilli, and obtaining a guide to the ruins, but no single man would go, so we were forced to pay two, taking, besides, the seruji; and Mr. Rassam, who at first proposed stopping behind, kindly joined the party.

CHAPTER XVII.

Viran Shehr.

Viran Shehr (Ruined City). Shohair (Little Town). Saracenic Road. Tunuz—ancient Tonoza. Black Sanctuary. Agricultural Armenians. Pass of the Beard-Stroker. Town of Gurun. Sources of the Tokmah Su—Melas. Derendah—ancient Ptandari. Christian Inhabitants. Castle. Historical Reminiscences.

May 12th. THE necessary arrangements being completed, we made an early start this morning, well armed, light, and unencumbered with baggage, for the rocky wilderness in which Viran Shehr was reported to be situated.

We first crossed the hills which constitute the crest of Anti-Taurus in this part, and are designated as Yel Gadugi, a Kurd name. They are at an elevation of 5400 feet above the level of the sea, and still had patches of snow upon their summits and acclivities.

From the crest of these hills, we observed an extensive plain of chalk stretching before us, about twenty miles in length by ten in width. From the elevation at which we stood, this plain appeared almost as an uniform level; but when travelled over, not only presented slight undulations, but was cut by the tributaries of the Sihun into ravines, with nearly perpendicular cliffs, varying from 50 to 200 feet in depth.

Passing an artificial mound with ruins, called Kushakli Uyuk (the Mound of Winter Quarters), we crossed the head-quarters of the Sihun, here a rivulet three yards wide by two feet in depth, and said to have its origin at a place called Cheralik, three hours' distance. This was an important point to establish in the hydrography of Asia Minor, because, as we had traced up the tributaries to the Halys to the foot of Anti-Taurus on the opposite side, and found them immediately succeeded on this by tributaries to the Sihun flowing into the Mediterranean near Tarsus, it is evidently impossible that there can be any stream flowing from the foot of Mount Argæus, or any point to the westward of this, into the Euphrates.

A short distance beyond, we passed the ruins of a village, the peaceful inhabitants of which had been driven away by the Kurds, who have long since arrogated to themselves these districts. We crossed the upland for two hours, when we came to a deep ravine, containing another tributary to the Sihun, and down which we travelled about an hour, during which w roused a hare out of its covert, almost the only living thing we had yet met with. We then turned up the valley of a larger tributary to the same river, whose waters were remarkably clear, and flowed onwards in a swift stream, having their origin, as we were informed, from a cave, a little beyond Viran Shehr, and abounding in fish, which having been so long left to themselves, had in many cases attained a very large size.

At this period of our ride, our guides began to show many symptoms of anxiety and watchfulness, looking out ahead with evident distrust, and scanning the surrounding heights with suspicious looks; but it was certain that the Kurds were not at this time in this quarter of their migratory establishments, for not a living being was to be seen.

After pursuing our way some distance up this stream, we came in view of the ruins that we were in search of. Their appearance at a distance was rather imposing, and led us to expect great things. As we approached, however, (and in our hurry Russell and I had forded the river to be at them sooner,) we found only a large, open, and in some parts rocky space, nearly square, traversed by the river, and surrounded by a wall which fronted the four points of the compass, but extended further on the west side of the river than on the east, on which side it was also most dilapidated.

This wall was about seven feet in breadth, was defended by several square towers, and still although in a ruinous condition, in many places upwards of twenty feet in height. There were also four gateways, corresponding nearly to the four cardinal points.

The interior space was for the most part rocky, and presented few ruins. One or two buildings, the remains of which still existed, appear to have been the only ones that had been constructed of stone; the rest of the space was probably occupied by mud huts. There also existed the remains of a stone bridge.

It was evident that this station was formerly traversed by a great road, which came in at the east and west gates, and was carried over the river by the bridge. There is still a horse-path following the same line, but the road is little frequented on account of being unprotected.

The architecture of the place, the character of the walls and towers, and the style of its gateways, at once satisfied us that it was not a Cataonian or Byzantine relic, but the ruins of a Mohammedan fort and town, erected for the defence of a line of road described by Idrisi as extending from the city of the Khalifs by Malatiyeh to Koniyeh, the capital of the Seljukiyan Sultans of Rum, and which in its latter part no doubt fell in with the road previously described as extending from Ak Serai to Koniyeh.

According to the distances given by the same Oriental authority, this place would correspond with Shohair (the Little City), placed by Rennell at fifty-seven geographical miles from Kaiseriyeh, and eighteen from Tonoza.

On our return, after leaving the ravines and gaining the upland, we overtook a caravan of asses, laden with corn, and guarded by about twenty Christians, carrying long-barrelled guns. We could not resist the temptation afforded by meeting this formidable convoy in the wilderness to give them an alarm by galloping down suddenly and as if furiously upon them, a game in which our guides joined heartily, firing their guns in the air, and hallooing out. It was quite ridiculous to see the trepidation with which the little body of armed

Christians formed in the rear of their laden donkeys, and the hurry and anxiety with which they endeavoured to prime their guns, unwilling to go off. On coming up we laughed heartily at them for their fears, and then joined in conversation for an hour or so.

It rained hard all the afternoon, and we arrived late in the evening at Abasilli well soaked, after a ride of thirty-six miles, but without having met with any interruption or annoyance whatsoever.

Quitting Abasilli the next morning we pursued our way along the foot of Anti-Taurus, and afterwards down a ravine, at the end of which was a poor and small village, beyond which we entered upon the plain of Tonos, or Tunuz.

On our arrival at the village of the same name, corresponding to the ancient Tonoza, we could find no one to give us a house or apartment, or to recognise, or pay the slightest attention, to the seruji's demand for a relay of horses. These are the customary evils of being off the post roads. At length, during our perambulations of the village, we perceived a goodly-looking house that was uninhabited, so we quartered ourselves in it, nor did any one come to dispute with us our temporary possession; on the contrary, confidence was gradually established between the inhabitants and ourselves. First an old woman picked up courage to bring us an egg, which being, contrary to all expectation, paid for, she brought us another; then another brought us milk, and a third, bread,—the men all the while looking on in a listless group at a distance. After our repast, we had to go forth in search of barley for the horses; this was a more difficult matter, but was ultimately effected when the peasants found that we really meant to pay for it, a treatment which from travelling tatars, khawasses or other persons who claim to belong to government, they never meet with, and hence are distrustful of all travellers.

The proprietor of the modern Tunuz is a Turkoman, who resides near Yuz-Kat, and the taxes were collected, as in many other places, under the flattering falsehood of their being devoted to the support of the sacred temple of Mecca.

May 14*th*. Quitting Tunuz, we again crossed Anti-Taurus, here called Kara Tunuz (Black Tunuz), a little beyond the crest of which was a knoll of basalt, crowned by a ruined Mohammedan monument, and designated as the Kara Ziyaret (Black Sanctuary, or Place of Pilgrimage).

Proceeding onwards over the upland, we came to another ruin, situated at the sources of the Baloklu Su (Fishy River), a tributary to the Tokmah Su, or Melas of antiquity. It was an extensive oblong space, formerly surrounded by a wall, the foundations of which now alone remained.

We descended from this upland by a grassy, but uninhabited vale, reascended by low chalk hills, then down a basaltic ravine with a rock fort, called Kara Saki; then up hill again, and again down a long vale, with a rivulet, which brought us at a late hour in the evening, and after a long ride through a desolate country, to Manjulik, a large Armenian village.

These agricultural Armenians lived in large dwelling-houses, the centre of which was devoted to cattle, horses, and carts, while at the corners were apartments for the different members of the family. There were about fifty houses in the village, and much appearance of industrious wealth. Upon the heights above was a good-looking church, where we attended service previous to our departure in the morning, and on another adjacent height were the ruins of a monastery. The road beyond this was described as rocky and bad, but we were luckily enabled to raise here eleven good horses and two sturdy drivers, so that the baggage being more divided was lighter and less exposed to accidents.

The first hour's ride, the ensuing day, was over a black stony upland, which led us to the foot of a range of mountains, sometimes covered with shrubs, but more generally naked and void of all verdure. We entered this range by a narrow and difficult pass, rendered still more so by the smooth and slippery nature of the stones. It is called by the Turks Sakal-i-Tutan (the Beard-Stroker), from the patience required to get through it, the act of stroking the beard being expressive of that quality among Asiatics. Russell and I having dismounted led our horses on first to explore the difficulties, Rassam followed on horseback, and the muleteers took care of the baggage. Rassam had first a rude fall, which more than warned him of the necessity of walking, and this was followed, to our horror, by one of the baggage horses, loaded with instruments, and to which the attention of the muleteers had been especially directed, being allowed to roll over the mountain side. We did not, however, exhibit the patience of Orientals, for the serujis on this occasion got a whipping to make them more attentive, and we then got through without further accidents.

The pass continued narrow for about five miles, when it suddenly expanded, and was backed by a range of hills, the ruins of a fort being observable on a nearly isolated summit to the left. There were no habitations, but a few way-worn pedestrians were reposing on loose stones, which marked the graves of other travellers who had perished in the pass.

We now began to ascend again, amid patches of snow and an early and brilliant spring vegetation of sweet-scented hyacinths, blue anemonies, star of Bethelem, squills white and yellow, ranunculuses, and red tulips. These flowers sometimes almost carpeted the rocks, just below the melting snow, and enlivened the stony sterility around, where steep and barren cliffs were thrown into deep relief by a clear sunshine, and their shadows darkened by contrast with long ridges of snow.

After a further ride of two hours from these hills we came to a narrow ravine, down which we kept descending for upwards of an hour more, when we reached the valley of the Tokmah Su, replete with the verdure of trees, and everywhere occupied by gardens, in each of which were cottages, the summer abodes of the inhabitants of Gurun. We turned up this beautiful valley, the more captivating to our eyes from having now travelled for so many days over bleak stony districts, almost without a tree or shrub, to reach the town itself, which we found to be built along the foot of a slaty chalk cliff, in which were some occasional grottoes, and on one point the ruins of a castle. We had ridden about twelve hours this day, and were happy in obtaining a room in a Christian's house, a little outside of the town, where we had greater chance of repose and quiet than when exposed to the intrusion of the curious.

The next day (May 17th), being a day of festival (St. Gregory) with the Armenians, we visited their church, and some of their houses, which were generally whitewashed and very cleanly. The Armenians constitute the chief population of the town, being 2400 souls to 1800 Mohammedans. Their merchants trade with Aleppo, Marash, Sivas, and Constantinople. They were at this moment about to build themselves a new church. The taxes of Gurun are devoted to the Haramein—the two sacred edifices at Mecca and Medineh.

The castle is an irregular building, of which the front has fallen with the cliff, while the remaining two sides meet at an acute angle, and are defended by round and square towers of rude construction. This edifice is built of slaty limestone, put together without mortar, and with little art. It constitutes, with the caves, the only remnant of antiquity we found in the town, which, from various circumstances of distance from other sites in Commana Cappadocia, and its relation to these, appears to correspond to the ancient site of Arabissus, called in the Theodosian tables, Arcilipo-popolis.

The second day Russell and I started, accompanied by a seruji, to visit the sources of the Tokmah Su. Immediately beyond the town the river is shut up in an impassable glen, which obliged us to ascend a ridge of steep rocky hills. We gained the river banks on the other side of this, which is there called Injeh Su (Narrow Water); and following it up above successive tributaries, it diminished to a mere brook, which had its sources in the village of Kopek Viran (the Dogs' Ruin).

We returned after a ride of about seven hours by the same road to Gurun, having lunched at a Kurd village, where we were hospitably received.

May 18*th*. Quitting Gurun, we travelled down the delicious valley of the Tokmah Su, presenting at almost every step a varied scenery; summer-houses, embowered in groves, shady vineyards, Mohammedan and Christian villages, with excavated cliffs; the valley itself at times open, with gardens, when it is often swept by the sudden rising waters; at others shut up amid rude and precipitous rocks, a fragment of which here and there stands out isolated in the midst of the stream, as is the case with the rock of Tanil.

Not far from Gurun, we passed a rivulet, Gök Bunar (Blue Spring), flowing from a cave which is celebrated for containing fish without bones, and consecrated to Ali, perhaps a species of Proteus. Beyond the large Mohammedan village of Tanil, we passed a large tributary, called, from the ridge of rocks which it forces its way through, Sach Aghz (Hair Mouth). On the right bank, and at the foot of a rather remarkable hill, is the village of Tokmah, whence the river receives its name.

Below this we crossed the river by a bridge of one arch, where it enters a more rocky country, and in the midst of which is a recess, called Sari Kaya (Yellow Rock), with some grottoes; and to the south a ravine, with a rivulet shut up by rocks, with sepulchral grottoes on their face, and which afterwards opens to where, amid some romantic cliffs, is the village called Orta Keuy (Middle Village), said to be founded on an ancient site, apparently the Zoropassus of the Tables.

Beyond this the river enters Dereh Jik (Little

Valley), which is approached by paths carried along the face of fearful-looking precipices and perpendicular chasms, and having a cliff nearly isolated in the midst of the stream, to where it washes the walls of a first portion of the town of Derendah, containing two jamis, with their tall menarehs, and a few houses with gardens; and forcing its way by a dark, deep, and narrow ravine, it separates the Castle Rock from the opposing precipices, and issues forth from its narrow chasm to water several miles of gardens and country houses which stretch in beauty down the then expansive vale of the river, and constitute the summer residences of the present inhabitants of ancient Ptandari or Tanandaris—the modern Derendah.

The town itself is situated on the south face of the Castle Rock, or that opposite to the one cut by the river's course, and, like Gurun and Malatiyeh, is abandoned in summer time, the inhabitants retiring to the gardens lower down the valley, and this gives to it an appearance of population that exceeds the reality. At Gurun, at an elevation of nearly a thousand feet above Derendah, the inhabitants had not yet left the town, but here they had quitted it a fortnight ago, and to us a great and almost incredible inconvenience resulted from this, as all the cloacas had been opened upon the streets, and the passage through the town was sickening beyond the power of expression. Is it to be wondered at that plague should be endemic in countries where such loathsome abominations are practised? It looks as if done out of some old superstition, from such a practice having been successfully resorted to, to drive away an enemy from the siege of the citadel.

We were quartered in a Christian house in the gardens, and where they showed a great degree of ill-will and still more of jealousy at our presence. They not only carefully shut up the females from our sight, but were also extremely fearful of our having any communication with the children, whom when they saw us inclined to propitiate, they immediately locked up. It was sometimes quite amusing to observe how far this jealous surveillance was carried; for, upon occasions, it was absolutely necessary to call the females to meet some of our demands, when they were followed at every step, and their business accomplished, they were again shut up under lock and key before our eyes. We felt a little hurt at this want of confidence, but said nothing about it, till, in the evening, while Russell and I were observing in the garden, a parcel of Osmanli khawasses came from the governor's to get the customary bakshish (present) for obtaining us a lodging, and rudely seized upon the instruments, whereupon we at once drove them out of the garden and house, to the great astonishment of the Armenians, who scarcely venture to answer a government official, and who in consequence became afterwards a little more civil towards us. They appear, however, to have thievish propensities, for at Gurun they stole my carpet from me, and here they robbed Russell of his waistcoat.

The ensuing day we visited the mutesellim, a polite, well-behaved Turk, who sent a khawass with us, with the keys of the castle. The inhabitants then again, with wonder, saw us picking our way through the town, the loathsome streets being rendered the more intolerable by a bright and warm sunshine. The approach to the castle was defended by a square tower and other outworks, and the point at which the rock is ascended is defended first by a gateway of Saracenic structure and style, with an inscription, which was so high as to be, unfortunately, illegible to Mr. Rassam; following a winding ascent, there is another portal of a similar character, and at the top of the rock a ruined bastion.

The extent of the rock is 662 yards; the width is various, but it in no place exceeds 150 yards. Upon the platform there are about forty houses, where the governor and his attendants reside in winter. The extremities of the rock are defended by towers with walls and curtains in advance, but the cliff is in general so steep as to require no outworks.

All these ruins evidently belonged to the Mohammedan era; and we find in Osmanli history, that Derendah was first reduced in the time of Bayazid I., but it afterwards fell under the power of Alai Doulet (soldier governor), or the Syro-Circassian military government, from whom it was again taken by Selim I.

A site so eminently remarkable, and a rock presenting such great advantages for defence, were not neglected by former nations. We have seen that it corresponds with the Ptandari or Tanandaris of antiquity, and it appears also to have been known in the middle ages by the name of Singa, given in the Theodosian Tables, an identity rendered the more evident from the fact, that there were in olden times two roads from hence to Melitene; one along the valley of the river, the other over the hilly country to the south, as there are also in the present day.

CHAPTER XVIII.

Laviasena

Start from Derendah. Akjah Kurds. Resistance to the Osmanlis. The Salep Orchis. Arka—ancient Arcas. Aspuzi, summer quarters of Malatiyeh. Discussion on road to be pursued. Town of Malatiyeh—Melitene. Start for the Taurus. Persian Pilgrims. Viran Shehr (Ruined Town)—the ancient Laviasena.

May 20*th*. We left the valley of the Tokmah Su, by that of Ashik Derehsi (Lover's Valley), having a rapid river in its centre, and being even more beautifully wooded than that of Derendah, and crowded with country houses.

Crossing some low hills, we came again upon the valley of the Melas, which was now expansive, less wooded, but generally cultivated and replete with villages. I have already noticed, that in olden as well as in modern times, there were two roads from Singa or Derendah, to Melitene, one following the course of the river, which was fifty-one Roman miles in length; the other was carried over the mountains, and was only thirty-nine. The first site on the river road was Arega, eight Roman miles from Singa, and at a distance corresponding to this, was also now a large village on the river side. At the same distance on the upper road was Osdara, and we found corresponding to it, a large village, chiefly of Christians, and which like Gurun and Derendah, had its winter and summer portions. This olden site is now called Yeni Jah (Little New Town).

We ascended hence among limestone hills that abounded in fossil shells, beyond which were long black ridges of volcanic rocks, of dreary and repulsive aspect, where long platforms and table-lands, with rock terraces rising in steps one above the other, terminated at the crest in stony conical summits.

At the foot of these hills was a well wooded and fertile valley, with a rivulet, which watered first the small village called Yokari Setrek (Upper Setrek), and then, about a mile and half below, the larger village of Ashar Setrek (Lower Setrek), both villages of Turkomans; while below, and near the junction of the rivulet with the Tokmak Su, was a large Christian village, the site of the ancient Nocotessus.

After an ascent of about two hours, we gained an upland on the crest of the hills, and at an altitude by barometer of 5625 feet. There were many conical and rocky summits around us, each of which bore the remains of rock forts, and had its own separate designation, as Kilisa Kalehsi (Church-like Castle), Kara Kaya (Black Rock), Chi Chakli (Little Point), Sarichi chek (the Topmost Point of all), etc. The prospect beyond comprised a great portion of the nearer groups of Taurus, with the great plain of Al Bostan beneath our feet, and nearer to us the snow-clad summit of Akjah Tagh (Little White Mountain).

We kept along the mountain, till we came to a terrace on the acclivity, where was the encampment of the Bey of the Bekr Ushaghi tribe of Kurds, more commonly Tagh known as the Kurds of Akjah Tagh.

This encampment occupied one of the usual peculiar sites selected by the mountaineers: a mere shelf on the acclivity of the hill receding far enough to allow of the dusky tents being pitched in a line in its remotest part, with only the customary cross poles in front of each, on which the skins are swung, by which the women churn their butter, and this without a fragment of the camp being visible from below.

We rode up to the bey's tent just as it was growing dusk, and he came out to meet us. We briefly announced ourselves as travellers, and that having to sleep in the mountains we placed ourselves under his protection. After the customary compliments he sent a man with us into the valley below, where we pitched our tent, and shortly afterwards another, with a present of bread, butter, and buttermilk.

A short time ago the Akjah Kurds acknowledged no authority but that of their own beys, but after two harassing campaigns, carried on the last year and the year before that, they had been subjected by Hafiz Pasha. We did not on this account, however, claim any thing from them on the score of our firman, but simply on that of hospitality, which always answers better with these haughty and independent tribes. After the battle of

Nizib, they all rose again to a man, and reasserted their independence, which I suspect has not since been ventured to be called in question, and it will be some time ere a traveller can follow the same road.

Slumber in a tent is always more sweet and sound than in a room in the East, where there are so many things opposed to rest, and we rose early in the morning refreshed and light, to pack up, load our horses, and pursue our journey. We had not gone far before we met a Kurd chief, travelling with his harem, family, and attendants. His wives were two in number, and they rode in advance of the chief. They were both good-looking, stout, healthy women, their faces were uncovered, they rode astride, and with an air of dignity as if they had been mothers of heroes.

Crossing some rocky hills, we came to an open valley, one of the most central of the Akjah Tagh, partly cultivated, and with here and there cypress-trees rising gradually, till lost in dark forests that encircle the mountain immediately below the snow line.

In a rocky glen at the bottom of this vale was a small village with ruins and hewn caves in a limestone precipice. This was the site of Dandaxena, another station on the road to Melitene.

The next valley to this, which it took us two long hours to reach, was not so wide, but more picturesque, being bounded by lofty rock terraces. We passed on our road several villages and khans, and the vale was throughout pretty well cultivated.

The Kurds of this part of Akjah Tagh told us how long and how resolutely they had fought against the troops of Hafiz Pasha, taking refuge ultimately in the castle of Kurnak to the south, which corresponds to the ancient Lagolassus on the Melas, where they were besieged for four days, and ultimately forced to capitulate. On this occasion many of their young men who were not slain, were sent to Constantinople to the public works or to be made soldiers of, their old men returned to their farms, and many of their wives and women were taken for a time by the soldiers to Malatiyeh, "and these are are some of them," said our narrator, turning round to two or three healthy-looking peasant woman, with babes in their arms, and who had been standing by sympathising with the tale of woe which was related to us.

It took us three hours to cross this long valley, from whence another rocky ascent led us to our first view of the great plain of Malatiyeh, extending as far as to the valley of the Euphrates, and almost beyond the reach of vision. We descended among shrubs of dwarf oak and banks of flowering orchis, the same which affords the salep (*O. mascula*), till we reached the village of Arka, built on a high artificial mound, all that remains of the ancient Arcas, except the name, which has been only slightly altered. Strabo calls it Argus, an elevated fort near Taurus.

The ayyan of the village visited us in the evening, and from him we first learnt that Hafiz Pasha had crossed the Taurus with warlike intentions, but to which report we did not at the present moment attach much importance, as we did not think that he had collected in so few years an army large enough to cope with the Syro-Egyptian army of Ibrahim Pasha, and were not aware of the reinforcements which he had received that spring from Constantinople and the surrounding pashalics.

May 22nd. From Arka to Malatiyeh was a plain, occasionally cut into deep valleys by running streams, and extending along the foot of the Baghli Khanli Tagh (Mountain of the Garden Khan). At this season of the year the plain was covered with a luxuriant vegetation of flowering plants, among which it was interesting to observe how many were common to England. Plants, however, of our shadowy hedge-sides, as the greater and lesser periwinkle, and plants of warm stony acclivities, as the viper's bugloss, were here mingled with the vegetation of plains and meadows.

We passed first the Sultan Su (Sultan's River), and at a distance, the Shakmah Su (Flinty River), which we crossed on a bridge, with a single well-constructed elliptic arch. Beyond this we entered the beautiful gardens and vineyards of Aspuzi, along which we rode full seven miles before we came to the habitations, and where we obtained permission to pitch our tent in a shady garden attached to a large house tenanted by several families of Christians, and commonly known as the Tailor's Khan.

Aspuzi is the summer town of Malatiyeh, from which it is distant about six miles. While the town, or rather fort, itself is situated on an exposed plain, cold in winter and hot in summer, and unsheltered by a tree, the summer quarters lie amidst groves, orchards, vineyards, and gardens, that are propagated over an extent of from eight to ten miles, by a careful and refined system of irrigation, that probably dates from a remote antiquity.

We stopped some days here, engaged in astronomical observations, in making excursions to Malatiyeh, to the junction of the Euphrates and the Melas, and still more especially in endeavouring to obtain from the pasha, then at Malatiyeh, horses to go by the Pass of Euphrates to Someïsat. While we were here, a Polish general, of the name of Janowski, accompanied by two other officers, arrived, on his way from Baghdad to Constantinople. This gentleman was in the confidence of the British ambassador, and gave us much information as to the actual state of Turkish politics, and among other things, of the support that Hafiz Pasha had met with from the Sultan, and that he had undoubtedly passed the Taurus with the view of exciting Ibrahim Pasha to hostilities, but that it was still to be hoped that the influence of the European powers would avert a calamitous war.

Under these circumstances our future movements became a matter of serious consideration: five different plans presented themselves to us. First, to turn back again, which was scouted unanimously. Second, to remain at Malatiyeh till the fate of the war was determined. This, considering the uncertainty of events in the East, that Hafiz Pasha's army had not crossed the frontier, that it was not at all certain that a battle would take place, and that such a delay might be prolonged to an indefinite period, did not meet with a better reception. Thirdly, we might get out of the way and proceed towards Erzrum, carrying on our researches in that quarter; but there was a decisive objection to this, even if our feelings and judgment had been in favour of it, in the state of our funds, which we had endeavoured ineffectually to get replenished at Kaiseriyeh, and which were now so low that we were glad of the opportunity of giving General Janowski a cheque on Constantinople for his spare gold. Fourthly, we might strike out for

Musul by Dyarbekr, but here, as the General himself remarked, we ran great risk, as should the Turkish army be defeated, the whole country would be in a state of insurrection, and there would be no chance of saving our instruments, even if we should get through ourselves; and this was fully shown afterwards, for a long time after the battle two American missionaries attempted this line, when they were robbed and so maltreated that one of them only reached Musul, and the other returned on his steps. Fifthly, there remained for us to proceed onwards, examining the Pass of Euphrates, as pointed out in our instructions, and reaching Bir, to leave our baggage there, and merely visit Hafiz Pasha in order to obtain the further assistance we should want to proceed onwards to Sinjar, while, upon the occasion of a reverse happening to the Turkish army, we resolved to bury our instruments in some forest or secret place till the storm had blown over. I moved, as an amendment to this last plan, which was the most favourably received, that we should go to Urfah and there leave the baggage, previous to our going on to Hafiz, but this was negatived, chiefly by the influence of Mr. Rassam, who objected to four days' additional riding to and from Urfah and Bir for a mere uncertainty; besides that, such a measure would probably, as things turned out, have been of little avail to us. The result of all these cogitations, as will be told in the sequel, was unfortunate to us, and I have only mentioned them, because after the evil had occurred, each and every one of them were placed before us as a course we ought to have adopted. Our reasons for not doing so are put as they occurred to ourselves, sitting in discussion, previous to the event, and are an answer therefore to the objections afterwards made to our mode of proceeding. It is in human nature to err, and when the error has become manifest, it is so easy to point out how it could have been avoided!

The modern town of Malatiyeh contains about 500 houses, of which every other one is a ruin, and it is surrounded by a rampart of considerable strength, but in many places level with the ground, with here and there crumbling towers and the remains of a handsome but battered gateway, besides the still more extensive ruins of a palace or a citadel.

Hafiz Pasha had now for two winters made this unfortunate town the head-quarters of his army, obliging the Mohammedan and Christian inhabitants to remain in their summer town of Aspuzi, and this is what had reduced it to its present fallen condition.

Independent of this, its ruined citadel, battered gateway, and dilapidated walls, attest its various fortunes. It is related by Strabo, that Melitene sprang up from a Roman encampment on the river Melas, whence its name and that of the province. A great battle was fought here between Justinian, the Greek general of the Emperor Tiberius, and Kusru Nushirvan, A.D. 572. Diogenes Romanus led his army to the same place, but in the days of Manuel Comnenus it was in the hands of the Turkoman Sultans of Rum. It was conquered from them by the Syro-Circassian government, but restored by Hulaku the Tatar, and ultimately reduced by the Osmanlis under Bayazid I., who, leading his troops eastward, reduced Derendah, then Malatiyeh, and afterwards Bexene (Besni), and Divrigi.

In the middle ages Malatiyeh was a principal stage

on the great commercial road from Europe to India. In the days of Lucas and Schellinger it still contained from 12,000 to 15,000 houses, but which never could have been within the walls of the old city, and probably extended from thence towards the summer town. In modern geographies, as Maltebrun's and Bell's, especial regrets are expressed at the want of information as to the actual position and population of this interesting town, which is sometimes placed on the Euphrates, at others on the Melas, but is at some distance from either. It is also written of sometimes as a cold city, at others as a very hot one, having an extreme climate; the mean temperature appears to be 55°. The population now amounts to 11,000 souls, of which 8000 are Mohammedans, and 3000 Armenians.

The Mohammedan inhabitants are proverbially luxurious, affect gaudy-coloured dresses—being chiefly Turkomans—and, as the old governor of Arka said to us, "Having little money and still less care, they fill their pipes, and sit by the fountain's side." Hafiz Pasha had also so little gallantry as to say that the ladies of Malatiyeh lay under the mulberry-trees to let the fruit fall into their mouths*.

Malatiyeh and Aspuzi are both very unhealthy in autumn, when fevers assume a very fatal type. Out of a brigade of 3000 troops that were first quartered here, 400 men were lost in a single autumn.

After considerable delay, the Kurds of Kaktah (who had only been reduced the year before and their town

* In Strabo's time this place was celebrated for its fruit-trees and wine, called Monarite.

stormed,) being in open rebellion, the pasha refused to grant us horses by the river side, so we were obliged to start by the pass of Taurus, now called that of Erkenek, but anciently of Perre, being determined to reach the Euphrates, if possible, at Gergen Kalehsi, immediately below its passage through the mountains, which it enters south of Ilijeh (the Warm Baths), the Elegia of Pliny, Al Hammam of Idrisi, and probably the Tomisa of Strabo*.

We had thus on starting to retrace our steps to the valley of the Sultan Su, up which we travelled for some distance to the village of Goz Khana (Khan at the Head Spring), corrupted to Goseneh, and situated in a little recess in the mountains. Part of a caravan (kerwan) of Persians returning from pilgrimage was encamped in the little hollow, so that we had some difficulty in finding an open place to pitch our tent. The variety of costume, diversity of occupations, and strange people, that were grouped together in this motley assemblage of pilgrims, afforded us much amusement. We took care to get as near to the head of the spring as possible, for as many pilgrims were, regardless of the *inconvenance* resulting from it, washing themselves bodily in the small rivulet, there were several advantages to be obtained by such a position.

May 31*st*. The ensuing day we met with the other half of this Persian caravan, in a deep and rocky valley, where the Sultan Su issues from the mountains

* The Prussian officers attached to the staff of Hafiz Pasha's army discovered at or near this place a remarkable inscription in the Persepolitan character.

to the west. This party appeared to contain some pilgrims of a better class. Among others we observed a mounted lady, in a cloth riding-habit, laced boots, and straw-coloured kid gloves, but her physiognomy carefully concealed. A black-bearded Persian did not appear to relish our surprise at such an apparel. Upon inquiring of some of the lagging members of the caravan, they told us that she was a beautiful Georgian, who had once belonged to an infidel Frank, but was now the wife of a Persian, who had made her perform the pilgrimage to wash off her sins and to strengthen her faith.

Ascending hence, we travelled through a forest of oak, to the point where the plain began to widen, near the head waters of the rivulet, and where we perceived at some miles' distance to the right, the ruins of a city or town to which the seruji gave the usual appellation of Viran Shehr (Ruined Town.)

Leaving Mr. Rassam and the seruji to proceed with the baggage, by the mountain side to Surghu, Russell and I struck across the country to examine these ruins, and we were rewarded for our pains, by finding the undoubted evidences of the existence of a former town, of considerable size, great antiquity, and which had contained many edifices of goodly structure.

This town was encompassed by a double wall on all but the south side; the walls were very thick and defended by towers, which still remain, although dilapidated, for the most part upright. In the interior were the remains of a chapel of chaste and elegant structure, 28 feet long, by 18 feet 6 inches wide, and having an arch with a span of 40 feet. There was also a large central mound, beneath which were a collection of arches meeting at the groins, the interior of which was now a place of refuge for cattle. We laid down a general plan of the town, as it at present exists, for all the buildings in the interior, with the few exceptions mentioned, are level with the ground. The tradition of the people assigns its destruction to Timur Bey, as the Tatar is called.

We identified this ruined town and stronghold with the Lacotena or Lacobena of the Tables, which is evidently the same as the Lavinianesina of Ptolemy. In the subdivision of Cappadocia into ten provinces by Strabo, Laviniasena is noticed as one, and further on, he mentions a prefecture of Cappadocia by the name of Laviniasena, both of which refer to the same district*.

Joining the baggage, we shortly afterwards gained the Kurd village of Surghu, close to which, at the foot of a limestone precipice, is a large stream of water, issuing from the rock by twenty-three different orifices. This spring and another near to it, form the Gök Su (Blue River), which flows to the south-west, and then makes a sudden bend to the south-east, through Taurus, ultimately joining the Euphrates in the valley of Adiyamán.

---

* The Rev. Mr. Renourd remarks upon this, that the MSS. both of Strabo and Ptolemy vary much with respect to this name: Laviasena is most favoured by those of the former; Laviniasena by those of Ptolemy. See Tzschucke, note on Strabo, p. 534.

CHAPTER XIX.

Castle of Besni.

Passage of the Taurus. Pass of Erkenek. Pelvereh—ancient Perre. Roman Roads. Town of Besni—ancient Nisus. Difficulties in fording the Gök Su. Town of Adiyaman—Hisn Mansur and Carbanum. Troubles with the Kurds. River and Town of Kakhtah. Kurd Bey of Tokariz. Evil habits of the Kurds.

June 1*st*. LEAVING Surghu, we ascended the mountain of Gök Tenah by a steep winding pathway; the bare precipices and rocky summits with long ridges of snow, which surrounded us, gave a truly alpine character to the scene. From this mountain we descended by narrow and rocky ravines, to a small but fertile plain watered by a tributary to the Gök Su, and passing thence over some low hills, entered the pass of Erkenek.

This pass exists in what constitutes the most central and alpine portion of Taurus in these districts. Starting from the Euphrates, the central chain is prolonged by the Ak Tagh (Snow, or White Mountains) to above Pelvereh, where colossal cliffs of limestone hem in the waters of the Gök Su, and constitute the pass in question, which was anciently called the Pass of Perre, after the town of that name, and by the Christian historians of Bayazid's campaigns, Pass of Ernitzane.

We entered by what was at once a road and water-course, but soon left the rivulet far below us, passing a spot where it received a tributary from the Ak Tagh, and where were several picturesque mills. Turning thence, and still keeping high upon the acclivities of the mountain, we arrived at the village of Erkenek, which is still what it has ever been, a mere station in the pass, consisting of a few houses with their gardens scattered on the acclivities, while the luxuriant verdure around, maintained by numerous sparkling springs and rills of waters, fills up the valley on both sides, and stretches downwards to the bottom of the ravine below.

The rivulet itself flows onwards, till it meets with obstacles in the form of rude mis-shapen masses of fallen rock, amidst which it tumbles along, hewing its way through narrow and lofty precipices, that opened beyond to afford a glimpse of a varied and boundless mountain scenery.

We stopped a short time at Erkenek, and lunched upon the roof of a house, in order to better enjoy the magnificent scenery by which we were surrounded.

The road led hence down into the valley and up again on the opposite side, and as we proceeded onward, and above the rivulet of Erkenek, which rolled as previously noticed along impassable and rocky glens below, we observed a considerable stream precipitate itself into it, from a cliff opposite to us, as a lofty fall of water. We took a sketch of this fine cascade, which was unfortunately lost.

Beyond this the aspect of the valley altered, the character of the rocks being changed from hard limestones to shingly schists, which here as elsewhere constituted the axis of Taurus. The valley widened considerably and was filled up with little round hills, upon which was a scanty clothing of fir and cypress trees.

It had been dark some time before we came to where the rivulet of Erkenek was joined by the Gök Su, which juncture takes place in the same valley, the united waters flowing through the mountains in a south-easterly direction, and we had some difficulty in finding a place sufficiently level and void of trees to pitch the tent upon. This accomplished, we set about picking up sticks, easily obtained on the river's banks, with which we lit a fire, by the bright glare of which we found our tent already filled with innumerable small creatures, among which frogs and crickets were, after the musquitoes, the most numerous; these were trifles to fatigued travellers, and did not prevent us sleeping soundly, when it was not our turn to keep watch.

June 2nd. We crossed the Gök Su by a modern bridge of two unequal arches, above which were the ruins of another of older date. From hence we began to ascend, passing the ruins of an aqueduct covered with travertino; at the summit of the hill we found vineyards, and a little beyond the large village of Pelvereh, where we were to obtain a change of horses, but it was abandoned by its inhabitants, who had fled to avoid the continual demands made upon them by the khawasses and military, in their journeys from Malatiyeh to the camp of Hafiz Pasha.

Pelvereh, the ancient Perre, is a situation of high interest, as being a connecting point in the Antonine Itinerary and Theodosian Tables, between the routes to and from Cappadocia, Mesopotamia, the Lesser Armenia and Syria, as it is in the present day, for although in the time of Rennell the existence of a pass in this part of Taurus was only deduced by that able geographer from ancient data assisted by some information obtained by Mr. Vaughan at Aleppo, it had in our days been the route followed by the Osmanli army under Hafiz Pasha, and through which the guns had been dragged with immense labour; the Baron Moltke, a Prussian officer attached to the staff, having previously floated down the Euphrates on a raft, expressed himself against their being transported over the rapids of Taurus, by the fragile skin-rafts of the country, which were hence only used for the transport of provisions and other lighter objects.

There were two Roman roads from Melitene through Taurus. The first led by Metita, a site not yet identified, to Claudius, now Kakhtah, with ancient walls and iron gates, and joined the Euphrates at Barsalum, now Bersel, half an hour from Tokariz, and followed the course of the river to Samosata, now Someïsat.

The second road led by Miasena, which appears from distances to be represented by Tchirmiktah; the next station was Lacotena, which we found at the head waters of the Sultan Su; the third station was Perre.

The great road from Ancyra to Zeugma on the

Euphrates, part of the details of which we have already given, reached Perre after six short stages from Commana Cappadocia, and was continued thence by Carbanum (Adiyaman and the Hisn Mansur of the Arabs) to Samosata.

The next great road that joined at Perre was from Germanicia (Marash). This, which followed the vale of the eastern Pyramus, was an easy road.

The third road led from Syria by Antiochia ad Taurum (near Aintab), and entered the pass of Taurus at Perre.

There was besides these a cross road from Perre to Samosata by Nisus (Besni), without going to Carbanum, and the same was continued from Nisus by the Pons Singæ to Zabothra (Rum Kalah).

At Pelvereh we observed the various springs that flow from the south side of the ridge on which it is situated united to form a small lake in the hollow below. This was succeeded by a second, and then a third, and all these lakes poured their waters into the eastern branch of the Jaihan (Pyramus), which had been seen, on a former journey in company with Colonel Chesney, to join the main stream a little to the south of Marash, and before the river enters the deep gorges of Cilician Taurus (Durdun Tagh).

On leaving Pelvereh the road became less mountainous and vegetation more varied. We travelled in a southerly direction round the foot of Khurkhun Tagh, a nearly isolated conical mountain, and then descended into the wooded Ak Dereh (White Valley) where we found another deserted village, and could get food neither for our weary horses nor for our hungry selves.

Crossing this valley we had a long journey up the Hamiyiyan Hills, an upland rather than a mountain chain. This upland lowered gradually to the south, and we kept descending to where it broke off suddenly into a narrow glen, at the base and on the sides of which were the houses constituting the modern town of Besni, rising in terraces one above the other, while on a fragment of the rock that towered up in the middle of the glen, were the crumbling ruins of the ancient fortress of Nisus, or Bexene.

We got accommodation here at the house of an Armenian seraf, or banker, and in this pent-up ravine it was so warm that we were glad, like others, to sleep on the exposed terrace, admiring and admired by all. The next morning early we had a delightful bath in an old mesjid, now converted into a hammam.

Besni we found to contain 2500 houses of Mohammedans, and 250 of Armenians. It has a very good market, but provisions were uncommonly scarce, on account of the demands of the army, and we had to pay three piastres, equal to sevenpence-halfpenny, for a cake of bread, in England not worth a penny.

June 4th. We quitted Besni by a suburb, inhabited by poor Armenian weavers, and advanced thence upon an upland covered with vineyards, and having a few naked-looking country houses. About seven miles from Besni, we descended to cross the Ak Dereh, on the other side of which we visited a village to get some milk, which the peasants offered us with a good-will and kindness that we rarely met with in our travels. The remainder of the day's ride was through a beautiful country, generally clad with vineyards, and we spent the night in a grove full of birds, that made the valley resound with their varied song. As with us, the nightingale bore away the palm, and we had the advantage here of hearing it sing all the evening as well as the night.

The next morning we took some villagers with us to assist in crossing the Gök Su, which flowed past not far from the village, and the fording of which was represented to us as being formidable to laden horses. On our arrival at the banks of the river the Kurds stripped to carry over the baggage, a small quantity at a time, lifted above their heads, crossing the rapid stream with a kind of jerking running step, and returning by swimming over a deeper part. Mr. Russell and I must fain try this experiment, but in doing so the rapidity of the current carried us off our legs, and although for a time we were able to swim, we were soon carried down to where the water was so shallow that we could no longer do so without striking the stones, nor yet stand up from the current, which had gained additional swiftness in the rapids we now found ourselves in; so we were rolled over and over again, till (there is nothing like companionship in misfortune) we were both brought-to in a deep eddy, from which we had nothing but to make a quiet exit, not a little bruised and knocked about, shivering with cold, and very crest-fallen at the result of our attempt to imitate these practised and hardy mountaineers.

On the left bank of the river was Bur Konak, with a very old-looking ruin of a khan, and in the plain beyond were the tents of the Kochanli tribe of Kurds.

Our road now lay over nearly level grassy plains,

which extended along the foot of Ak Tagh (the White Mountains), down to the banks of the Euphrates. This chain is composed of various summits, having a more or less conical form. They form the loftiest portion of Taurus in these districts, and constitute the snowy ridge which is seen from the greater part of northern Syria, and down the course of the Euphrates as far as Balis.

After a ride of seven hours we arrived at the town of Adiyaman, which is circularly disposed round a large artificial mound, appropriately called the castle hill. In the present day this town contains 800 houses of Mohammedans and 300 of Armenians. It has several mesjids, one jami, three ruinous khans, and one bath; this is but a small remnant of its former prosperity. The Christians have no church.

We ascertained, from existing traditions, that this town is the same as the Hisn Mansur of Idrisi, which Rennell places on the Euphrates. It was also known to Oriental geographers by the name of Cholmodara, and was by the Romans designated as Carbanum.

It is surrounded by gardens and groves, in the midst of which we pitched our tent. Not far from us were two rocky eminences, on which were the tombs of two eminent men, Mahmud el Ansari and Ibn Zaïr Ansari.

The mutesellim of Adiyaman happened to be the same person who was governor of Birehjik at the time we were at that place putting up the boats of the Euphrates Expedition; he was very kind and attentive to us, but strongly urged our proceeding on to Someïsat, and giving up our intended visit to Gergen Kalehsi, the Kurds of which he said were very bad, and would certainly rob, if not kill us. We, as usual, thanked him for his advice, but persevered, when, finding us resolved, he kindly offered us the company of a khawass, who would at once act as a guide and be a protection.

June 6th. Our road lay through a country of the same character as yesterday, only with deeper valleys and larger rivulets. The soil was of a red clay, much broken up by the heat of the sun, and out of the large fissures thus occasioned, there issued innumerable mole-crickets of a gigantic size.

We turned off near the Black Mound (Kara Uyuk), to visit a Kurdish encampment and obtain a drink of milk; and we passed in the course of the day a good many small villages, which enlivened the otherwise monotonous grassy plains, by their little groups of fig-trees and pomegranates, but the inhabitants were at this season in their tents, pasturing their cattle. They did not appear to cultivate the ground, and, beyond the produce of their cows, had nothing but a little dry fruit from their gardens. Some of them told us, that they had not tasted bread for many weeks.

We arrrived, just as evening was coming on, at the village of Kerkunah, and pitched our tent, not to give any trouble to the inhabitants, in an adjacent orchard. Our demands upon the village were very few, consisting merely of eggs, bread, and milk, which we willingly paid for, yet the Kurds furnished these with ill will, and with an unrestrained exhibition of dislike and hostility, which, as the evening advanced, and fresh arrivals momentarily took place, grew more open and manifest.

I had just been taking the altitude of Spica Virginis, which passed over the meridian shortly after sunset, and

Russell was recording time, when we were alarmed by discordant yells, and the seruji came to us breathless to say, that the Kurds had attacked Mr. Rassam, the khawass, and our servant. We hastily buckled on our swords, and taking up our guns, ran to the rescue; but on our arrival in the little square, in the centre of the village, we could scarcely help laughing at the scene it presented. It was full of men and women, amid whom Rassam and the khawass were expostulating with vehemence, while the boy Peter, who had hitherto shown nothing but the more patient qualities of his nature, had seized a pole, with which he was industriously belabouring the crowd, having positively strewed the ground with turbans. The first thing we had to do was to arrest such desperate valour, after which we managed to enforce Mr. Rassam's cause, which we found to be a question of driving us out of the garden in which we were encamped, and we then returned to our tent.

Later in the evening a party, who had been brooding mischief ever since, came and told us we must move away immediately. Their object in this, which was to rob us the moment we struck our tent, was too plain to be misunderstood, and we accordingly peremptorily refused to stir. They ultimately retired, promising to cut our throats during the night, so we kept a good watch, but were not again disturbed.

The next morning we made a start before daybreak, ere the inhabitants of this inhospitable village were abroad, reaching soon afterwards a ravine which led us down to the banks of the Kakhtah river. The walls of rock on both sides were clothed with wild fig-trees, mulberry, and shrubby Cercis, (*C. siliquastrum*), the budding leaves of which have a refreshing acidity, and form a pleasant salad.

The river of Kakhtah was at this point spread over a wide space, being divided into three branches, and hence easily forded; when swollen it must be a large river, as its bed was upwards of a quarter of a mile in width. Its waters appear to have been much valued by antiquity, for they were carried to the capital of Commagena (Samosata), by an aqueduct that followed the banks of the Euphrates.

The town and castle of Kakhtah was about four hours' distance from us up the river. I wished very much to examine this interesting stronghold, of whose iron gates the Kurds speak much, but its mountaineer inhabitants were in rebellion, and the khawass and seruji positively refused to go or let the horses go with us. It is mentioned among the places reduced by Bajazid after Besni. During the same reign, however, fell into the hands of the great enemy of Osmanli pride, the Tatar Timour, who crossed the Euphrates at Gergen Kalehsi, and sacked in these countries, one after the other, the new conquests of the Osmanlis, who did not regain them till the time of Selim I. Kakhtah has not yet found a place in our maps, which it would have done, as well as Lacotena and other sites, had we been fortunate enough to visit it.

As we crossed the river we observed the piebald kingfisher hanging over its waters, and the delicately shaped tern of the Euphrates winging its way up the stream. The waters are as much sought for by the fish of Euphrates, as they formerly were by the luxurious countrymen of Lucian and of Paul of Samosata.

Groves of fig-trees and pomegranates on the river banks were filled with sparrows, here, as on Euphrates, a social bird living apart from the habitations of men.

Beyond the river of Kakhtah we continued traversing uplands covered with a most luxuriant vegetation of corn-bearing grasses (oat-grass, rye-grass, &c.), a character of vegetation which renders these districts, like certain parts of Cappadocia and Cilicia, peculiarly favourable to the rearing of horses.

In the afternoon, after passing several other villages, we arrived at Tokariz, surrounded by a mud wall, and the residence of a Kurd bey. There are three such governors in this part of the country; one resides at Kakhtah, the other at Tokariz, and the third at Someïsat.

We pitched our tent a short distance from this Kurdish stronghold, and in the evening the bey paid us a long visit, with a numerous suite, of which only a small proportion could be accommodated within the tent. He showed himself extremely suspicious of our intentions, and our statement that we had come there from mere motives of curiosity was totally disregarded, and only made things worse, by leading him to think that we wished to conceal the objects we had in view. He could not conceive that strangers would come into such wild districts for the mere purposes of exploration, and did not scruple to tell us so. He was exceedingly curious to hear everything that concerned ourselves and our country, with which he appeared to be somewhat acquainted. He said, among other things, that Russia and England were disputing between themselves the possession of Turkey. He asked to see our watches and some of our instruments, but we endeavoured to make as little show as possible; for from the side looks which he gave his attendants it was quite evident, that if there was a general scramble for our property, he intended to come in for his share.

These Kurds are perpetually engaged in strife, which appeared, indeed, to be an essential part of their existence. The day before a skirmish had taken place between two villages (Murdessin and Sevan), close by, when several of the combatants were slain. Shortly after dark this evening there was a robbery committed close to us, and a party turned out from the fort, but finding that the people robbed did not belong to them they returned without interfering. They, however, gave us no inconvenience beyond stealing our dog from us. In the morning we went and searched the houses in the interior of the fort, where we found the poor beast, and took him away without wasting words in useless remonstrance*.

On preparing to start we found that our khawass, who, instead of taking his turn at the night watch at the tent, had followed the safer plan of sleeping at the bey's house, had heard such accounts of the present state of the Kurds at Gergen Kalehsi, that he positively declined accompanying us upon any consideration. The muleteer also rebelled, and said he would not expose his horses, nor could we quiet him till we promised to remunerate him in case of their loss; he started, never-

* They also stole our tent mallet from us here, and the mollah was detected in the act of secreting an instrument in his bosom.

theless, very much discouraged. But with us it was not so; the morning wind, fresh and cool from the mountains, sweeping in our faces, the determination to gain the point we had started for, the hope, that, as long experience had taught us, the evil was exaggerated, and, above all, a firm trust in a kind Providence, lent us on the occasion rather a buoyancy of spirits, than the contrary.

Our seruji did not know the way, and we travelled from village to village in a general north-eastern direction towards Taurus. At one of these, by promises of remuneration, we obtained a Kurd guide, but he ran away as soon as he had got half a mile from the village.

On arriving at the foot of Taurus, we descended into a deep vale, having the Swiss name of Chamuni, and we ascended hence by a very steep and rocky height, passing which we gained the large village of Oldish, containing about forty houses of Armenians and the same number of Kurds.

We were now rendered aware that we were in a district of Kurds who were in the vassal, but not the subject state. The ragged garb of the rustic was supplanted by a handsome highland and military costume, a waistcoat of brown cloth, surmounted by a braided jacket of the same material, open, with loose sleeves. The wide trowsers of blue stuff, open to the knee but tight to the legs, were upheld by a narrow waistband, so as not to impede active or prolonged exercise, and the feet were protected by good laced boots. Every man carried his gun on his back, and his pouch by his side. The latter was made of the same coloured cloth as his jacket, and adorned by two or three black tassels.

The features of the men (who as usual with the Kurds, were strong, muscular, and sinewy, any one equal to two such Osmanlis as constituted the army of Hafiz Pasha,) were regular and handsome, and more expressive of reckless daring, than of that low deceitful cupidity which so often characterizes the Arab. The women were also very good looking, and had generally fine heads of glossy black hair. They did not cover their faces. We had an excellent opportunity of contemplating these villagers, for we rested ourselves half an hour by a fountain side, in the middle of the village, and under the shade of a great plane-tree, where we were soon surrounded by almost all the inhabitants.

CHAPTER XX.

Gergen Kalehsi.

Vale of Gergen Kaleshi. Rupture with the Kurds. Castle of Gergen. Prospect from the Castle. Armenians of Taurus. Muleteer runs away. Visit from a Kurd Chief. Bribe the Ayyan. Dangerous Mountain Road. Passage of Euphrates. Syrian Village. Cataracts of Samosata. Aqueduct. Difficulty of procuring food. Deserted Villages. Someïsat—Samosata. Ruins of Syrian Villages. Curious Cavities. Ecclesiastical and Monastic Edifices. Arrival at Birehjik.

Leaving Oldish, we followed a rude path on the side of a rocky acclivity, and we had not gone far, before a handsome young Kurd, in his military costume, overtook us, and addressed Mr. Rassam in a mysterious manner. It appeared that he had made up his mind that there must be a hakim, or doctor, among so many Europeans, and he was not blessed with a family; this was a misfortune for which, however, we had no patent remedies, and we were obliged to leave our new friend much dissatisfied at the useless march he had taken.

The reflection of the sun to day, from the bare surface of the rock, produced so intense a degree of heat, that one of the horses fell down as in a swoon, and the dog's feet were so swollen, that he could not proceed any further, and we were obliged to put him across a saddle.

At length we came to a small pass near the crest of the hills and where the beds of rock were curved in so irregular and fantastic a manner, that it appeared as if the waves of the sea had been turned into stone. This pass was defended by a wall, now in a ruinous condition, and also two square towers, quite dilapidated.

When we passed there, the open wooded beautiful vale of Gergen Kalehsi, lay before us in all its mountainous seclusion, hemmed in by the giant Ashur Tagh and other heights, at no great distance; at the foot of the rocks to the right was the small town of Gergen Kalehsi itself, and above it on a rocky height, detached as if by accident from the adjacent range of hill, was the castle of Juliopolis.

The first thing on our arrival was to see the mutesellim, but he had only a deputy here, who communicated to us the not unanticipated, but still not very agreeable intelligence, that the Kurds had thrown off their allegiance to the Porte, that the governor had gone to Hafiz Pasha to obtain assistance, and that it was not in his power to protect us from any ill feeling which the Kurds might entertain towards us. We had already made up our minds, however, that our visit should be to the Kurds, and not to the Osmanlis, so we pitched our tent near the village, and exerted ourselves in conciliating such as came to see us.

The modern town of Gergen, although the seat of a mutesellim, is only a small place containing about 150 houses, and there are thirty more in the castle. The chief population is composed of Kurd mountaineers, but there were also a few devout Turks, besides twenty-five houses of Armenians. This small congregation has a priest and a church.

The next day being Sunday, the Armenian priest came to visit us, and brought some communion cake. We requested him to be seated within the tent, which was nearly filled with visitors. Among these was the mollah of the Mohammedans, whom we had not recognised as such, he being merely dressed as an ordinary Osmanli. A party present were indulging in scurrilous epithets towards us, when the priest took our part, upon which he was assailed so fiercely and outrageously by the mollah, that we took the latter, not then knowing who he was, by the shoulders, and put him out of the tent. This was the commencement of our troubles, for by this untoward event, we had unintentionally openly attached ourselves to the Armenian party, and set ourselves against the Mohammedans, and a short time afterwards the mollah made his reappearance, accompanied by some stout armed Kurds, who let us know, in language loud, and not to be mistaken, that to insult their priest was to insult them. We were now obliged to mount guard outside the tent, which preparation for active hostilities for a time quieted our opponents, and also cleared the tent of visitors.

The same morning we visited the castle, an interesting remnant of antiquity. The castle hill is separated from adjacent cliffs by an excavated way, which is crossed by a wooden bridge, supported by central square pillars. The gateway is very handsome, and of Saracenic architecture, having an Arabic inscription over the portal; it leads into a covered way with three arches, and then by an open way, along the side of the rock to a second gate. Here the passage is cut out of solid rock, in which there is a recess like a frame, which may have contained a statue, or head in bas relief, that has now disappeared, and round this frame was a long inscription in Greek letters of the middle ages, of which only a few words here and there remained legible.

Beyond this we entered upon that part of the fort which contains the houses, and which is in a more dismantled condition. On the highest part of the rock, there is a mass of solid stone masonry; there was also in the castle three small pieces of ordnance of curious workmanship, which appeared to have belonged either to the Arabs of the Khalifate or to the Tatars, who, under Timour, crossed the Euphrates at this point.

The view from the castle is one of great beauty, and in one direction, that of the plain of Suverek, very extensive, being only limited by the Karajah Tagh to the east, and extending beyond the reach of vision to the south. The great slope of the Kurd district towards the Euphrates, is, however, hid by limestone cliffs. In other directions was a varied mountain scenery, amid which the rocky pass of Kakhtah, the high conical mountain of Ashur, and other bold mountain ridges, formed the principal features; but the most attractive objects were the adjoining green valleys, and the rich sloping hills, in districts often supposed to be uninhabited, but where villages are met with, and cultivation is extended in almost every direction.

The Euphrates sweeping round through Taurus, attains a few miles beyond the ferry of Dirisko, in the vale of Gergen Kalehsi, its most easterly curve, rolls over the rapids immediately above the village so named, and then turning again below the cliff of the castle of Gergen, passes through a very narrow gorge above 400 feet in depth, of which one third is formed by nearly perpendicular cliffs; from this it emerges below the valley of Chamuni, and its banks become for a time productive and luxuriant. The summits of the mountains around are, for the most part, bold, rocky, and barren; the declivities are also rocky and uneven, but well wooded, with much breadth and depth of shadow.

The whole effect is one of dark mountain scenery, with occasional glimpses of light, from winding rivers, white cliffs, smiling villages, crops and vineyards, which still belong in this, as in almost all Taurus, rather to a subalpine than to a mountainous region of the first order.

During our visit to the castle, although we were accompanied by a goodly crowd, more especially anxious to see, if by the perusal of the inscriptions, we should be led to find any treasure, we were not subjected to any personal inconvenience. Within the castle, the women were the most noisy, and did not fail to heap plenty of epithets, such as the domestic language of Orientals is particularly rich in, on our infidel heads.

In the evening, after our return, the Armenians kindly offered that two of their tribe should watch for us during the night, and we accepted their offer, for the Armenians here did not resemble their heartless, prostrate countrymen of the plains, but were accustomed to fight for their rights with the hardy predatory mountaineers, and had acquired manly and martial attributes; they were also armed and willing, and we felt that we could put confidence in their proffer of friendship.

June 10*th*. The next day we wanted to start, but our muleteer had absconded during the night, the Kurds would not furnish us with mules, and as we could not leave the baggage, Mr. Rassam kindly offered to go to Dirisko, and see if a raft could be constructed.

During his absence, the whole time was spent in keeping the Kurds at bay. They sneered and insulted us, even in the interior of the tent, but forbearance prevailed, and we kept ourselves and property safe without coming to an open rupture. The manner they showed that they would shoot us if we came to active hostilities, from behind a heap of stones, did not add much to our opinion of their courage.

During the morning a chieftain of the tribe of Murderli came with a party of armed followers to pay us a visit; he knew whom we were, "English, not Russians," he said, and seemed pleased. This party was well received and behaved with great decorum, touching nothing but our arms, which a Kurd can never resist, and possessing too much manly hauteur to side with the harassing persecutions of the half-bred Kurds of Gergen.

Mr. Rassam returned with the intelligence that he had not succeeded in obtaining a raft, so after a short consultation we deemed it wisest to bribe the deputy-governor of the town, and try how far his authority would extend. This plan, although costly, answered, and after a little further delay we had the pleasure of seeing sundry mules come out of their hiding-places, for a short time before they had positively asserted that there was not one in the town, and striking our tent we were truly glad to take our departure.

Another happy circumstance for us was, that our muleteers, who were very numerous, nearly one to every mule, were willing (to make the journey answer two purposes) to go on with us to Birehjik, where they could convert the money they would receive from us into a load to take back to the mountains, but as the Serasker's army was at that town they did not dare to take any arms with them beyond their daggers; and thus, noisy, obstreperous, and ill-willed as they were at starting, we fairly reduced them into submission before night, though not before Rassam had been obliged to deal out many hard knocks.

We left the valley of Gergen by the same pass that we approached it, and descending due south from this, reached the borders of a deep glen, both sides being almost vertical and from 300 to 400 feet in depth, while the Euphrates rolled below, much diminished in size by its rocky barriers.

The road was carried down the sides of this precipice, sometimes among detached rocks, at others in front of the cliff, and so narrow, that the slightest push would have hurled a mule below; at times the descent was an actual staircase, but Kurd mules appeared as accustomed to these as a human being. The baggage had to be carried up and down, and as there was but one small raft on skins to take us over, notwithstanding that we all lent a hand, still we were the whole afternoon in effecting the passage. We had only one mishap; the tent equipage rolled off the bearers' shoulders, and did not stop till thrown by a projecting crag nearly into the middle of the stream; one of the men engaged at the ferry, however, took to the water and brought it ashore again.

Just before sunset we arrived at the village of Masro, tenanted by a small congregation of Syrians, who were peaceful and prosperous agriculturists. We felt at once at home among these quiet Christian peasants, and pitched our tent in the stubble of a corn-field by the village, gathering mulberries as long as sufficient light lasted. It was a great change from our position at Gergen, and while we felt grateful for it, we could scarcely believe that it had been effected by merely passing the Euphrates.

June 11*th*. Our road now lay with the general course of the Euphrates. Passing Hadro, with groves and gardens, we came, after three hours from Masro, to the river of Zengibar, or of Negroes, in a limestone ravine. This river abounded in fish, and before it joined the Euphrates formed a large muddy pool, which contained numbers of the Euphrates turtles (*Trionyx Euphratica*), being the most northerly point at which I had observed them.

We now descended the banks of the river Euphrates, and an hour below this were some islands and rapids in the river, at the ferry of Misibin. We rested ourselves a short time at Kantarah, a very miserable village of Kurds.

We soon started again, along the banks of the

river, passing Cham Chaye (Fir River), flowing slowly through a deep ravine in chalk.

Beyond this we turned a little inwards, and arrived at another ravine, with rivulet, which we followed a short distance, till joined by another, on the cliffs of which were sepulchral caverns; and a little beyond the village of Hoshun, built on an artificial mound or teppeh, and evidently an ancient site.

We had rode this day about thirty-five geographical miles, and after pitching our tent in a field below the village, there still remained light enough to go and shoot pigeons, which abounded in the artificial caves in the cliffs below.

June 12th. Our road lay still along the banks of the Euphrates, over a country very little cultivated. Two hours from Hoshun, and above the junction of the Kakhtah river, are some rapids, which appear to be the cataracts noticed by Pliny as being above Samosata, for we saw no others from hence to that town.

Below, the Kakhtah river flowed into the Euphrates by three different mouths. From hence to Someïsat the remains of an aqueduct, which carried the water of this river, as previously noticed, to the capital of Commagena, are every now and then visible. Its lofty arches, supported either by strong walls or piers, show that it must have been a work carefully executed.

Below this, and at a village called Nahr Laga, we came to groves of mulberries and pomegranates, where we did not hesitate to refresh ourselves awhile. These gardens continued by Bakchi (the Village of the Gardener), for several miles along the course of the river.

At Kesan the river turned to the south-west, and we

continued more or less in this direction till we arrived at the village of Ledar, situate about two miles north of Someïsat, by the side of an artificial mound, in which there was much pottery, but of Mohammedan origin.

We did not go on to Kantarah, the village opposite to Someïsat, where I had slept on a former occasion, becausewe thought that as the Serasker's army was so near, and this was a government station, the vexatious demands to which the inhabitants must be daily subjected by travelling khawasses, would either make them unwilling or put it out of their power to furnish provisions; but we were scarcely better off at Ledar, for the most tempting offers procured us neither bread, nor milk, nor eggs, till we threatened, if they were not forthcoming, to help ourselves, and they were then quickly produced, for they had plenty in store, but fearful of it being known, lest they should be subjected to exaction.

Such is the fear or unwillingness of the Orientals to give information, or such their ignorance of what is going on around them, that to-day was the first time that we heard that the Serasker had removed from Birehjik, and was gone with his army to Nizib.

June 13*th*. When we passed by Kantarah we found that the inhabitants had fled, a short and common way in this country of avoiding extortion. Someïsat is on the right bank of the river*, and a little lower than

---

* Strabo (lib. xvi. p. 749) describes the ferry here as the actual Zeugma of Euphrates. Opposite to Samosata was Seleucia, a fortress of Mesopotamia, added by Pompey to Commagena, and in which Tigranes caused Cleopatra, surnamed Selene (Moon), to perish (B.C. 70), after having kept her some time in prison.

Kantarah. All that remains of this once celebrated city, the seat of the kings of Commagena, the birth-place of Lucian, and an episcopate in the middle ages, is a partly artificial mound, with the fragmentary remains of a castle on its summit. The modern town is a poor place, of about 400 houses, peopled by Kurds and Turkomans, with an occasional Osmanli and Armenian, and governed by a Kurdish boyahbeg.

At Jemjemi, with a ziyaret or sanctuary, we left the river side, as it had been already explored from Birehjik to Someïsat by Captain Lynch, when I accompanied him on a former journey. Ascending by a pass in chalk, with superimposed gravel beds, we reached Yasinjah, where were large flocks of the locust-eating thrush (*Turdus roseus*).

Our road lay hence across a fertile plain, and fine corn country, only rather in want of water, till we arrived at Yailash, a large village built round an antique-looking artificial mound or teppeh. By position and distance this corresponds to the ancient Porsica. It is now the seat of a boyahbeg. The surrounding country is well cultivated, water being drawn from wells. We pitched our tent in a field near the village; and in the evening shot a beautiful green ibis.

June 14*th*. Travelling over the plain as before, we approached some low limestone hills with ruins of houses, which, unlike others in these countries, had been carefully built of stone, and had once been edifices of some pretensions, both as regarded size and style of building; these were situated in three groups about half a mile from one another; the central group was the largest, and contained the remains of two churches, still in a good state of preservation, having been solidly built after the fashion of the Cappadocian churches, with bold semicircular arches, and roof of large slabs of stone. These churches evidently belonged, however, to a Syrian community, for the altars were level with the floors; whereas, in the Armenian churches they are raised, and in the Greek are placed in a sanctuary.

Accompanying these were some curious cavities, hewn in the solid rock, in the form of a pear, the base varying from eight to twelve feet in diameter, and the depth from twelve to twenty feet or upwards; but the aperture is small and round, and generally covered up with a single large stone. They are coated on the inside with mortar, and some of them being broken down are used as stables for mules, others are filled with tibbin, or chopped straw, the usual food for horses in these countries.

These cavities have been supposed to be tombs, and their perfect make, and occasional proximity to the churches, would appear to favour such a supposition; but they may also have been repositories for corn or water. The mortared walls favour the idea of their having been reservoirs, but that they were granaries is rendered the more probable, from the circumstance of cavities of similar character, although less carefully constructed, being still in use in many parts of Syria for such purposes.

This spot is now called Utch Kilisa (Three Churches), and there are still the houses of a few poor villagers in the neighbourhood. A little beyond this we came to the ruins of another village; a single wall with two windows was all that remained of the church.

The soil was now formed of indurated chalk, appearing often on the surface, like a rude but nearly level rocky pavement, at times covered with a slender vegetation of grass. The outline of the country was undulating, but there was an almost continuous barrenness, and a total want of water.

As we continued to travel over this inhospitable district, we were constantly discovering traces of early Christianity, ecclesiastical or monastic edifices, often of great beauty; remains of large villages, with deep cisterns or reservoirs hewn out of solid rock, arches isolated on some lone rocky summit, or fountains deserted and broken up.

We were evidently passing through an interesting district, it having been the seat of one of the early Christian communities in these countries, and,—as in the somewhat similar circnmstances already noticed respecting the Greeks in Garsaura,—it was impossible to travel through such a scene without asking oneself, was it from fear of persecution—to avoid jealousy or envy—or, which is most probable, to practise severe exercises and austere self-denial, that here, as in the Syrian hills of Reïha and Edlip, and amid the rocks of Sheikh Barakat (Mount St. Simeon), the early Christians retreated into stony and sterile districts, without soil to cultivate, without shade from the sun, and even without spring-water to quench a summer's thirst.

After a ride of nine hours we descended to the plain north of Birehjik; the tents of the Osmanlis were now seen lining the heights above the river north-west of the town and on the right bank. A further ride of an hour and a-half, and having in all made about thirty geographical miles, brought us to gardens of mulberry, fig, and pomegranate-trees, about a mile north of the town.

Here we pitched our tent, as we expected to find the town full of soldiery, and as, further, we could from hence best take our measures for visiting the Serasker without taking our baggage to the encampment.

CHAPTER XXI.

Retrospective. Views of the Sultan Mahmoud. Hafiz Pasha, Serasker. Dyarbekr. Campaign of Sinjar. Campaigns in Taurus. Campaign of Akjah Tagh and Kakhtah. Preparations in other Pashaliks. Prussian Officers. Passage of Taurus by the Army. Camp at Nizib. Policy of Ibrahim Pasha.

The magnitude of the events which took place shortly after our arrival at Birehjik demands some previous explanation. I therefore quit for a moment the journal system of recording our travels, to glance at the circumstances which had gradually paved the way to the denouement which we so unfortunately and so unintentionally arrived just in time to witness; and it is certain that, although people in general, and the author in particular, were almost to the last moment ignorant of the real objects of the warlike preparations of the Turks, still these preparations had been going on for six years, before the day which witnessed the toil, trouble, and expense incurred during that period of time swept away, in two brief hours, at the foot of the dusty hills of Nizib.

The Turks had never forgiven the reverses of Syria and Karamania, and the loss of so fine a portion of their country was not more vexatious than the superintendence of the great road to Mecca passing into other hands was humiliating to their religious pride. Sultan Mahmoud, resolute and heroic, but whose genius and abilities were too much wrapped up in vanity and fatalism to succeed in any great undertaking, except that which his heroism alone accomplished—the sudden destruction of the Janissaries—meditated at once the recovery of his lost possessions, the overthrow of Mehemet Ali, and the regeneration of an European fame for the Osmanli, by the institution, to a large extent, of the Nizam Djedid, or regular troops, in the interior of Asiatic Turkey; and subsequently, when it was still doubted if this would answer all the purposes desired, by the raising of large bodies of militia, which were incorporated and disciplined in great part by European instructors, in the interval between the treaty of Kutayah (1833) and 1839, by which time they were brought to a considerable degree of perfection in their drill and discipline.

As serasker over the new troops, and successor to Reshid Pasha, an officer was appointed, who, by birth a Circassian, was well known for his personal strength and address, and had also served in the previous unfortunate conflicts sustained against the Egyptians at Homs and at Koniyeh. Hafiz Pasha combined with the qualities of some experience of his opponent, and undoubted courage, considerable judgment and discrimination, individual sensibility and consequent refinement of manners, and a real enthusiasm in the cause in which he was engaged. He was further possessed of a liberal and enlightened spirit, far beyond that manifested by the generality of Turkish pashas, which rendered him open to all innovations that promised good, and led him to avail himself more freely of the assistance of Europeans and Christians.

To insure the attainment of the objects in view, the command of two leading pashaliks, besides the control over some minor ones, was given to the new Serasker;

but these, though populous and flourishing provinces, are little regarded by European nations, who, from Brusa to Erzrum in one direction, and from Erzrum to Mosul in another, had then no recognised agents and no mercantile residences; so that the long detail of the gradual progress by which the army of Nizib was collected, remained almost unknown, or at least little attended to, by either diplomatists or governments.

At first Hafiz Pasha established his head-quarters at Sivas, the ancient Sebaste; from whence he afterwards removed to the more central position of the plain of Mezireh, close to Kharput, renowned as one of the four great cities of Armenia (Carcathiocerta), and at no great distance from a second, Arsomsata, or Arsomasata. Here, on the fertile plain that extends at the foot of the bold rocks from whence the castle of Carcathiocerta appears to overlook at once the Euphrates and the Tigris, and in the centre of the great district of the Imperial mines, the direction of which is attached to the pashalik of Dyarbekr, he erected commodious barracks, from which the Seraï was not far distant, and while husbanding his resources, he introduced into these districts the use of something like European carriages; for the Owah, or plain of Kharput, covered with picturesque Mohammedan and Armenian villages, and carefully tilled and cultivated, is traversed by roads upon which (a rare thing in Lesser Asia, and still more so in Taurus,) the labours of agriculture are assisted by the use of carts.

This productive district, a part of Armenia as a kingdom, included the best portion of the province designated as *nobilissimam regionem Sophenen.* Its resources for the support of a large population, or an army, are as great probably in modern as in ancient times. The whole country is covered with villages surrounded by gardens, while its soil, deposited by the loaded tributaries of the Murad Su, appears never to have known what niggardness was towards any population, which, under varying names and varying faiths, was inclined to be industrious.

From hence the Serasker repaired to Dyarbekr, and in the winter of 1836-37 he had already fifty guns, though badly mounted, and a force of about 25,000 regular and irregular troops. The beautiful and durable walls of the ancient Amida used to excite his admiration. He saw that they were superior to anything done in the present day by the Turks, and he would ask over and over again, when riding beneath the lofty arch of a Roman gateway, who were the architects? but his historical knowledge of the power and the refinement of the former possessors of Western Asia was not sufficient to enable him to remember their name, or policy made him wish to appear ignorant of the works of infidels.

At this period commenced the campaigns against the Kurds of Kurdistan Proper, which originated in the rebellion of the natives against a governor appointed by Reshid Pasha after the siege and capture of Jezireh Ibn Omar, and the erroneous belief that one of their old chieftains, who had been sent to Baghdad, was on his way with a large party of followers to re-establish their independence; being mingled up besides this with family broils. The tranquillization of the disturbed districts was intrusted to the Pasha of Dyarbekr and other generals, and was to all appearance accomplished.

But the resources of Dyarbekr, although a considerable place of trade, are not of themselves great, and soon became exhausted. Mirza Pasha, general of cavalry, had also been for the last eighteen months quartered with two regiments upon the small town of Mardin, in this district, which, naturally ill-disposed, and unable to bear the burthen, was in a state of passive revolt.

In such an emergency, in order at once to employ the soldiers, to recruit means, and to conceal the real objects of the drain continually going on, an expedition against the Kurds of Sinjar was resolved upon, and for a time absorbed all attention, as the Serasker was himself to assist in the campaign. Every one was anxious for the subjugation of these people, who have so long troubled the peace and impeded commerce in Mesopotamia. Assistance thus came the more voluntarily, though a stout resistance was expected, and being at Dyarbekr on the business of the Euphrates Expedition, I often heard the question seriously put as to the chances of success against an armed banditti, who could only muster from 4000 to 5000 firelocks, and to whom discipline and military tactics were unknown.

It is not my object to detail the progress of this campaign: suffice it that the villages were reduced, the women given over to the soldiery, and the men hunted even into their caverned fastnesses, in which many were slain. Hafiz Pasha was bit by a centipede, from which he suffered severely, and after leaving a mutesellim and several inferior officers to govern the country, he retired to Dyarbekr, stationing Mirza Pasha, with a small force, at Nisibin, which is on the centre of a fertile plain, watered by the Mygdonius, and sufficiently near, to keep Sinjar in obedience.

The restoration of the antique Nisibis, where Trajan and Severus had held imperial banquets, and the Bacchanalian grape is seen entertwining the emblem of Roman power in the exquisite friezes that still remain,—from whence a fleet of boats descended to the Euphrates, from thence to overrun Babylonia and the magnificent Ctesiphon,—which witnessed the triumph of Lucullus, and the disgrace of Jovian, and which was one of the great points whence early Christianity was promulgated, was a noble enterprise. No love of antiquity nor regard for classic ground, however, urged the present labours, and their duration will be as frail as the power that begat them. In 1837, the author passed a night at Nisibin, in a hovel attached to the post-house; there were a few other cottages near it, and the whole were inclosed in a small quadrangle to keep off marauders. In the month of October, 1838, the Kurds having been subjugated that spring, Dr. Forbes* found Mirza Pasha at Nisibin with a regiment of cavalry, and a troop of artillery, numbering altogether 900 men; a strong and commodious building, called a kasr, or palace, had been erected, there were a hundred well-built houses, inhabitants had been enticed from various parts, and there were a dozen shops kept by Christians.

In January 1840, I again passed through the same place. The kasr still existed, but was untenanted; near it were also a mud barrack and a mesjid, and a few trees were withering in the sun. There was also

---

* *Journal of the Royal Geographical Society*, vol. ix.

a village in which were a few irregular soldiers and a zabit (inferior civil officer), but it was difficult to find an inhabitant; of the shops, there was already no trace left. Such is a page in the history of Nisibin, the proud Antiochia Mygdonia of the Greeks, and it is truly illustrative of what is seen every day in this unsettled and ill-governed country.

Taking advantage of the troops being withdrawn into Sinjar, the Kurds of the northern parts of Kurdistan rose in revolt; they had been misled to suppose that the destruction of the Osmanlis in the plains and hills of Sinjar was certain, but, nothing daunted, the autumn of the same year saw the Serasker and his troops marching to a more fatiguing and laborious campaign than that of Sinjar. In the former, two English officers, Colonel Considine and Captain Campbell, had arrived too late to give their assistance; in the present, the Serasker had the company and aid of the Prussian officers. Tribe after tribe was reduced, the castles at the head of the tributaries of the Tigris fell before the victorious troops, and Hafiz Pasha returned covered with glory, but the results have been the same as in every attempt to subjugate these hardy mountaineers; the battle of Nizib freed them from the new yoke that had been imposed upon them, and the Kurds of Sinjar at the same time re-established their independence.

Notwithstanding these successes, partly from necessity and partly from certain advantages which the position presented, Hafiz Pasha removed with his staff to Malatiyeh, and having ensured the permanent residence of the inhabitants of that town at their summer quarters, a market sprung up in the middle of the gardens, while Malatiyeh itself was abandoned, the soldiers burnt shutters and frame-work for firewood, and tore off roofs or pulled up floors, and the old city became a ruin. But the Serasker worked steadily at his object: a powder-mill was now established, and wrought with success, forges were built, guns repaired, and new and efficient carriages were made.

Few, if any, of his predecessors had made themselves so well acquainted with the resources of the provinces under his control as Hafiz Pasha, nor knew better how to turn them to account. The great post road had especially been looked to, and (excepting that, from a wish to gratify the Sultan, who took about this time a sudden enthusiasm in favour of quarantines, a vexatious stoppage was effected between Malatiyeh and Sivas,) never was the road more safe nor the interior of the country more bustling, than at the moment now in question. Agriculture flourished, nor did the pasha neglect the mines. His brother was appointed to the superintendence of the lead and silver mines of Kapan Madan; he had engaged an European, who unfortunately fell a victim to the climate at Sivan Maden, and he was anxious to render more efficient the rich copper mines of Arghana, and to avail himself of the abundant iron ores of Divrigi. The ordinary equipments of his soldiery were made under his own immediate inspection, except the shoes, which were obtained from Russia and the bonnets from Constantinople.

The spring and summer of 1838 witnessed two new campaigns against the Kurds. The first against the Kurds of Akjah Tagh, of which notice has already being taken in traversing that remarkable country; the second, to which greater difficulties were opposed, was against the castles in that part of Taurus where the Euphrates forces for itself a passage through the mountains, and which had for many years been in the undisputed possession of the mountaineers. These would be in the rear of the army that was about to penetrate into Syria, and policy as well as actual necessity dictated their subjugation. Among these places were Kakhtah and Gergen Kalehsi, both previously described. They were reduced, but the Kurds repaired to their mountain fastnesses, where they were as safe as the native ibex, and the result we have already seen.

Misfortunes, however, began now to overtake the Serasker in his labours. Malatiyeh is renowned, even among the natives, for its unhealthiness. The soldiers fatigued and harassed, and withal not over well fed, soon began to sink under the climate, and in the autumn of the same year perished by hundreds, so that the army was at the moment most of need, rendered no longer efficient. This was a severe affliction which tended much to retard the measures in progress, but Sultan Mahmoud had from various circumstances become more firm in his resolution than ever; and that nothing might prevent his general commencing hostilities against the Egyptians by the next spring, he began to reinforce him from Constantinople itself, whence two regiments of guards, besides guns and amunition, were sent to join from the port of Samsun, and other succours came with an activity that delighted the heart of the Serasker, and raised to the highest pitch the hopes and the enthusiasm of the Turks.

The secresy which had been observed at head-quarters could now no longer be preserved throughout the empire. The Sultan, while he was assuming so warlike an aspect in the interior, was devoting almost all his resources in the capital towards the equipment of his fleet, and it became what it was to the last moment—a crowd of noble ships without sailors and without officers—a sword of state which no one could wield.

While the events which have been detailed were in progress, Izzet Pasha of Angora, and Haji Ali Pasha of Koniyeh, had also been long engaged in the collecting and drilling of troops. The levies had no longer, as at first, been confined to the provinces of Dyarbekr and Sivas, but extended to near Smyrna on the one side, and as far as to the interior pashalic of Boli on the other.

The pasha of Erzrum was active on his part. Ali Pasha of Baghdad had also undertaken extensive plans, which were not, however, followed by success; he erected barracks at Erbil and Kerkuk. Suleiman Pasha of Suleimaniya, in Southern Kurdistan, had long had a few regular troops, and they were incorporated with what was now intended to form a *corps d'armée*. The pasha of Amadiyah was applied to in vain. The pasha of Mosul erected barracks, and succeeded in raising an efficient force of 3000 men, besides a small park of artillery. These troops in the extreme east did not, however, co-operate in the campaign of 1839.

It was impossible for European diplomatists to close their eyes any longer to the progress of events, and assistance in the way of instruction was asked for, and given, on the part of the powers friendly to the Turkish empire, but political intrigue thwarted these measures at an early period, as it also did others, at a later hour. Two English officers of known abilities and talent, after their assistance had been sought for by the Sultan, were neglected, and a strong remonstrance was made to Mahmoud by the British ambassador; but what could the Turk do against the urgent insistance of a power which so short a time before had a fleet and camp at the head of the Bosphorus?

I am not aware if assistance was sought or offered on the part of the French government, but it was accepted at last from an admitted neutral power—Prussia, who sent several able and experienced officers to their assistance. Barons Moltke and Mulbach, of the Prussian staff, and Captain Lauer, of the artillery, were appointed to the head-quarters at Malatiyeh. M. Fischer lent his services to the pasha at Koniyeh, and first put the defences on the Turkish side of Taurus into an available condition. Baron Wincke, another well-qualified and industrious officer, repaired to Angora, to the army of Izzet Pasha.

Men so intelligent as the officers who had now come to superintend the instruction of the Turkish army could not fail to observe in a very short time that there existed, in the division of command over that army, a principle opposed to all success.

Izzet Pasha could never concede the justice of appointing over him a man of less standing and less military reputation than himself, one of whom he used to speak as a young and inexperienced pasha, perhaps with some degree of truth,—but Hafiz was the favourite of the Sultan. The aged Haji Ali also held himself aloof enshrouded in comfortable and never-failing Osmanli pride; and thus there was no real co-operation among parties jealous of one another.

The Prussian officers urged in the strongest manner the union of the command under one, but they did not at first agree as to the choice of the individual to recommend. Whether the diplomatists in Constantinople had before this seen and urged the necessity of such a measure I cannot tell, but if they did, it is much to be regretted that the Sultan did not at once acquiesce in the arrangement, as to the neglect of so important a point, the failure of the ill-arranged campaign of 1839 is in great part to be attributed.

It is certain, as I have had means of assuring myself since on the spot, that, so far had Ibrahim Pasha drained his resources to oppose the Serasker's sole army, that there were not 3000 men to impede the progress of the 15,000 troops of Haji Ali through the Cilician Gates, or Golek Boghaz; and, besides Suleiman Pasha at Marash, there were 20,000 men bearing arms and in rebellion in the Amanus (Gawur Tagh), ready to join the army of Izzet Pasha, had he received earlier orders or been more active in his operations. If Ibrahim Pasha had been so skilful and prompt in his movements as to have fought these armies in detail, still there would have been a diversion in favour of the Serasker or any one of the remaining armies, which, combined with the good will that then existed to the cause of the Sultan in Damascus and Aleppo, as well as in the inferior towns, must have led to the loss at least of his Syrian possessions to Mehemet Ali.

Early in the spring of 1839 Hafiz Pasha commenced the passage of the Taurus; in order to effect which, notwithstanding previous preparatory labours, there were still rocks to be cut through, stones to be removed, and bridges to be built, and a constant and fatiguing exertion to be kept up for nearly two months. The Serasker in part superintended these operations, and for several days took up his position near the cool fountains of Surghu.

But the welfare of the army required a separation; and leaving the artillery to pursue their arduous course by Erkenek and Pelvere, the pasha moved with the cavalry and part of the infantry by a more difficult road to the fertile plain of Adiyaman.

From hence the banks of the river Euphrates by Rum-Kalah to Birehjik were easily gained; the point of reunion was established on the large and level tract of sand and gravel which has been deposited by the river opposite to the latter town, and every day for some time saw new parties arrive, more or less fatigued with their journey through the mountains; and, according to the spirit of the parties, more or less rejoiced at the broad bosom of waters that now extended before them, and the promises of more regular supplies, which generally attend upon head-quarters.

After considering the position of the country and the direction whence the enemy were likely to come, the Prussian officers began to lay out lines of defence upon the heights above, which, when completed certainly presented a very formidable front, and in which, in after-times, much reliance was still placed, not from the natural advantages of the position, but because with a river in the rear (no very complimentary arrangement), they thought the Turks might be more firm to their post.

But this position presented a disadvantage, which at the first could scarcely have been contemplated. As the warm weather came on, the troops used to bathe in the Euphrates, whose waters are here both deep and rapid, besides having frequent quicksands, which are extremely dangerous. The loss of lives which occurred from what would appear at first such a trifling cause, and which it would have been thought good sense and a natural caution would also have soon put a stop to, was so great as to render it desirable to the pasha to change his quarters. There was no other rivulet or river nearer than the Kesrin, and on its banks there were no villages, but a little higher up the country, and at the foot of the hills, nearly due west of Birehjik, were the pleasant groves and large village of Nizib, at once an agreeable and good site for a camp, offering some resources and not a disadvantageous position for defence. While the preparations were making for departing to this spot, a new accident came to discomfit the troops and bring dejection into the army; a depôt of powder, placed improvidently in the very centre of the camp, was by some accident exploded, and the result filled the hospitals with wounded, and entailed the loss of many hundred lives.

The Serasker having pitched his tent at Nizib, the encampment was effected in a more orderly manner, and with a more efficient and comfortable distribution of its parts and of the different services, than on the banks of the Euphrates, where it had been allowed to accumulate almost according to the accidental arrival of the parties; and here commenced those first petty hostilities, for which the Egyptian general was anxiously waiting, in order that he might be able to say to the other powers that he did not begin the war. With the same view he kept the garrison of Aïntab, which has a strong citadel, capable of standing a long siege and with accommodation for 10,000 men, with only 1,500 men in it, and fomented rebellion among its inhabitants, that so promising a bait might be, as it was, taken by the Turks, and thus afford him at once a clear and prominent excuse for hostilities; for it is to be observed, the Turks had not passed the frontier established by the treaty of Kutayah, which was at the river of Sagur, four hours on the way to Aleppo beyond their present position.

CHAPTER XXII.

Town of Birehjik. Prospect around us. Ferries on Euphrates. Road to the Camp. Reception by the Serasker. Birehjik at night-time. Return to the Camp. Aspect of the Camp. Curious Whirlwinds. Village of Nizib. Defences of the Camp.

THE spot at which we had pitched our tent, to the north of Birehjik, was equally pleasant and remarkable for the beauty of the scenery by which it was surrounded. A continuous and nearly level plain, covered with meadows and feeding many flocks, with here and there an encampment of pastoral Turkomans, or a village of herdsmen, stretched to the north, to where the Euphrates breaks from its rock-bound channel by a huge gap, which is visible far away along the course of the river. The direction of the latter, as it issues from the hills, is southerly, but sweeping round the foot of Tel Balkis, a high mound of chalk, whose name, that of the Queen of Sheba, and existing ruins, attest it to have been once the seat of a temple, the waters come in contact with the prolongation of the hills of Nizib, and are forced away to the east, whence curving round to the spot where we were, the silvery expanse turned and glided away to the south, washing in its course the marble walls and white stairs of the town of Bir or Birehjik, and a little beyond on the right—a speck on the plain—the brown intrenchments of Port William, where the boats of the Euphrates Expedition were put together, and where several of our adventurous countrymen lie buried.

The appearance of Birehjik, with its noble castle,

where paintings of the time of the Crusaders still exist, its caverned houses and climbing ramparts*, its rocky shelves studded with green ibis, and its cleanly mosques with their broad marble steps, for the frequent ablutions demanded by an Arab prophet, ought to be familiar from the sketch given by Mr. Buckingham, if not from the more accurate drawings of the officers of the Euphrates Expedition; but, although not so comprehensive, the view from the north is far more striking, the outline of the hills and walls is more distinct, and the bold irregular form of the castle perched upon its craggy rocks, advances into the rapid and resistless stream like an armed warrior of by-gone times, ready to dispute its further progress.

On the green slopes which extended like a lawn, and then rose like a terrace over the right bank of the river, and opposite to the town, was a small encampment, while another detachment of troops occupied the more picturesque point of the peninsula, which stretched like a dry and thirsty tongue to lap the waters opposite to us.

The immediate position of our tent was in a garden at the foot of a radiant chalk cliff. There, under the shade of a wide spread fig-tree and masked in front by a dense foliage of pomegranate, we found some shelter from the glaring heat of a midsummer sun, and as much repose as the infinitude of flies and insects, and clouds of dust, raised into whirlpools by every passing breeze, would permit us to enjoy.

The next day we mounted our horses, and pursued

* "Muris velut sinuosis et cornutis." Ammian. lib. xx. cap. 18, who by mistake writes Virta for Birtha.

our way along the foot of the cliffs, which on approaching the town only allow of a narrow path between them and the troubled waters below. Birehjik was nearly deserted; the castle had been converted into an hospital, and was tolerably full, but in the streets scarce a person was to be seen, and the shops were shut; here and there an European hakim was hurrying with careworn and anxious face to his duties, and there were besides only a few houseless Arabs, with long lines of weary camels which had lately brought wheat, rice, or barley, from the rich granaries of Harran and Seruj.

At the ferry there was more bustle: the boats had been taken into government pay, and were engaged in constantly passing and repassing all day and the greater part of the night with sheep and cattle, camels and horses, and grain of various kind.

The ferry-boats of Someïsat and Birehjik, the great thoroughfares from Syria and Arabia to Mesopotamia, do not possess very high claims for convenience. They resemble a great coal-scuttle with a flat bottom and the stern a little pointed. The steersmen are two in number, for the boat being at once steered and propelled by a long sweep like the tail of a fish, it requires two men to work it, and there are four more in front, occupied, with loud bursts of exclamation, and groans innumerable, in clumsily beating poor Euphrates with two awkward oars. In the interior, camels, horses, sheep, and men are huddled together, and if the passenger, up to his ankles in water, stretches himself to free his foot from the heavy pad of a camel or the iron pressure of a struggling horse, ten to one he receives a thump from the delicately managed sweep, which he may consider, according to his philosophy, either as a mere practical summons to crouch again, or as an emblem of the evils of life.

The pleasures of the ferry had an end, and were succeeded on gaining the outposts on the top of the hill by a detailed examination of our papers; luckily the official employed in the capacity of Turkish secretary of police was an old friend, and after a few expressions of kindness over the customary finjan (cup) of coffee, we were allowed to pursue an uninterrupted progress to the camp, two hours, or from seven to eight miles, distant from the river. The road is carried along an almost level plain with two hills to the right, and a gradual slope towards the valley of the Kesrin to the left. Vegetation had now, for more than a month past, lost the freshness and vigour of spring—the flowering plants were withered and dry; the grass had assumed a russet-brown hue, which was not enlivened by the feathery blue of the olive groves; the fields were wasted, the crops having been cut when green for fodder; and the heather on the hills was buried in dust, which covered every thing, greensward, trees, and hills, and saddened the whole aspect of nature.

The carcasses of camels and horses, some newly dead, but others emitting most noxious effluvia, were encountered in numbers, and fully shewed how severe were the tasks to which the animals were put in order to supply the wants of an army. Nor was the loss on the part of the Egyptians less in this department; for on a subsequent journey, made some time after the battle from Aleppo to Birehjik, I saw the skeletons of nearly a hundred camels on various parts of the road. When soldiers, occupied in the commissariat, had a horse drop upon the road, they ripped up the skin and cutting a bit, carried it to the camp, as a proof that the animal was really dead. We saw a party engaged in this operation; the animal was panting with thirst, heat, and exhaustion, unable to proceed or to die, and writhing under the knife.

Parties driving their loads to the camp, others hastening with unladen horses for further supplies, a few craven laggards slowly progressing to join the martial band, khawasses on their way to hurry tardy peasants or construct rafts up the river, tatars bound to the mutesellims of distant towns, and the aghas of districts, and officers upon various duties, gleamed through the sun's misty glare, and lent life to the great open furnace in which we all moved.

The teskereh we had obtained at the outposts was asked from us on entering the camp, and crossing the valley and rivulet of Nizib, we ascended a low hill, riding round which we dismounted in front of the pasha's tent, easily distinguished by its superior splendour, and by a guard and two guns placed on its threshold. The servants took our horses, and the General, against the Mohammedan law, which forbids rising to infidels, rose to receive us.

After many friendly congratulations, inquiries were instituted as to our objects, which were briefly but sufficiently explained, and our requests for letters, &c., put forward. The Pasha received them with a serious and thoughtful air, and when our explanation was finished, he endeavoured to dissuade us from our journey, which he strongly insisted upon was now fraught with insuperable difficulties, and rendered full of danger; he had endeavoured to raise supplies and men from among the subjected mountaineers, but without the least success, and he was at that moment exceedingly irate and vexed with the rebellious inhabitants of Sinjar.

After some further conversation, he promised to assist us, but only on condition that we would consent to spend a day or two with him in the camp. It was in vain that we represented the distance at which our tent was pitched, that we had instruments to carry, and altogether there would be much inconvenience to us in coming out of our way to the camp. These arguments were of no avail: the Pasha appeared rejoiced at having some English friends with him; our things, he said, should be sent for immediately by a trust-worthy person, and we must stop. Finding further objections useless, if not detrimental, I at first proposed that one of us should superintend the transport of the instruments, while the others remained as a sort of hostage, but considering that it was growing late, and whoever went upon the mission could hardly return that evening, I determined upon all going together, and coming back in the morning, and expressed my wishes to that effect to the Pasha. He was not much pleased with this new arrangement, and appeared afraid of losing us, but after a moment's consideration he sent for a colonel of irregulars, and put us under his charge. We accordingly started for Birehjik, and reached the water-side just as the dim veil of night was creeping over the town, and towers and menarehs rose out of the obscurity, like giant forms rearing themselves above ruined piles, dark covered ways, and solemn arches. The outline was beautiful, even in its indistinctness; and it required very little imagination to people the castle walls with crusaders armed cap-à-pie, or to convert a white menareh into the the pontifical robes of a successor of the apostles*.

Our companion had orders to find supper for us, and beds in the castle and at the house of the governor, and he was not a little surprised to find us resolved upon still proceeding to our tent; we pursued our way, however, along the foot of the dark cliffs, lighted by troops of stars, and welcomed by the low hooting of the owl, to our tranquil recess, where we roused the weary servants, and were ourselves roused shortly after by the arrival of a caravan of donkies, bringing supper ready made, and a dozen live fowls, for a midnight feast, and as a present from the mutesellim of Birehjik.

At sunrise, that is to say, at three in the morning, when life is truly an enjoyment in the East, an age-struck member of the Serasker's household, who had travelled with me on a former occasion, when we had had some sharp work with the Kurds of the Kara Bel, came and threw himself into my arms, and before I could prevent it, covered me with embraces. Our colonel came with him and drank coffee, during which time our tent and traps were loaded, and a few hours saw us once more seated in the camp of the Osmanlis.

At this period no hostilities of any importance had taken place: Ibrahim Pasha was quiet at Aleppo; some skirmishes had occurred between the irregular troops, but it was impossible to say which party was to blame;

* Birtha, with Edessa, Callinicum, and Batnæ, which succeeded to Seruj, was one of the oldest episcopates of Mesopotamia.

there had been a few predatory movements on both sides, and many inhabitants of the territory of Ibrahim Pasha, at Aintab, in Amanus, and in other places, had risen in favour of the Sultan, and had been supplied with arms from the camp; against which proceedings the Egyptian general had remonstrated in form, through the person of a military envoy; yet, notwithstanding these preliminaries to open hostility, this appeared, at the moment, as far removed as ever. The Turkish troops had on no occasion crossed the frontier, where the Osmanli advanced guard was stationed, and Ibrahim Pasha remained quiet in the great city of Aleppo.

After a short visit paid to Hafiz Pasha, his brother, Ibraila Pasha, accompanied us to the tents of the Barons Moltke and Mulbach, where we also met several of the European officers engaged in the Turkish service: M. Lauer, of the Prussian artillery, M. Chateauneuf, attached to the instruction of the same branch, M. Petit, an officer of infantry, who had served in the campaign of Algiers, and a M. Tournami, a native I believe of Tuscany.

These visits concluded, we were taken to the tent prepared for us by the Serasker, which was one of the most luxurious in the camp. It was circular and very capacious, being divided into two parts, the outer canvass walls at a distance of about four feet from the inner, and a circular gallery thus left, in which water being continually poured upon the parched soil currents of air were originated by rapid evaporation, which swept round the sombre and shady precincts, and were allowed entrance to the interior by openings left in the front and in the rear. The central space, besides its canvass walls, was lined with a pretty pattern of red print, on the floor were carpets, and in front a double row of cushions, with variegated yellow and red silks, on which flowers of gold were exquisitely wrought. Besides our own attendants, two of the pasha's private servants waited upon us, and his kitchen was also made to contribute to our comforts.

Ibraila Pasha was bowing inquiringly, "Did we like the residence appointed for us?" we were delighted with the splendour of our imprisonment, but were still more anxious to contemplate the scene around us; so seated upon the divan, and getting rid of the intrusive servants from the front, we had a few minutes,—and only that,—for visitors soon thronged to the new arrivals,—to eliminate from the crowd and bustle the peculiarities of a Turkish camp.

It certainly was a gay and varied scene, to which the inequalities of the ground, the distribution of the tents among groves and gardens and on the bare hills above, batteries on outstretching peninsulas, guns on upraised mounds, and long lines of horses, added in no small degree. Every thing was here made to answer two or three purposes at once,—a convenient distribution, a strong line of defence, and a picturesque display.

If the vegetation was burnt up, and the soil was sandy, and there was a red-hot glimmer in the air, and a rather oppressive sense of stifling heat in the frame, still a pleasant illusion was produced. The soldiers had become amphibious, and were almost as much in the water as on land, and their green tents gladdened the scene, the more from their contrast with the parched but glittering leaf of the olive groves which extended to the right and left. But even the shroud of decay which enveloped all vegetation was rendered more dismal now and then by a tall column of dust, that remained whirling round and round with extraordinary tenacity in the same spot, but sometimes advanced fiercely from the heights, breaking over the devoted camp, frightening horses and tearing up tents. There appeared to be something electrical in this phenomenon, which was of frequent occurrence, for the pillars of sand often came on in the still hot evenings, when there was scarcely a zephyr abroad.

We were upon the eastern brow of a low hill, on the summit of which was the tent of the Serasker; by its side were those of his secretary and treasurer, and on the western slope of the same hill, a large tent, which served as a place of prayer and home for dervishes, besides other tents of officers, household, &c.

To our right, and close by, was a small grove, in which most of the Europeans had had at once the precaution and the influence to quarter themselves, while immediately in front was a portion of land, occupied by farriers and workmen of various kinds, more especially a large body of Armenians, who were the sappers and miners of the army, and the chief constructors of intrenchments.

This irregularly-occupied space extended about 500 feet to the rivulet of Nizib, immediately beyond which, to the right, was a level appropriated to the artillery. The guns were chiefly in the batteries, but as there were two sets of ammunition cars, or near 400 rounds of powder and hollow shot to each, this was the reserve, arranged in a great parallelogram, the tents of the men on the outside, the horses picketed in lines in the interior, and the neatly painted cars in the intervals between.

Beyond this the ground rose gradually, and here in the centre, opposite to us, was the great road to Birehjik, at the foot of which on one side was a fountain, on the other a menareh and a few houses, with a burial-ground above. At this point a guard was placed, and teskerehs required to go out or enter into the camp, and it was at this point also, that the camp was first gained by the enemy, and a small battery opened upon the inoffensive tents and retreating multitude. Beyond this to the north, and up the course of the valley, extended the village and gardens of Nizib, more particularly characterized by a huge pile of building, which had once been a Christian church, but the style of which was Saracenic. There was also a mound of ruins between the village and the rivulet, to which the timid peasants used to repair to watch events, and perhaps even to speculate upon chances, for no soldiers were to be seen among them.

To the south and to our right, the scene was more animated. The valley of the rivulet extended about a mile and a half to where it joined the Kesrin river. About a mile down, was one of those mounds called tells by the Arabs, and teppehs by the Turks, upon whose summit were three guns and a guard. From the point where we were to this teppeh, was a continued succession of tents on both sides of the rivulet, but chiefly on the right. To the left the tents were also distributed on the hill-side, and occupied even a portion of the upland, while beyond, and near the extreme of the cape, which advanced over the junction of the rivulet of Nizib with the Kesrin, were two batteries, which were destined afterwards to become the defences of the extreme right of the Turkish line, as they now constituted those of the extreme left of the camp.

The line of front was formed, first by the batteries on the heights now alluded to, secondly by the guns on the teppeh near the rivulet, then by three main intrenchments, with, in each, from ten to fifteen guns, the intervals between which were defended by columns of infantry, whose muskets were left piled up, at the point which they were to occupy in case of attack.

In front of the hill occupied by the General and his staff, was another vale of small dimensions and without water, in which was a vineyard; further on was a plantation of young fig-trees, and another vineyard, and then a waterless vale, in which were encamped the Turkish guard, under Sadallah Pasha, who formed the extreme right of the army. Beyond this was a dense grove of olive and fig-trees, on the outskirts of which were two more batteries, and above the grove a bold rocky hill, called that of Nizib *par eminence*, and which advanced from the chief range into the plàin. Three pieces of ordnance were placed upon a jutting crag, high up upon its acclivities, and the extreme summit was made a place of observation.

Such was the distribution of the camp of Nizib. The Kurdish and Arab irregular troops had quartered themselves partly upon the village, but mainly on the banks of the rivulet, near to the teppeh and below the camp. Many of their horses had perished from want of food, and the over-exertions to which they were put, during nocturnal predatory expeditions; and this did not render that neighbourhood particularly pleasant.

The Turkish forces, combined with the two battalions which afterwards came up on the morning of battle, under Suleiman Pasha of Marash, consisted, as far as could be proximately ascertained, of

Seventeen regiments of infantry, of three battalions of 400 men each, which complete would have given 20,400 men, but in reality - -	17,000
Seven regiments of cavalry (musasiyah), six squadrons, each 100 men, incomplete - -	3,600
Four regiments of sipahis, four squadrons, each 100 men - - - - - -	1,600
Gunners and waggon train (160 guns) - -	3,000
Irregular infantry (1000 came the morning of battle)	3,000
Irregular cavalry - - - -	6,000
	34,200

There were also about 2000 Egyptians on the field, on the day of the engagement, one battalion of which, of about 800 men, there was not time to distribute, and it remained a short time in the rear previous to disbanding, but without firing a musket.

The advance guard was placed about two hours and a half in front, at the village of Niksar, on the Kesrin, and consisted of about 800 to 1000 irregular horsemen, and a few gunners with tents, and three pieces of ordnance.

CHAPTER XXIII.

Hafiz Pasha's Tent.

Prisoners of War. Arrival of the Egyptian Army. Thoughts suggested by our present position. Mohammedan vespers. A Reconnoissance. Skirmish of irregular cavalry—Interrupted by cannonade. A Martial Dervish. Conflagration of the Plain. Fate of Isaïd Bey.

The day after our arrival (Tuesday, June 18th), while sitting with the Serasker, a peasant came running on foot with the news of the surrender of Aïntab. He was immediately ordered a backshish, or present, and all were delighted at what they did not understand to be but the trumpet-note for hostilities.

The next morning (Wednesday, June 19th), at an early hour, several Bedwins were brought prisoners into the camp. They had made a descent during the night upon a village near Niksar, which they pillaged, and had wounded several men and women, as a weeping female was allowed to corroborate. We expected that they would have their heads cut off, but nothing was done to them; there was nothing barbarous in the treatment of prisoners. One of these was a celebrated Bedwin chaoush, or captain, originally from near Tripoli, by name Haji Batran, and an officer high in the esteem of Mohammed, commonly called Majun Bey, the chief of the irregular troops in the Egyptian army. By the result of the battle of Nizib, this man regained his liberty, and was, when I last heard of him, employed upon a mission to the Zor, or tamarisk woods of the Euphrates, to rouse the Anazeh for a Mesopotamian campaign. These Bedwins had fallen into bad hands, for they were in a state of nearly complete nudity.

Early the next morning a battalion of Egyptians, about 800 strong, that had surrendered at Aintab, were marched into the camp. The little drummers, with eyes askance, and a curious expression of half apprehension and half merriment, came in front beating away, but their thoughts elsewhere than with their drums; they were followed by a party of Albanians, dressed in the showy costume of their country, and behind marched the dusty soldiers. The officers appeared to have many acquaintances, for there were embraces and congratulations exchanged. I may have been mistaken, but they appeared to me to be aware of the part they were playing, the soldiery not. Having been drawn up in front of the Serasker's tent, Hafiz Pasha went out to greet them by a nominal inspection, after which a mollah uttered prayers for the Sultan, and an attempt was made to obtain a general cry of Allah, but it was a signal failure. The soldiers were then promised the arrears of pay due to them for the last eighteen or nineteen months, which was soon afterwards made over to them; a great part were then distributed among the ranks, but many preferred acting as grooms and servants, and I believe all the officers were allowed to remain neutral.

In the mean time, the news of the pre-ordained surrender of Aïntab had reached Aleppo, and the same day Ibrahim Pasha reviewed 40,000 troops on the plains of Abu Bekr, immediately after which they started on their march to Nizib. So rapid was he in his movements, his army unencumbered by baggage or tents, with only a little biscuit for all supplies, that the third morning (Thursday, June 20th) from the time when we learnt the surrender of the castle, the Egyptians, driving the Turkish advance guard before them, merely by firing a few guns, and so quickly that tents and ordnance were left in their hands, came down to the banks of the Kesrin, and reposed themselves near the village of Niksar, which had been occupied the same morning by the Turkish troops.

We rode out in advance of the lines to have a peep at the new arrivals. Baron Mulbach was busy in rallying the irregular troops, who were retiring in a confused manner into the camp; but he brought them to order, and made them turn their horses' heads the other way. "Voilà l'ennemi, messieurs," he said, pointing at the same time to a black-looking mass that lay like a huge tortoise upon the dusty brown land. With a glass, however, we could distinguish the soldiers reposing in lines upon their knapsacks, while others were cooking; but there only appeared to be three or four tents (perhaps those which had been captured the same morning,) in the whole army. It would have required an experienced eye to say what the force of the enemy was. We have previously said, as is now well known, that 40,000 were reviewed at Aleppo, at the moment of departure; but the news of the rebellion in the Amanus had reached Ibrahim on his march, and he was obliged to detach a few regiments to Cilicia, where his possessions were most threatened; and I believe the following is pretty nearly a summary of what remained to fight at Nizib:—

Twelve regiments of infantry, four battalions, each of 500 men - - - - -	24,000
Eight regiments of cavalry, 500 men each -	4,000
One regiment of cuirassiers, 800 men - -	800
Gunners and waggon train (120 guns) -	2,000
Four companies of engineers - - -	2,000
Anazeh, about 1500 - - - -	1,500
	34,300

Thus the amount of forces was not far from being equal, but many hundreds of Turks were labouring under diarrhœa, from which same cause there was also a considerable daily mortality; many were boys scarcely able to carry a musket. Above all, the courage and abilities, as well as the constant successes of Ibrahim Pasha, gave a degree of zeal and enthusiasm to his soldiers which was quite unknown among the troops of the Sultan.

We had now arrived at what constituted truly the picturesque part of the campaign; the infantry were ordered to their arms, and the cavalry, all lancers, were grouped in part round the teppeh at the extreme left, while to the right long lines of glittering banners indicated where other squadrons were filing through the olive groves, dim at noon-day. On every side staff officers and pashas were galloping up the hills, or sweeping along the forest of tents, bearing further orders for precaution against surprise, or to reconnoitre a now visible enemy. It was a moment of exciting interest, and a moving panorama which lent beauty and favour even to so sad a thing as war. I could not help thinking of Akenside's reproach:

Come, then, tell me, sage divine,
Is it an offence to own
That our bosoms e'er incline
Towards immortal glory's throne?

But is there glory, it may be said, in military triumph, or even in death on the field of battle? Most certainly so, if the cause is a virtuous one. There are many sources of national grievances, which lead to war, for they take their origin in the imperfection of our natures, and when such cases do arise it is undoubtedly glorious to see the new duties imposed upon us discharged with unshrinking resolution.

In peace, there's nothing so becomes a man
As modest stillness and humility;
But when the blast of war blows in our ears,
Then imitate the action of the tiger.

True, it is all vanity, and the victor himself is vanquished by the worm; but that when the passions are called into play by an injury done to the nobler sentiments, or to the intellect, man will be roused to become an offensive being, is founded upon his unchangeable mental constitution. And according to his various capacity for harm his incentives will be the greater the more noble is the feeling that has been injured,—his sense of right and wrong, his patriotism, his love to his friends or kindred, his religion! And is philosophy so niggardly as to deny a tear or a branch of laurel to one who dies fighting for his hearth, his home, or his faith? rather, it is no philosophy at all; for when there shall be no honour in defending that which is good, then will there be no dishonour in doing that which is vicious. The rolling cycles of generations yet to come will witness the same effects produced by the same causes; man will remain as he is now, a breathing creature made up of elements of good and evil, and nations will continue to prosper or fall as the one predominates over the other.

It is pleasant to ride out and come in to our shady tent, to picket our horses at the threshold, and to sit and thus reflect upon the position in which events have placed us; but a little more, and, like a friend who saw a sword and decoration accompany the gift of rank to an officer kneeling before the Serasker, we shall be almost inclined to wish to become warriors ourselves; but the passing hour is not so agreeable to the soldiers, —they are left all day exposed to the hot sun and with little food, for as flour is served out instead of bread, every soldier had to make his own, and now that that is out of the question, one is employed for many, and his progress is generally felt by the others to be very slow and unsatisfactory.

In the cool of the evening we again went out, and advanced to within a couple of miles of the Egyptian forces. The outposts were within gun-shot, and two Egyptian officers, in their white summer dresses, were examining our position close to us. A terrified tatar came galloping from Aintab, but nobody offered him any molestation. Both armies and scouts were grouped, where possible, under trees or reclining in the sun; the one fatigued with two days' and nights' march, the other with watching and the suspense of fight. Ibrahim Pasha's position was compact and good, with a ravine on one side and the valley of the Kesrin on the other, and a village and vineyards in his rear.

The last tints of a summer sun stained the top of the hills before we retired from our ride; Hafiz Pasha had left his tent, and taken up his station in a central position in front of the lines, and under an olive-tree somewhat isolated from the remainder. The troops called to arms shouted the name of Allah, like a solemn and warlike melody. Three times it resounded along the line of guards, and was then taken up by other regiments one after another till it died away in the distance; a glorious hymn chanted to God, before the setting orb of day, by 30,000 voices. The silence that followed was as suddenly broke by a hundred drums beating from various quarters, which were again succeeded by the loud but more musical inflexions of the trumpet's blast.

We repaired to the Serasker to talk over the events of the day. He was seated upon a carpet and surrounded by his pashas, and a paper lamp swung from a branch over his head diffusing a softened light around. Neither his aspect nor his conversation was at all hopeful or joyous, yet the enemy he had long expected, and even wished for, was there! Perhaps he felt anxious on the score of the behaviour of his soldiers.

The stars had long ago twinkled into space, watch-fires were lighted upon the hills, and a deep, almost palpable darkness, enshrouded everything; trees, and tents, and horses were blended in the same invisibleness, and the two great armed congregations of men forgot their passions in the obscurity of night, and endeavoured to sleep away anxiety for a morning pregnant with evil for so many.

Friday, June 21st. The longest day in the year. Early in the morning the Egyptian army left its quarters near Niksar, with the exception of a regiment with two guns left at the station, and a small party that was detached towards the foot of the hills of Nizib as a diversion to cover the reconnoissance which Ibrahim Pasha was about to make. The main body advanced in three columns over the rising ground which extended along the right bank of the Kesrin. From these heights Ibrahim Pasha was enabled to obtain a good view of the disposition of the Turkish camp, and to discriminate its intrenchments. We were watching his intentions as closely, and with the glass could perceive the Pasha and his staff; Ibrahim himself and many of those around him having telescopes in their hands.

After some time spent in this distant contemplation of one another, some doubts and discussion appeared to arise among the Egyptian officers; and to cover this their irregular troops were ordered to advance and commence a skirmish, while the division to the right, having gained the wood, opened an irregular fire upon a detachment of cavalry which was placed there, and upon whatever stragglers happened to be within reach.

At half-past seven, A.M., the first collision took place between the Anazeh and some of the Kurd irregular horsemen who had crossed the Kesrin to meet them, but they were not sufficiently seconded, and the Egyptian lines being much the nearest, from whence new horsemen issued forth every moment, they were forced to retire on this side the Kesrin, where, forming into a line upon the heights above the river they opened a fire of musketry, which was observed to put many of the enemy *hors de combat.*

This, however, was not long continued; the greater part of our Bashi Bozuk, or irregular cavalry, had now mounted their horses, and sped out to the engagement. They soon crossed the Kesrin, and for some time the curious system of tactics, pursued by these undisciplined warriors, was displayed to great advantage, in presence of both armies. A horseman gallops, as if towards the foe, an opponent advances to the rencounter; when sufficiently near they discharge their pistols at one another; Kurd followed Kurd, and Anazeh, Anazeh; and the second pistol of the first Kurd was fired with the first pistol of the second Anazeh, while the second pistol of the first Anazeh was fired at the first pistol of the second Kurd, and so on in succession; horsemen continually relieving one another, and each cavalier sweeping round, so that by the time his pistols were unloaded he was in the rear to load again. Success in these manœuvres depends considerably upon the horse, which must be very quick in turning round, or else the cavalier would come unarmed upon a third opponent; and also upon the horseman in the rear, who must be quick enough to take new opponents off the hands of an old antagonist. The horses were, indeed, so well trained, that they often performed their part of the service after they had lost their rider, who had been shot on the first or second rencounter, but the relief from behind was frequently uncertain and ill regulated.

There was in the staff of Hafiz Pasha, a young man of prepossessing exterior and gentle manners, by name Isaïd Bey; we had formed his acquaintance in the Serasker's tent, and had learnt part of his history; he had once, from mere momentary irritation, been disgraced by an appointment among the mines of Taurus, in those bleak and barren stony districts, where only men as brown and as rude as their own employments take up their residence. But tardy justice had removed him from a position so little congenial to his ambition, and, ever anxious still to show his master how he had been wronged, by a generous devotion, bidding his black servant follow him, and taking a glance at his pistols, he left us and galloped away to join in the fray.

But about this time the affair in the woods to our right became more serious; two regiments of cavalry had moved off to the support of the irregular troops, and the three guns that were on the cliffs of Nizib hill had been frequently discharged. On the part of the Egyptians, Ibrahim Pasha, to support the irregular cavalry, moved forward three regiments of infantry in columns, at some distance from one another, having each a small park of artillery in front. These having gained the summit of a chalk hill, opened fire upon the Kurds, and compelled them to retire to this side of the Kesrin; at the same time (9 A.M.) Mahmud Pasha, who commanded our left wing, moved forward with a small body of infantry, and upon the demand being made, two pieces of ordnance were also sent off on the same service, and four more were dispatched in front or to the right of the enemy.

Hafiz Pasha also wished apparently to amuse himself; so riding from the tree, round which we had all been hitherto gathered, he went to one of the central batteries and ordered a gun to be fired, but even the valley of the Kesrin was at least 3000 yards off, and the shot buried itself in the ground, scattering around a cloud of earth and dust, while the nearest sharpshooters of the enemy were on the opposite side of the valley. Notwithstanding this, two or three more guns were fired with similar results, until M. Lauer, a stern common-sense Prussian, who could not understand this sort of thing, interfered, upon which occasion the Serasker got very angry at his amusement having been put an end to, and the two interchanged expressions of rather haughty contempt for one another.

The guns which had been sent to the left having by this time opened fire within range, the Anazeh were soon dispersed, as, independently of a natural dislike both Kurds and Bedwins have to artillery, they are always quite as anxious for the safety of their horses as for themselves, as these are their own property, and often their only means of livelihood.

The musquetry still continued in the wood, but was distant, the guns that had advanced to the right also opened a fire, which was returned from the Egyptians, when suddenly the grass, withered by a hot sun and long drought, caught fire and spread with vast rapidity, forming a dense mass of fire and smoke, amid which nothing could be distinguished except now and then a horseman still in stern pursuit of an enemy.

There was a martial dervish in the camp who wore a sword, and being tolerated for his many oddities used to take great liberties with the Pasha; to-day he afforded us no small merriment by his prowess. Drawing his sabre he rushed forward, as if to the enemy, but took care to turn round before reaching the scene of action; he then came galloping up to the Serasker brandishing his weapon, and proclaiming that he had challenged Ibrahim Pasha, as the enemy of God, the prophet Mohammed, and his vicegerent the Sultan, but that no one had dared to fight him. He performed a variety of other equally ridiculous antics. There was also another more harmless idiot in the camp, who was deformed, and subject to religious hallucinations; this man had followed the soldiers from Malatiyeh, he was a great favourite with them, and had received a good Nizam dress. He was admitted into the Serasker's tent, where one of his frequent amusements was to come and stroke me behind when engaged in conversation, on which occasions I could scarcely preserve my gravity, but the Mohammedans considered this as a token of favour and success. I never saw either of these camp oddities after the battle, and almost doubt if they effected their escape.

There was a moment in the present day, when affairs wore a very threatening aspect, and it appeared probable that Ibrahim Pasha was not merely engaged in a reconnoissance, but wished, as he had done with Reshid Pasha on a former occasion, to draw the Turks from their intrenchments. It is generally attributed to Suleiman Pasha (Selves) that the attack upon the Turkish lines was deferred, and the position of the camp was turned; but if Ibrahim Pasha had intended hostilities on this occasion, he would not have advanced his troops along the right or far-off bank of the Kesrin; he would have come with his customary fearlessness in front of the cannon, and when I consider the display of boys that filled up the intervals between the intrenchments, and the little energy shown in the final combat, I have little doubt but that he would have been equally successful had he attacked the Turks in their much vaunted position.

As it was, the Egyptian army retired behind the smoke of the conflagration that now spread over great part of the plain, the troops and ordnance were called in, and the fire being stopped by the river a light breeze carried the smoke away, and evening saw the Egyptians in their position of the morning, and the Turkish troops a little more encouraged by the day's reprieve that had been obtained, and by the advantage that was taken to make the transactions of the day appear as acts of cowardice on the part of the Egyptian commander.

We retired to our tent to see if anything would be forthcoming from the culinary department, for we were not a little apprehensive that amidst these stirring scenes the attention of the Serasker's cook might have been taken away from its proper objects; but we were in reality more anxious on our horses'* accounts. They had been out with us all day, and there was no barley, nor even chopped straw, to be got, so we were at length obliged to send two servants to cut barley in a field, at a distance from the camp, which was carried into execution with some success after nightfall.

* The Serasker had presented us with three horses, one for each, the day after our arrival.

Panting with heat, but too excited to feel fatigued, we had thrown ourselves upon our cushions of yellow and gold, when there came, rather dancing by than walking, and carrying a dead body, four of those indescribable beings who devote themselves to the last offices of humanity, and are to be found in cities and in the camp. The body they were now carrying was at once seen, by the dress and European boots and spurs, rare things in the Turkish camp, to be that of a superior officer. I could not find heart to speak to the wretches that bore it, but after the Osmanli fashion shook my head inquiringly. "Isaïd Bey," growled, rather than answered, one of the amiable porters, still hurrying on. Poor young man! We subsequently learnt from his servant, that he had killed two opponents, but on sweeping round to re-load was himself shot through the body. It was scarcely two hours since he had parted from us full of life and vigour, and he was now extended between his bearers, two to his head and two to his feet, motionless as the reclined statues which repose upon the gothic tombs of our own brave ancestors.

CHAPTER XXIV.

Position of the Turks turned by the Enemy. Hafiz Pasha's Irresolution. Position of the two Armies. Midnight Cannonade. Personal arrangements. Preliminaries to the Engagement. Arrival of Reinforcements. The Kurds pillage the Tents. Egyptian Prisoners disband. Progress of the Battle. Right and left wings driven back. Final defeat of the Turks.

Saturday, June 22. This is the third day, and the past night is the second, that the troops have remained under arms outside of the camp, exposed to sun, under which the thermometer rose to 125°. During the night a small detachment of cavalry came over from the enemy; great secresy is preserved regarding the desertions that occur on our side, but they are said to be numerous. The Serasker gives each deserter 100 piastres, or about one pound sterling, and orders them food and repose.

A report also came during the night that the Egyptian army had left its position, and moved off in a retrograde direction. At the same time Reshid Bey, a Turkish officer, who had been educated in France, and is now Pasha in Syria, received a letter written in French, and announcing that Ibrahim Pasha had retreated on the road to Aleppo, leaving tents, cattle, &c. on the field.

The early dawn of morning cleared up the meaning of these feints to draw the Turks out of their intrenchments; soon after daylight the Egyptians were discovered at a considerable distance. They had gone off truly to the south, but only to get round a hill which was necessary to be encompassed to enable them to travel out of the range of our guns, till they got into the rear of our position, which the indefatigable Egyptians performed in one long day's march, which began two hours before daylight, or at one in the morning, and was completed one hour before sunset, without, by some strange and inexplicable infatuation, any one thing being done on our part to prevent it.

Finding themselves now observed, and their object no longer to be hidden, they set fire to a village, and their progress was partly hidden by the smoke; at the same time a detachment of our cavalry, that had been sent out at an early hour to support a reconnoissance, returned, and stated that about a thousand men and two guns still remained in the position of the night before. The batteries at our extreme left now received reinforcement, and two regiments of cavalry, and a party of irregulars, were sent out beyond the Kesrin to support a further reconnoissance. For our parts, we repaired to the batteries at the left, and for some time watched the progress of the enemy; tired of this, we joined the Pasha's staff, and with him visited the lines and batteries; during this progress a chief mollah, for there were two about the Serasker's person, knelt down in prayer in front of one of the batteries, and this caused a general stop for a short time. This mollah had great influence with the Pasha, and was generally consulted upon all matters. There was also in the staff a Russian agent, a native I believe of Aderbijan; he wore the kalpac, as also did his servant, who always followed him, and both in true Oriental style were ridiculously over-armed. This man was well received by the Pasha, but was silent and haughty. There was another Russian in the camp, also much in favour with the Pasha, of a more jovial and courageous temper, and who sometimes came near us to interchange ordinary civilities.

The Prussian officers came in from various recognitions, and strongly recommended the Serasker to attack the Egyptians during their march, for if they were allowed to gain a position between us and Birehjik the intrenchments of the camp would no longer be of any use; but the Pasha did not appear to coincide with them, or could not make up his mind to leave a place he had taken a great fancy to. At one time he was assured by the same gentlemen that the enemy were in a ravine, a position most favourable for cutting off a large body of troops, but it was to no purpose.

At length, three hours before sunset, the advanced guard reached the valley of the Kesrin, by a ravine, beyond which was a bridge. The Kesrin is a small river, and is nearly everywhere fordable in summer, but still the bridge presented an easy and important point of defence, and was only about a mile from the batteries of our extreme left; but the passage was left undefended, and company after company, and squadron after squadron, filed along close to our camp, as if at a parade.

When we saw circumstances in this position, it became necessary to take some definite steps to secure at least our baggage. I had taken every little occasion that presented itself of late to urge to the Pasha the necessity of our departure, and I now determined to come to a definite explanation as to whether or not he would allow me to leave the camp, while the road to Birehjik remained open, which we could scarcely suppose it would be a few hours longer. Accordingly, Mr. Rassam and I started for the now well-known olive-tree, and on our road we met Baron Mulbach with his interpreter, bound to the same quarters. I told him my intentions, and he said he also was going to speak upon serious matters, and he would be glad if I were present. I accordingly hurried on before him, and, certainly under no pleasant circumstances, urged the necessity of our immediate departure. The Pasha was much affected at what looked like a not very honourable desertion. I felt it my duty, however, to be firm to my purpose, and offered that Russell and I should remain with him, if he would only let Mr. Rassam go away with the baggage.

At this moment, the Barons Mulbach and Moltke came up: the latter had had some previous conversation; he was angry and did not sit down. Mulbach's interpreter was as timid as dragomans generally are, and Mr. Rassam was kind enough to lead the conversation. It consisted, on the part of the Prussian officers, in a simple and definite statement of only two alternatives: an immediate attack upon the Egyptians, or a retreat to the intrenchments of Birehjik; the attendants and officers around the Serasker recoiled, and stared to hear the Europeans in what they deemed an unnecessary hurry. The mollah grinned ghastly. Hafiz Pasha looked perplexed, and turning to me, asked my opinion. I at once said I was no soldier, but Baron Mulbach had fought at Jena and at Auerstadt, and was an officer of much experience, as Baron Moltke was of acknowledged ability, and their opinions ought to have great weight. He struck his breast, and his eyes were suffused with tears. "I cannot retreat," he said, "I am ashamed to retreat!" This was at once overruled, and led to a long conversation on predents, which history did not fail to provide us in superfluous abundance; amid which, however, the truly distressed and wavering Pasha rose from his carpet, and walked quickly to and fro. After leaving him for some time to his thoughts, I again approached him, and asked, "Will you give the teskereh?" "What, have you so little trust in the Osmanlis?" he said rather peevishly. "No, I remain, but Mr. Rassam goes this evening. May your secretary write out the teskereh?" He softened, and, stopping a few minutes, said, "Await: the example of your departure will do much mischief; I will go with you myself at midnight." I hastened to inform the Prussian officers of the Serasker's resolve; but the mollah had overheard it, and approaching him, whispered something in his ear: there is no doubt of what his words were. "If you attempt to retreat, your army will disband." Poor Hafiz Pasha had no alternative left, so rousing himself as a man, he buckled on his sword, became cheerful, as his determination was taken, and calling to the Baron Moltke, he mounted his horse, and, followed by a numerous staff, went out to choose a new position in front of the enemy.

Baron Moltke was joined by M. Lauer, and they were so exceedingly irate against the Pasha, that they would hardly speak to him; but he persevered in his intentions. The troops were moved from their stations, the heavy guns were dragged up the hill side. Armenians were set to dig new intrenchments, the moon shone brilliantly over the arduous labours of the night, and by two o'clock in the morning, and an hour before day-light, the distribution of the troops was effected. The cavalry occupied the wings, the infantry was disposed in columns or lines according to the necessities of the soil, and batteries were placed at the most promising intervals. The Serasker had a tent pitched in front of the lines at day-break, and taking advantage of the circumstance, one of the Prussian officers tried to remove his effects to Birehjik, but they were sent back, and profiting by the example I did not attempt to do any thing surreptitiously.

Sunday, June 23rd. The position now occupied by the Turkish forces formed part of the upland that extended from above the rivulet of Nizib to the river Euphrates. At its northern part, and at the foot of the hills, were groves of olives, the trees of which were diffusely dispersed, while to the south the plain, sloping slightly towards the valley of the Kesrin, was broken up, and denuded into numerous ravines with gentle acclivities, which stretched down to the banks of the Kesrin. Ibrahim Pasha and his army were gathered together, like a lion and his whelps, in a confined space formed by the meeting of two or three ravines on the camp side of the river. His troops appeared to have been much fatigued with the very long march of the day before, for he allowed them to rest all the day; this was also advantageous to the Turks, who had for the most part been in arms all the previous night. Mirza Pasha, who was now in the dangerous post of our extreme right, informed me of a reconnoissance which Ibrahim Pasha had made of our new position, in front of the line to-day. I saw several

Turkish lancers go over to the enemy; the desertion from the enemy which took place during the march had also been considerable. I smoked a pipe with some of the pashas; except Sadallah and Mirza Pasha, they appeared to have no zest for the fight. "Praise be to God and we shall beat them," was the most prevalent doctrine that obtained in the army.

A long line of camels arrived to-day with wheat and barley. "For how many days?" asked the Serasker, for the camels came up to the lines instead of going into the camp; "For two," was the answer; he looked dissatisfied, and yet it was one day more than was wanted.

In the evening, Suleiman Pasha of Marash, an intrepid and courageous man, came up with a reinforcement of cavalry; his infantry was to arrive in the morning.

This officer, on his arrival, urged in the strongest manner, as had been done by the Prussian officers, an immediate attack; not only as the initiative is always more favourable to an army than the defensive, but because the position of the Egyptians was easily assailable. Ibrahim Pasha had felt this all day, and, impatient at the repose of his soldiers, had pranced up and down in the waters of the Kesrin for hours together.

The only steps, however, that Suleiman could get the Serasker to take, was a feint to be made under cover of night, the chief object of which was, by throwing confusion into the enemy, to facilitate the desertion of troops; for Hafiz Pasha had got it into his head, that if an opportunity could be given, the greater part of the Egyptian army would come over to the Sultan.

It was midnight, and we had retired half dressed to

take a little repose, for the night before had been one of bustle and disturbance, when we were roused by the long deep booming of distant cannon; a rolling fire was kept evidently from two different quarters, and the dark veil of night that spread over the two armies appeared as if lit up by a conflagration. This continued for a short time, and then as suddenly ceased; we waited on the tiptoe of expectation for further symptoms of hostilities, but none occurred, and it was only afterwards that we learnt the objects of this midnight cannonade. It was reported to have thrown the greatest confusion into the enemy's lines, and only to have been stopped by the earnest entreaties of the mollah to spare the lives of the faithful. From the Egyptians I heard another tale; that for one shot sent among them, they returned twenty, and that it is rather to this that the discontinuance of the firing was to be attributed; but when I saw the encampment in the day, the guns were distributed around it by pairs, and it would have been difficult to bring many to bear upon a new point in so short time, nor do I think, from all I could hear, that Suleiman Pasha was a man to be so easily silenced without an order from the too-confident Serasker, for coming events had not cast their warning shadow before him.

At the very earliest break of day, when light was just creeping over the chalk hills of Birehjik and the sun was tardily following in the van, almost every tent in the camp of Nizib was already emptied and abandoned. Every man had crowded to the field of battle, and there only remained the Serasker's secretary and treasurer, who, with a few soldiers and khawasses, were left to keep guard on the money, and a party of horse artillery, busy in harnessing and preparing the reserve ammunition for the demand of the moment.

By singular good fortune, Mr. Russell had secured during the night, the services of a seruji, belonging to the post, with six horses. He belonged to Birehjik, but now no longer able to get there, was prepared to make himself useful in a flight, in any direction that might save himself and his steeds. Every thing was carefully packed up, but as there was a chance that our large travelling bags might still be lost, two small bags were entrusted to the care of our faithful Greek servant, containing the sextant and Kater's circle, and one of the post horses was placed at his command for an emergency. Another Arab servant had charge of Mr. Rassam's desk, which contained our reserve money and some of his private things. We each lashed a great coat behind our horses, and in addition to our arms and ammunition, we had a shirt, a pair of stockings, and a comb in our pockets, besides a small sum of money distributed, in case of accident, to each.

Things appeared thus tolerably compact for a flight; so mounting our horses, we all rode out to see the preliminaries of the engagement. Day after day of postponement and reprieve had succeeded to one another, but after the midnight salutation, which had been given to the Egyptians, it was not to be expected that another sun would set, without witnessing an issue to events so long pending. We directed our steps to the extreme right, from whence we were nearer to and could better see the movements of the enemy. They were to our surprise breakfasting very quietly on biscuit dipped in water in the hollow below. Taking advantage of the further delay thus afforded them, the Turks were also running down to the rivulet to fill their cans with water. In the battery on the headland we found M. Tournami; he was a brave old man, and although very eccentric, was still most anxious that every thing should go off well; he was running to and fro on the battery, and I wished him success.

The old man survived the battle, but I know not if he has survived his indignation. I met him afterwards in the retreat, when he amused me much by his *naïve* recital of the part he took in the engagement. "Monsieur, c'etoit comme de la pluie, comme la grêle! Oh! les poltrons! je ne me battrai plus pour les Turques, non je mangerai de l'herbe dans ma patrie!" and he stretched out his hand to suit the action to the word.

After a few minutes' conversation with Mirza Pasha, we rode along the lines to see how the soldiery appeared affected. They were totally buried in destructive inertness, a mixture of apathy and pride, which no gleam of hope and confidence came to illumine like a moral sunshine. The scene was quite heart-breaking; but the evil of the war (besides that it might have been prevented, by a timely interference,) was also that it was founded on circumstances in which the numbers took no interest. What was it to the soldiers, if the Sultan had one great province more or less, in his vast dominions? The enemy was also of the same faith as themselves, and few that were on the field had ever met them before, or bore rancour or hatred, or even ill-feeling towards an Egyptian. There had not even been any of the usual little incentives put into play to excite their feelings, and there existed nothing but the sense of duty, and a decent regard for honour, to keep the men to their posts. The Egyptians, it might be said, had not greater incentives to the struggle; this is true,—but they were perpetually talked up to a contempt of the disgraced of Homs and of Koniyeh, and they were now deeply irritated by the occurrences of the past night.

Our reflections thus indulged in, in front of the Turkish lines, were interrupted by the appearance of the Serasker and his staff: "Aha, bey," he said, "so you are come to assist at our wedding!" a man always jokes when he has something vitally serious upon his mind. Ibrahim Pasha, the day he left Aleppo, requested our consul there to be particular about a certain *flower*, which he wanted. Napoleon was very fond of these little effects, and immortal Shakspeare has pourtrayed them with his usual truth and energy.

A few moments after our joining the Serasker, two battalions of infantry from Aintab, about a thousand irregular Kurdish musketeers, and a battalion of Egyptian prisoners, came round the foot of the hill of Nizib, and filed over the bridge of the rivulet to join the Turks; it was a gay sight, their guns glittering in the morning sun, their red tarbooshes and silken tassels waving in the wind, and drums and trumpets mingling their martial sounds. Hafiz Pasha went a little out to meet them, but he did not speak a word of encouragement. There was no time to distribute the Egyptians, so they were left in the rear, the Kurds were sent off to the extreme left, and the infantry was marched to the rear of the lines. A reinforcement, however small, coming at such a time, would, with any other people, have been a source at least of a momentary agreeable sensation, but the same sombre indifference was persevered in as ever, an indifference which sprang from the dogma of fatalism, which trampled upon the energies of the soldiers and officers, and prostrated, as such a doctrine must naturally do, all incentives to good, and all the nobler sentiments that can inspire the human mind.

Baron Mulbach had addressed me in the course of our ride, to request, that his secretary, who had charge of his effects, and his dragoman, might be allowed to put themselves so far under our protection, as to follow whatever steps we thought it prudent to adopt with the course of events. I, therefore, got Mr. Rassam to ride back to the camp, and to see that they were like ourselves prepared for any sudden emergency. Mr. Russell and myself proceeded to explore the extreme left, where we wandered among fields of barley newly cut or trodden down, and groves of olives, behind every tree of which was a Kurd, while the irregular cavalry was gathered in more open spaces. There was loud and harsh quarrelling going on among these people, the natural result of having no acknowledged commanders.

Weary with suspense, and wishing to feed the horses, we returned to our tent; but at the same moment the Egyptians left their quarters and advanced steadily up the ravines, trying to get as much as possible to the left and in front of our lines before the battle should commence; this was not to be done, however, without exposure, and we had scarcely dismounted, when the sound of cannon once more brought us to our saddles, and leaving Mr. Rassam and the servants to load the mules, we rode off to see the progress of events, it being understood that upon the first symptoms of our party giving way, Mr. Rassam was to start, and Aintab was to be our place of meeting, but we fully anticipated being able, when there were any signs of retreat, to rejoin the baggage ourselves.

It appears that shortly after we went away, the Kurds at the extreme left having returned in confusion to the camp, which they immediately began to pillage, our friend very properly made an attempt to depart, but he was opposed and surrounded in his tent by the bayonets of the Kurds, as was also the secretary of Baron Mulbach, and it was only some time afterwards, when the attention of the robbers was occupied by the tearing up of the treasury-tent, and the distribution of its contents, that he and the other gentlemen and the servants were able to mount their horses and to effect their escape.

In the mean time, Russell and myself having gained the hill-side, came upon the rear of the army just as the action was becoming general. We observed M. Petit at this time part from a German doctor and make off to the left, whence, as the troops in that quarter were soon after driven back, it appears that he became at an early hour a prisoner of the Egyptians. As we advanced over the hills, we perceived that the main body of the cavalry was drawn up in columns under Sheriff Pasha, in rear of the Turkish guard, and where the Serasker had taken up his position. It has been said that the Turks committed a great error in firing too high, but if so, the Egyptians appear to have been equally to blame, for balls were falling plentifully around us who were in the rear of the cavalry. There was a ravine to our right, in which was a road, and up this the drivers were hurrying with the reserve cars of ammunition; we observed that the heights above this commanded a better view, and crossed the ravine, which was, however, made very hot by a battery that had come up the acclivity, and opened a sharp fire immediately in front; many of the cars were struck and exploded in the air, sending up a tall dense column of white smoke, while the affrighted horses, throwing their riders, or these being killed by the explosions, sped without guides along the ravine, rushing to the water's brink, where the cars buried in the mud, and their own panting thirst, made them bring up. At this time the battalions of Egyptians in the rear disbanded, and also retired to the banks of the stream. Already also by this time, a common trick in all engagements, four to five men were to be seen going away with one wounded; they were passing in abundance. I asked the doctor what was to be done with them: he avoided the question; in fact, there was not one out of the many hakims that had long enjoyed the Sultan's pay who gave any assistance on the day of battle. He soon after left us to go and save what he could of his baggage, while we remained at our station immediately behind the Turkish guard.

M. Petit, who certainly had means of observing the movements on the side of the Egyptians, has described them as having persevered in their attempt to reach the extreme left of the Turkish lines, but that in doing this they were so severely galled by our batteries, that they were at length forced to turn round and march upon their enemy, manœuvres which they accomplished, amidst a galling fire, with the greatest coolness and discipline. To the truth of this statement I cannot attest; the firing appeared to us to be pretty equal on both sides from the moment that the engagement set in, and the extreme right was certainly exposed at once, and at the beginning, to a bold and determined attempt at dislodgment. M. Lauer assisted in one of the batteries in this part of the field, M. Tournami in another; and Mirza Pasha, one of the generals commanding in the same quarter, fell early in the engagement. The service in the batteries was either unskilfully or too hurriedly performed, for every now and then an ammunition car blew up, scattering death-fragments around, and almost clearing the whole side of an intrenchment.

The Kurds we said had retreated at the beginning of the fight; and when two battalions of Egyptian infantry, with a small park of artillery, came up to the woods, they found no enemy, and proceeding on and on, they gained without opposition the point in front of the village, where the teskerehs were taken on entering into the camp. Russell could hardly be brought to believe that events had already (it was about an hour since the fight had begun) gone so far; but I could distinguish the Egyptian dresses, with which my eye was more familiar, as the troops came down the hill, which they did in the form of an acute angle, the point of which was formed by a tall man, who led with sword in hand. This person I since ascertained was a renegade Maltese, and he obtained the rank of kaïmakam for his services on this occasion. At the same time, a detachment of Egyptians had been despatched up the bed of the Kesrin, so as to bring them, under cover, in the rear of the batteries of our extreme right, but on turning into the valley of Nizib they were opposed by the three guns upon the teppeh, which were, however, carried by the bayonet.

Grieved as we were at the progress of events, and anxious for the success of the day (and amidst all evil forebodings we had never ceased entertaining some latent hopes), still it was now fully time to beat in retreat, and give assistance to the baggage department; but we had already deferred this too long, if it had ever (which it could not) have been of any avail.

Long before we had gained the valley of Nizib, the flight had almost become general, guns and cars were rattling across the encampment, and there was a dense multitude of soldiers, baggage-horses, and camp-followers, that rendered it impossible to proceed in any direction which was opposed to the stream of living and flying beings. It was curious to observe the different excitability of the Egyptian and of the Turk in the present position of affairs. Many of the latter were riding away almost as unconsciously as if nothing had happened; an officer we were acquainted with, calumniating his now unfortunate leader, said as an excuse for his retreating, "Hafiz Pasha is no pasha!" but some Egyptian officers were hurrying away, shouting, sword in hand, as if leading to an attack.

The dust and consequent obscurity created in the valley by this mingled host, was now broke through by the flash of guns and the discordant cries of the wounded, of persons run over by the affrighted horses, and the rattling din of the cars was half smothered by peals of cannon close to us, while the whirling shot came sweeping by, ploughing earth and dust from our feet. I began to doubt if my poor horse would remain to carry me away, or have perchance a master to carry. We persevered, however, in endeavouring to force our way to the vineyard at the foot of the Serasker's Hill; here we could distinguish the battery which the Egyptians had opened near the fountain, and which was answered by the two guns from the front of Hafiz Pasha's tent, firing away right across our point of repair, which was in a line between it and the enemy. We felt that our friend could not, unless dead, be any longer there, so we turned round, and gaining the grove of fig trees, there waited the progress of events. The firing from the Pasha's tent was soon put a stop to by the customary termination of a grand explosion of ammunition, after which the few that remained made off.

All around was one great expanse of flying men and horses; some drivers, no longer able to take their guns and cars along the unequal ground and through the wood, were cutting the traces and effecting their escape upon the horses; the hill of Nizib and the heights beyond were covered with large bodies of mounted Kurds, who had long ago provided for the safety of themselves and steeds; but, on the battle-field, the strife still continued between the Turkish guards and the Egyptians, and a last effort still remained to be made. It was a most painful thing to see the brave Guards left without support to battle against a whole army. My friend felt as keenly as myself, but was more excited; several times he attempted to rally the fugitives, but I saw an expression in their countenances such as only dastardly cowardice can give birth to, and there was no possibility of mistaking its meaning. It was evident that all interference was fraught with imminent danger, and I persuaded him to be quiet. Poor Hafiz Pasha had seized upon the standard of the Guards, and endeavoured to urge this small remnant of fighting men to a decisive charge; but abandoned on all sides, and nearly surrounded by the enemy, they could do no good, and stirred not. The cavalry under Sheriff Pasha had withdrawn itself in the most shameful manner at the time that it ought to have supported the left wing. A determined and well-sustained fire of musketry was kept up a short time longer on both sides, and then all was swept away as if a hurricane had been in movement across the plain. The Pasha was carried away by the mass of fugitives who fled along the valley of the Kesrin and towards Niksar. It was a quarter past ten o'clock in the morning when firing first began, and it was half-past twelve when we turned, with heavy hearts and an uncertain future before us, up the side of the hill and away from the plains of Syria.

CHAPTER XXV.

Line of Retreat. Turn off for Aintab. Attempt at Robbery. Descent of a Ravine. Night's Bivouac. Retreat obstructed by the Kurds. Sufferings of the Disabled. Pons Singæ. Reach Besni. Renewed opposition from the Kurds. A Murdered Christian. Arrive at Malatiyeh.

As we proceeded on our melancholy way, we found knapsacks, cartouch-boxes, accoutrements, muskets, and portions of dress, strewed plentifully along the road-side; some had taken the precaution to arm themselves with bayonets, but others had thrown down the whole machinery of war, as uncongenial weapons, and especially troublesome on a long foot journey. Luckily a few held by their firelocks, and others took advantage of a stray horse or donkey, or of a steed whose owner lay low, to make it carry the arms of a multitude. The number of muskets that fell into the hands of the enemy was very considerable; we saw at Aleppo, some months after the battle, a pile at least containing six thousand, most of which had been taken out of the rivulet of Nizib, for the Kurds got the greater part of what were left on the road. One of the peculiarities of the battle of Nizib was, that there was no pursuit.

One poor creature had died with his chin resting upon his hands, and his elbows upon his knees; and he sat in this position by the road-side; another fine young man turned pale and fell from his horse; he was carelessly put off the road into a bush; his trowsers were bathed with blood, and it was evident that he had been mortally wounded in the thigh. He recovered for a moment, opened his eyes and gasped for breath, but soon fainted for the last time.

The chalky soil reflected the powerful beams of the sun, and lent further intensity to the heat. The fine dust rose in clouds, sometimes veiling the crowd from sight, then again leaving banners of white and red, and the tassels of black ostrich feathers attached to the spears of the Kurds, to toss above the flying multitude. Few spoke to one another. We observed close to us a young officer, upon whose carpet we had the day before smoked the chibuk of Eastern sociality—he now avoided recognition. Every one seemed engaged in securing his own safety, with as much secresy as possible, all avoiding to shew the least perturbation or dismay, and none appearing to have doubt or distrust towards another, for fear he might be supposed to have something to lose, but on and on, in silence and in selfishness, the great crowd of pashas and officers, Kurds and khawasses, priests and soldiers, doctors and camp-followers, servants and slaves, made their way regardless of one another. All ties were rent by disgrace and misfortune; the servant knew not his master, nor the soldier his superior; there was no distinction of persons or rank, the best mounted and the strongest sped foremost, and especially no one regarded the fatigued that tarried, the incapable that lagged, or the sick and the wounded that dropped in sad succession.

Thirst already began to be felt in all its horrors; we passed one small puddle—a mere solution of dirt—but it was surrounded by so many, that to wait our turn would have necessitated us to stay all night. We had picked up a soldier's can, as we thought it might be useful, but it had such a greasy odour, that, although not fastidious under existing circumstances, we were compelled to throw it away again. At length we came to a village, situated in a valley watered by a rivulet. Our horses and ourselves got a long and apparently unfinishing drink, but the villagers had fled or hid themselves, and no bread was to be procured.

We had hitherto been carried away, almost without reflection, by the onward course of the multitude. From the present village there was an ascent by a gentle slope to a stony upland of basalt; the road was becoming difficult, and evening was fast approaching, when we observed towers as if of a castle, a few miles to the right, and upon the same level as ourselves. I knew there was no castle on the road to Aintab, and a moment's reflection convinced me that it must be the castle of Rum Kalah, on the Euphrates, that now presented itself to us. After inquiring of two or three soldiers without their condescending to answer, we at length learnt from one more amiable than the rest, that our suspicions were just. Now our rendezvous was Aintab, and as we naturally concluded that Ibrahim Pasha would either march himself or send a detachment the next day to that town, it was necessary to go there that night or not at all; and more particularly as Mr. Rassam, not reflecting upon these circumstances, might remain there till entrapped by the Egyptians, we resolved to leave the road and bear off in what we thought to be the best direction.

There was no path, nothing but huge blocks of basalt and a few shrubs of prickly oak, amid which the horses made their way with difficulty. We had not proceeded far when we saw a Kurdish tent thrown down, and near it some men and women busy in driving off cattle. We were not surprised at this, as they might be fearful of being plundered by a retreating army. On seeing us approach, they attempted to make their escape, but we rode up, at once to tranquillize their fears and to ask for a little milk. They pointed to two tents, which we now first saw standing in the distance, and said we could procure milk there. One of the men volunteered to accompany us, and we walked with him leading our horses. On our road we were soon afterwards joined by two more. These began to exhibit much restlessness, and looked frequently behind them. At length they made a dead stop as if to wait for somebody. We endeavoured in vain to get them on, for time was precious. At this moment two more well-armed men came running up almost breathless. The last that came was a tall stout man with breast almost bare; this fellow seized our horses which happened to be near to one another, and held them by the reins. We scarcely knew what to do—we doubted but that there was mischief in the wind, but still we thought there might be some mistake; at all events, if we commenced a fight without sufficient reason, the numerous Kurds who formed part of the retreat, if not the Turks themselves, would assist in slaying two infidels, and we felt that we were not out of hearing of guns, from the motley crew we had just left. Under these circumstances we attempted a sort of parley, they demanding who we were and whither bound, and on our stating that we were going to Aintab, they evidently looked upon us as persons about to make over to the enemy. In the mean time we had produced our firman to the chief, as he appeared to be, and its contents were discussed without the form of a perusal. This being terminated, a search was commenced of our persons, during which two watches, one from myself and one from my companion, changed proprietors, but it was in vain they sought for the customary belt round the waist; they were not acquainted with the mysteries of breeches' pockets. These proceedings had illuminated our understandings like a torrent of light, as to what we had to expect. The moment arrived when this became no longer a doubtful matter. Having in part completed their robbery, they hesitated about what further to do. They were all armed with pistols and swords, and the man who held the horses appeared inclined to urge their being had recourse to, but the hesitation of the moment decided the whole affair, for Mr. Russell observing that the man who had got his watch was skulking off, stole away to his horse's side, and cutting the strap which swung his gun to the saddle, had it in a moment bearing upon the fugitive. At almost the same instant of time I had jumped upon my horse, and seizing a pistol from the holster, was in the act of cocking it, when my friend cried out, "Shall I shoot that fellow?" "By all means," was the answer; luckily he did not hear it, for as he afterwards said, he would have pulled the trigger. The man, however, observed the gun remained steadily bearing upon him, and began to retrace his steps, while my pistol being upon the fine open bosom of the leader, led him to exclaim several times, *Zara yoke*, "Never mind." Our watches were returned, and as in the scuffle some papers had fallen from my breast, we made the Kurds gather them up, then turning our horses, but keeping our guns to bear upon the foe, we effected our retreat to the road, taking care when we arrived among our old friends not to look as if anything had happened. It turned out afterwards that this occurrence was more advantageous to us than otherwise, and that, as is often the case, there was a kind providence in an apparent evil. Immediately beyond this encampment of Kurds was a deep stony ravine, which it is very probable we should not have succeeded in passing, and if we did, it could only have been after a toil which would have brought on night, when, according to all chances, fatigued, and weary of watching, we should have fallen easy victims to the stern marauders of these lonely rocky wastes.

We continued for a short distance, along the same stony upland, till we came to a steep and narrow ravine, the sides of which were strewn with large irregular masses of rock, and clothed with a luxuriant vegetation of oak and hardy evergreens, that twisted their fibrous roots between rocks and into crevices. There was no road visible, and every one proceeded as he thought best. Our horses of high Cappadocian breed took the largest rocks at a leap, lighting sometimes upon a space scarcely a few feet square, or held up almost entirely by some gnarled oak, and we reached the bottom with only a few injuries; I myself had a severe kick on the shin; but it was even worse with the multitude, upon whom every now and then horses and riders came rolling over once or twice, before a footing could be recovered, while laden horses had much more awkward falls, and many a sad accident took place; still the scene was very picturesque, such a dense mass of men and horses descending in what appeared to be three distinct lines down a precipice, which might have been thought insuperable to a single man. On arriving at the bottom, every one began to seek, in the dry and stony bed of the ravine, for remnants of water. We were lucky enough to find a small cavity, by lifting up a stone, which contained enough for two, but had scarcely time to congratulate ourselves, when a fat general of cavalry (Sheriff Pasha), abandoned by his servants, leading his horse and covered with dust and perspiration, came up begging for a participation.

The ascent was more toilsome and laborious than the descent; the horses could no longer leap over the detached masses of rock, but slipped down their smooth surface. Every rider had to look out for himself and for his horse, to speed on at one moment, to wait anxiously at another. Some poor animals fell as many as three successive times before they could pass one short space. At length, the summit was gained, and again we found ourselves travelling along a grassy and partly wooded upland covered everywhere with large detached stones.

Evening was approaching, and the Kurds, who belonged to the irregular cavalry, began to stop, turn back, and then pass on, evidently hovering about in search of prey. They soon distinguished my companion and myself as Franks, and Franks generally carry watches, and sometimes money; but whenever we observed a set who particularly watched or followed us, we became equally careful in avoiding them, and still more cautious in not getting surrounded. An unfortunate European medicus, who was not aware of their tactics, was plundered the first evening. He thought he was travelling along very quietly and unregarded, when, suddenly at a turn in the road, a party of Kurds who were in front stopped short, and when he attempted to retreat he found that another party was in his rear. He was then immediately despoiled of almost all his wearing-apparel, and his horse was taken from him, so that he had to continue his march in a few tattered garments, and in shoes, which the jagged rocks soon tore to pieces. Seeing the poor fellow in this plight the ensuing day, and observing that he was an European, Mr. Russell, with a benevolence which none of the Turks exhibited towards one another, lent him his horse to ride upon.

Just as the sun was about to set we got a crust of bread from a soldier, but we could not eat it, our mouths were so parched. As darkness increased, we ceased to converse except in whispers; by this means we avoided being recognised as Franks, and got off the scent of the Kurds. After another hour's journey we came to a steep cliff, down which we had to lead our horses in the dark. The crowd was going in various directions. Discordant cries were heard on every side, and they were answered by shouts of triumph from the invisible depths below. This announced water, for the voices of those below were clear and full; of those above, hoarse and weak. Our horses exerted themselves wonderfully; leaping or sliding, as the necessities of the case demanded, down they went, regardless of rocks or trees, and after scarcely more than half an hour's perspiring toil we found ourselves on the wooded banks of a rivulet of clear water, and most lovely to our eyes. Already some advanced parties had kindled fires in the jungle, or grouped themselves in little spaces of greensward. We turned from these into a deeper gloom, and ascended a short way up the stream; after a satisfactory drink we tied our horses beneath a wide-spreading plane-tree, leaving them to sup upon its leaves. We ourselves divided the crust of beneficence; it was small, but the first food we had taken that long day, during which we had been on horseback from an hour before sunrise till two hours after sunset; and the most faithful dog is not more patient of suffering than a Cappadocian steed. There was no restlessness nor regrets on the part of our fatigued and unfed friends, so leaving them to their reflections concerning barley and oats, we made pillows of our saddles, and wrapping ourselves in our cloaks, after uttering a prayer to the Father of all, were soon unconscious of all mundane grievances*.

So soundly did we sleep by the rivulet's murmuring side, and shaded from the falling dew by the magnificent expanse of plane-tree, that, when we awoke, we found it was daylight, and ourselves almost alone. We were, however, soon mounted, and overtaking the laggards of the train; we also soon passed the main body, who were toiling up a rocky ascent to the right, and pursuing our way up a lateral ravine we ascended by a tortuous course, and gained, even before the multitude, a great plain,

* The horse given to me by Hafiz Pasha was originally intended for the Sultan. He strained himself so badly in the ravines, that he was a long time in recovering. At Constantinople I parted with him with regret to Admiral Walker, and when I last saw him, he was in good health and excellent condition.

at first covered with rocks and shrubs, but beyond, becoming cultivated, with many villages dispersed, and ultimately terminating in a long range of partly naked, partly wooded, limestone hills.

This we at once recognised as the Araban Owahsi, a district I had visited on a former journey from Marash to Rum Kalah, and whose inhabitants were identified in my memory with certain acts of lawlessness and violence; nor was their character contradicted by their behaviour on the present occasion. The villagers had uniformly deserted their abodes, and were congregated in two separate bodies. Those who were on horseback were on the plain, from whence they apparently watched our progress. The footmen had perched themselves on the rocky crags, not far from where we had to enter upon the hills, and were ready to dispute our progress.

Under these circumstances the Turks, without any one to give orders, adopted a tolerably good plan of defence. The horsemen remained on the plain, riding along parallel to the direction of the hills, while a party of infantry, who had still their muskets, approached under shelter of a village to the foot of the crags. They then kept advancing in skirmishing parties, maintaining a pretty sharp fire upon the Kurds, who were soon dislodged from their fastnesses.

By this means the road was cleared for the remainder, and after a journey of about ten miles we had crossed the plain, and entered upon a hilly district of limestones with occasional groves. The suffering. however, from fatigue, want of water, and exposure to the sun, now became very great, and many most painful scenes were presented to us on the road-side. Some were begging for water, others wept in grief as they dragged their sore feet and jaded limbs behind them, others fell down and shrieked in despair; still, almost regardless of these horrors, each and all sped onwards. Indeed, we ourselves suffering, what relief could be given to others?

At length, upon turning out of a grove of trees, just after mid-day, a river was seen slowly flowing along the bottom of an adjacent vale. The multitude appeared as if inspired with new life; some crippled by blisters and cuts began to run, others wept for joy. Upon this river were two or three ivy-clad arches of an antique bridge, which stretched half across its waters. It was the ancient Pons Singæ. Heedless of the depth, our horses, no longer amenable to restraint, precipitated themselves at once into the river.

I forget how we drank from our horses' backs; I only remember that one long draught was not enough, but that we remained a long time, over our knees in water, drinking and drinking again. This is curious, for we had water in the morning, and I was accustomed when travelling scarcely ever to drink, from morning to evening; but it was not only us, but every one was similarly circumstanced, and many so much more grievously; it was most probably owing to want of food.

Our thirst being quenched we repaired to a field of wheat, the first we had met upon the road. It was fully ripe, and while we ourselves fed upon a few ears we turned our horses adrift on the crop. At this moment a Turkish soldier came by, who happened to be driving a mule laden with biscuit; observing the simplicity of our repast, he was led to give us a little bread;

we tendered a piece of gold, equivalent to four shillings, for more; he was astounded, and brought us more, but refused the gold. We went down to the water again, and dipping the bread made a comfortable if not luxurious meal; but our horses were less fortunate; for, either by accident or wilfully, the field of corn was set on fire; the straw was dry, and the ground parched, and, breasted by a huge cloud of smoke, and crackling furiously, the flames came on like a galloping horse. Nothing was left but to escape before the road became impassable, and refreshed and re-invigorated we proceeded on our journey.

We soon entered upon more hills of chalky soil; the road not bad. Here we met many Kurds going in an opposite direction, and anxiously asking for the Serasker. These revengeful clans nearly got him into their hands during the retreat.

Towards evening we came to another field of barley; besides giving our horses a hasty feed, we cut the corn down with our swords, and made a bundle for emergencies. We shortly afterwards passed by a village where was a spring. The sheikh was standing with a few peasants by the road-side, begging for contributions to cover the depredations of the retreating soldiery: strange to say, he appeared actually to have received some money. We added our mite for the barley which we had been forced to take for our safety, but could get no bread.

After night had come on, we came to another river, which we forded. There were now few persons on the road, and we had some difficulty in making out our way. At this moment a small party of lancers overtook us, and we joined company. An hour before midnight we stopped at a field of barley, and fed our horses; here, during our rest, two horses were stolen from the lancers. We slept a wink upon the stubble, holding the bridle in our hands, and then starting again, arrived before daylight at Besni.

It was a strange scene to see the inhabitants and soldiers sleeping in groups upon the roofs of the houses, disposed like terraces upon the hill-side; the mesjids and sepulchral chapels were converted into stables, and there was not an inch of ground to spare. We lay down in the street and fell asleep, but were soon awoke by daylight, when we repaired to the same Christian house where we had stopped before; and here we were delighted beyond the possibility of expression by being afterwards joined by our lost friend Mr. Rassam, who, unable to reach Aintab, had also been borne along by the current to this place: so it fared likewise with our Greek servant, who dropped in, in the course of the morning; but the Arab, with the money, government post-horse, and Mr. Rassam's baggage, never made his appearance any more.

Many of the Europeans came into Besni in the course of the day, stripped to their shirts and trowsers. A German doctor had been sorely pressed by the Kurds, but having a double-barrelled fowling-piece had got off safe, for on firing one barrel without effect, a Kurd had persevered in his attack, when he received the contents of the other.

An attempt was now made to re-establish some sort of order, that the remainder of the retreat to Malatiyeh, which had still to be carried through the heart of Taurus, might be effected with as little loss as possible. Accordingly, no one was allowed to start till the ensuing day, when, a little before daylight, rendezvous being given outside of the town, all were to go off together. At midnight a Frenchman rose from an adjacent roof, and called for his horse and servant. I asked him where he was going. "C'est mon étoile!" he said; "I feel that I must go." In the morning we found him at the rendezvous; so he gained nothing by his fidgets.

On reaching the side of the mountain of Khurkhun, previously described, the Kurds opened an ineffective fire upon us from the heights above; this was speedily answered by the Turks, and the skirmish had a picturesque effect in such a position, heightened by the depth of sound which the mountain echoes gave to the irregular discharge of musketry. Pelvereh was deserted. In the valley of the Ak Su we were lucky enough to find some pastoral Turkomen, from whom we with some difficulty procured a kid. At night, as we were now a large party of Europeans, we took one great roof of a house to ourselves, in the village of Erkenek, situate, as previously described, in one of the most beautiful of the alpine glens in Taurus. A professional gentleman, with few remaining clothes, but who designated himself as a Neapolitan marquis, operated as butcher; barley was found for the horses, and great was the feasting at sweet Erkenek.

Next day saw us on the road again. We had the difficult pass of the Gök Tenah to get over. In some places the path is so narrow that only one person could proceed at a time. Weary of the delay which this occasioned, many clambered up the almost perpendicular cliffs by the side, and endeavoured to get round. I could not tell why the Turks were, against their usual practice, trampling over the body of a man which lay stripped in this narrow pass. When I came up, the explanation was offered to me at once: it was the body of an "uncircumcised dog," murdered and stripped by the Kurds; had it been a Turk, he would have been put on one side of the road.

We passed by Surghu, with its beautiful rocky springs, and drew up a short time on the outskirts of a forest, which fills up the valley of the Sultan Su, girt by the snow-clad and conical heights of the Akjah Tagh on the one side and the more rounded outline of the Baghli Khanli on the other. There were here a few pieces of ordnance, which had come from Constantinople, and were on their way to Nizib. The pashas present determined on conveying these back, the more especially as news had come that the Kurds of Akjah Tagh intended opposing us in the forest in front.

The troops accordingly formed in some sort of order, and the pashas went in front, but we passed through the forest without interruption, and arrived in the same order at Gozenek. Many efforts were made here to preserve the gardens and property of the peasants, and so energetic had Saadallah Pasha become, that he armed himself with a gun to enforce his orders. We dined after dark with Sheriff Pasha, who illuminated us by his sentiments regarding battles, which he thought would soon be fought with cannons only; we agreed with him in wishing it might be so, and that their movements and firing should also be executed by machinery, and battles fought by engines instead of human beings.

The next day we reached Malatiyeh. On the road Reshid Bey shot his white charger; he had had four horses the day of departure, only two remained, the rest having broken down upon the road; the white was his great favourite, and he would not leave it to be ill-treated by the soldiery.

END OF THE FIRST VOLUME.

LONDON: HARRISON AND CO., PRINTERS, ST. MARTIN'S LANE.

Lightning Source UK Ltd.
Milton Keynes UK
UKOW04f1601201217
314803UK00001B/16/P

9 781108 080989